LEGAL HISTORY IN THE MAKING

LEGAL HISTORY
IN THE MAKING

PROCEEDINGS OF THE NINTH
BRITISH LEGAL HISTORY CONFERENCE
GLASGOW 1989

EDITED BY

W.M. GORDON & T.D. FERGUS

THE HAMBLEDON PRESS
LONDON AND RIO GRANDE

Published by The Hambledon Press 1991

102 Gloucester Avenue, London NW1 8HX (U.K.)

P.O. Box 162, Rio Grande, Ohio 45672 (U.S.A.)

ISBN 1 85285 054 X

British Library Cataloguing in Publication Data
British Legal History Conference
(9th: 1989: Glasgow, Scotland)
Legal history in the making.
I. Title. II. Gordon, William M. (William Morrison), 1933– III. Fergus, T.D.
340.09

Library of Congress Cataloging-in-Publication Data
British Legal History Conference
(9th: 1989: Glasgow, Scotland)
Legal history in the making: proceedings of the Ninth British Legal History Conference, Glasgow, 1989/ edited by W.M. Gordon and T.D. Fergus.
Includes bibliographical references.
1. Law – Great Britain – History and criticism – Congresses.
I. Gordon, William M. II. Fergus, T.D.
III. Title.
KD606.B74 1989 349.41--dc20
[344.1] 91-19298 CIP

Printed on acid-free paper and bound in Great Britain by Bookcraft Ltd., Midsomer Norton, Somerset

Contents

Preface

At the invitation of the Faculty of Law and Financial Studies of the University of Glasgow, the Ninth British Legal History Conference was held at the Kelvin Conference Centre, Glasgow, from Tuesday, 4 July until Friday, 9 July, 1989. Some ninety persons representing twelve jurisdictions attended. Amongst them was a party consisting of several delegates from the U.S.S.R. who came to us through the good offices of Professor Butler of University College, London. Two of them gave papers and it has been possible to publish one of the papers delivered; others made summaries of papers available to interested participants. We were particularly happy to welcome this group to Glasgow as it was the first time that the Soviet Union had been represented at the Conference. It is to be hoped that the bonds forged at Glasgow will be strengthened at future Conferences.

The Conference could not have taken place without the generous support and sponsorship of a number of bodies, and the convenors would like to record their thanks here to: The Faculty of Law and Financial Studies of the University of Glasgow; The Faculty of Advocates; The Law Society of Scotland; The Royal Faculty of Procurators in Glasgow; The Bank of Scotland; The Stair Society; W. Green & Son Ltd.; Cambridge University Press; The Hambledon Press.

In addition thanks are due to the staff of the Kelvin Conference Centre for their arrangements and to Mrs. Betty McIver for her invaluable secretarial assistance, particularly during the weeks leading up to the Conference.

The publication of this volume marks the ninth in a successful series of British Legal History Conferences. For reasons of space, it has unfortunately not been found possible to accommodate between its covers all the papers delivered at Glasgow. To those not represented here, we express our thanks, as we do to our contributors. We also extend our thanks to Mr. Martin Sheppard of The Hambledon Press for undertaking publication of the volume and for invaluable help in its preparation.

The convenors were heartened by the response which the Conference elicited, by the number and variety of the papers offered and by the debate they stimulated. It is good to know that at a time when it appears to be necessary to justify all but the most severely practical, legal history can command such an impressive following.

Preface

List of Contributors

Dr. M.A. Becker-Moelands	Dutch Centre for the Documentation of Legal History and Legal Iconography, Amsterdam
Dr. R. Chadwick	University of Texas
Professor I. Dübeck	Institute of Legal Science, University of Copenhagen
Dr. V.G. Grafsky	Institute of State and Law, U.S.S.R. Academy of Sciences
Professor R. Gregory	School of Legal Studies, Wolverhampton Polytechnic
Professor T.S. Haskett	Department of History, University of Victoria, B.C.
Professor J.P.S. McLaren	Faculty of Law, University of Victoria, B.C.
Dr. A.H. Manchester	Faculty of Law, University of Birmingham
Professor P.L. Nève	Faculty of Law, Catholic University of Nijmegen
Professor D.J. Seipp	School of Law, Boston University
W.D.H. Sellar	Department of Scots Law, University of Edinburgh
F.A. Sharman	School of Legal Studies, Wolverhampton Polytechnic
Dr. K.J.M. Smith	Department of Law, Brunel University
Dr. H. Summerson	London
Professor R.S. Tompson	Department of History, University of Utah
T.G. Watkin	Cardiff Law School, University of Wales
Professor S.J. Yeazell	School of Law, University of California, Los Angeles

The British Legal History Conference

The first British Legal History Conference was held in 1972 at Aberystwyth, on the initiative of Professor Dafydd Jenkins. Since then there have been meetings at London/Cambridge (1974 and 1975), Edinburgh (1977), Birmingham (1979), Bristol (1981), Norwich (1983), Canterbury (1985), Cardiff (1987) and Glasgow (1989) and the Conference has become established as a leading forum for the discussion of all aspects of the history of law.

Proceedings of the first eight Conferences have been published as follows:

Legal History Studies 1972, ed. D. Jenkins, University of Wales Press, Cardiff 1975

Legal Records and the Historian, ed. J.H. Baker, Royal Historical Society, London 1978

Law-making and Law-makers in British History, ed. A. Harding, Royal Historical Society, London 1980

Law, Litigants and the Legal Profession, ed. E.W. Ives and A.H. Manchester, Royal Historical Society, London 1983

Law and Social Change, ed. J. Guy, Royal Historical Society, London 1984

Customs, Courts and Counsel, ed. A. Kiralfy, M. Slatter and R. Virgoe, in *Journal of Legal History* v, 1984, and as a separate volume, Frank Cass, London 1985

The Political Context of Law, ed. Richard Eales and David Sullivan, The Hambledon Press, London 1987

Legal Record and Historical Reality, ed. Thomas G. Watkin, The Hambledon Press, London and Ronceverte 1989

Chapter 1

Saints, Seaways and Dispute Settlements

Thomas Glyn Watkin

In his book, *Trial by Fire and Water: The Medieval Judicial Ordeal*,[1] Professor Robert Bartlett argues that there is what he terms a 'strong likelihood' that the ordeal in Europe was of Frankish origin,[2] and that it spread from the Frankish kingdom to other parts of Europe with the advance of Christianity and Christian kingship.[3] This thesis is primarily concerned with the protohistorical period, that is the period prior to A.D. 800, although Professor Bartlett also argues that the subsequent spread of the ordeal into Scandinavia and the lands of eastern Europe during the tenth to the thirteenth centuries was also connected with the conversion of these countries to Christianity.[4]

In the protohistorical period itself, Professor Bartlett notes that the only form of ordeal encountered is that of the cauldron, which institution is vividly described in the sixth-century *De gloria martyrum* of Gregory of Tours. According to Gregory, a fire was built up and a cauldron was placed upon it, which was left there until it was boiling fiercely. A small ring would then be tossed into the boiling water and the person whose oath was to be tested was required to bare his arm and plunge his right hand into the boiling water to recover the ring. Gregory notes that grasping the ring was a far from easy matter, not only by virtue of the scalding effect of the water but also because the bubbling of the water made the ring difficult to locate.[5] It was this form of ordeal which, according to Professor Bartlett, was to find a place among the native laws of the West Saxons, the Visigoths, the Lombards and the Frisians, in each case as a result of Frankish influence.[6] Professor Bartlett believes that there was one part of Europe where this form of ordeal was to be found during the protohistorical period which had no connection with the Frankish kingdom, namely Ireland. Here, Professor Bartlett believes, the tradition of the ordeal of the cauldron was distinct from that of the Franks, because he states, there

1 (Oxford, 1986).

2 Ibid., 4.

3 Ibid., 47, 153, 155.

4 Ibid., 43.

5 Ibid., 4; citing Cap. 80, *Monumenta Germaniae Historica, Scriptores rerum Merovingicarum*, i, Bruno Kisch, ed. (Hanover, 1885), 542–43.

6 Ibid., 7.

were 'few plausible paths of influence or suggestions of common ancestry which would link these two early bodies of legal material (unless we have recourse to the *deus ex machina* of the Indo-European heritage).[7] He sees the Irish situation as 'quite exceptional', a tradition uninfluenced by others and itself without influence. The Irish ordeal amounts in his judgement to 'an autonomous and self-contained story'.[8] The evidence for the existence of the ordeal by cauldron in protohistorical Ireland comes from the seventh or eighth century,[9] and the texts credit St. Patrick with the introduction of the practice to Ireland, interestingly stating that it was one among several forms of trial introduced by the saint.

The first purpose of this essay is to suggest that Professor Bartlett is incorrect in his view that the Irish version of the ordeal by cauldron was beyond the pale of Frankish influence. It is submitted that there was a plausible path of influence by which the ordeal by cauldron could have arrived in Ireland between the sixth century, when Gregory of Tours wrote his account of the institution, and the seventh century from when the information from Ireland comes. Moreover, as one would expect from Professor Bartlett's own views, that plausible path of influence is connected with the conversion of the Irish to the faith of Christ. Indeed it can be argued that if the tradition of ascribing the introduction of the ordeal to Patrick proves nothing else, it certainly connects the advent of the institution in the memory of the Irish people with the coming of Christianity.

Modern scholarship has decisively rejected the initial introduction of Christianity into Ireland as being the mission of St. Patrick. Professor Daniel A. Binchy, in his masterly survey of the biographers of the patron saint,[10] believes the first major Christian mission to Ireland focused upon the south east of the country and was led by Palladius, a deacon of the church of Auxerre in France, who had travelled to southern Britain with St. German in A.D. 429 and may have been recommended by St. German for the Irish mission of A.D. 431. Professor Binchy, however, notes that even prior to the Palladian mission of A.D. 431, there is evidence of Latin loan-words being borrowed into the native Irish language to cover such concepts as Christian, priest and church.[11] These earlier Christian influences are ascribed to contact with the Christian peoples of southern Britain and Gaul at the close of the fourth century.

The picture presented by this evidence, therefore, is not one of Ireland as a closed society during the fourth and fifth centuries. Rather it is of an Ireland which had contacts with and received influences from southern Britain both in Roman and post- or sub-Roman times, and which in part directly and in part

[7] Ibid., 5–6.

[8] Ibid., 6.

[9] See, *Ancient Laws of Ireland*, W.N. Hancock, etc., ed. 6 vols. (Dublin, etc., 1865–1901), i, 195–99; v, 457, 471–73; *Corpus iuris hibernici*, D.A. Binchy, ed. 6 vols. (Dublin, 1978), ii, 393–94; i, 233, 238; iii, 916; v. 1872–73; vi, 2232.

[10] See D.A. Binchy, *Patrick and his Biographers: Ancient and Modern. Studia Hibernica*, ii (1962).

[11] Ibid., 165–68.

through southern Britain was also in contact with what was still at that time Roman Gaul. The sort of travelling to which the incursion of Latin loan-words and the mission of Palladius and later Patrick bears witness was by no means uncommon at this time. There were, in fact, strong links between the lands on the western seaboard of Europe in the fourth and fifth centuries, links which were to continue during the succeeding centuries. The importance of these maritime links for the social history of the lands concerned has been demonstrated admirably by the late Professor E.G. Bowen, most notably in his works *The Settlements of the Celtic Saints in Wales* and *Saints, Seaways and Settlements*,[12] the latter of which has provided not only the title but much of the inspiration for this paper. Bowen brought to light a matter which had remained obscure to earlier writers, namely that during the sub-Roman period the lands of the western seaboard of Europe had not been divided but rather united by the seas which lay between them. Professor Bartlett seems to have fallen into the trap which Bowen warned against: as a result he has seen Ireland as a remote, isolated corner of Europe. This was not so. Once the Romans had withdrawn from southern Britain at the start of the fifth century, the crossing of the Narrow Seas, that is the English Channel, became by degrees more perilous as protection from marauders was lost. The action of Vortigern in engaging the Saxon fleet as mercenary protection in 426 suggests that the crossing of the Narrow Seas was no longer protected by the Romans. As the south east of Britain and the north east of Gaul became subject to disturbance at the hands of the barbarian invaders, so there was a return to the use of the western sea routes by the peoples of the western fringes of Britain. The results of this resumption of activity along the western sea routes have been well described by Bowen:

> The southern section of the major sea-route soon became active with particular emphasis on the links between south-western France and northern Spain with Ireland. Refugees from Aquitaine made their way across the seas to southern Ireland taking with them their culture and the last echoes of classical learning. These were the *alumni* of Bordeaux and other cities of south-western Gaul recorded by an anonymous author as leaving their homeland early in the fifth century. Literary experts have been able to detect the influence of the continental rhetorical style among the earliest Leinster poets, and there seems to be no difficulty in accepting the derivation of this style from the continental *literati* of the fifth century. It is thought that many of the rhetoricians of Gaul attached themselves to the native princes of southern Ireland and Britain at this time, but more particularly to the Irish chieftains, because Ireland was a safer refuge. They might even be responsible for the introduction of the Christianity that was known to have existed in southern Ireland in pre-Patrician times. The links of Ireland with Spain seem to be equally clear. Orosius writing in the early fifth century speaks of a city in Galicia, which he calls Brigantia, as having some kind of direct relationship with Ireland. Modern authors stress the presence in Ireland at this time of specialized art motives, like the marigold design,

[12] E.G. Bowen, *The Settlements of the Celtic Saints of Wales*, 2nd ed. (Cardiff, 1956), hereafter S.C.S.W.; E.G. Bowen, *Saints, Seaways and Settlements* (Cardiff, 1969), hereafter S.S.S.

> which must have reached the island by the same route from Spain or southern France. This motive is usually considered to be the most characteristic feature of Visigothic art. It is found all over Spain and again in Lisbon, while occasional examples occur in France from Poitiers southwards.[13]

Professor Bartlett's notion of an isolated Ireland is a far cry from this description by Bowen, who establishes that these western sea routes 'brought the Gallic, Spanish and even the North African world into contact with southern Ireland, Cornwall and Devon, south-east Wales, north-west Wales, the Isle of Man, the Galloway peninsula and the Solway area'.[14] These lines of communication were to remain open and of importance until the Islamic conquest of North Africa, Spain and finally Bordeaux and Aquitaine gradually severed the connection during the seventh and eighth centuries. After that, even though some contact was renewed as the tide of Islamic conquest ebbed, the routes never assumed the same importance that they had enjoyed from the fourth to the seventh and eighth centuries.[15]

The fact remains that the links between Ireland and France were in use in the centuries separating Gregory of Tours' account of the ordeal by cauldron from the Irish texts claiming its arrival to be connected with the coming of Christianity, centuries during which control of the French end of this link passed from the hands of the Romans into those of the Franks. This, it is submitted, is a sufficiently plausible path of influence to refute Professor Bartlett's view that the Irish ordeal is uniquely that land's own development, and to restore the Irish ordeal to the fold of those derived under Frankish influence with the arrival of Christian missions.

This suggestion solves one problem only to create another, for if Ireland received the ordeal from the Franks as a result of contacts forged along the western sea routes, it is pertinent to ask why Wales, which enjoyed similar links, did not witness a comparable reception. Wales, it is generally accepted, knew nothing of the ordeal until the coming of the Normans in the twelfth century.[16] The second purpose of this essay is to suggest a reason why the ordeal was not received into Wales during the protohistorical period, even though Wales was subject to much the same set of influences as was Ireland at this time.

Wales was quite distinct from Ireland in one very important regard. Wales had been part of the Roman empire. It has been noted by historians of the Roman period in Wales that Roman troops were withdrawn from this area of Britain speedily from the time of the Emperor Hadrian onwards, and this

[13] S.S.S., 51–52, citing Orosius, *Operae*, Book I, Cap. ii; A.W. Clapham, 'The Origins of Hiberno-Saxon Art', *Antiquity*, viii (1934), 50; V.E. Nash-Williams, *The Early Christian Monuments of Wales* (Cardiff, 1950).

[14] S.S.S., 57.

[15] Ibid., 76–77.

[16] Bartlett, op. cit., 47–48.

has been recognized as a sign of a fairly rapid degree of Romanization.[17] This has also been treated as an indicator that south Wales was relatively quiet in its acceptance of Roman rule, and that, within three generations of the Flavian conquest, the indigenous population had come to regard itself as in some way 'Roman'.[18] Such feelings could only have been strengthened by the grant of Roman citizenship to all the free inhabitants of Wales along with all free inhabitants of the empire in A.D. 212 by the *constitutio Antoniniana* of the Emperor Caracalla. With the withdrawal of the official Roman presence at the start of the fifth century, modern scholarship prefers to consider that Roman Britain went into a period of slow decline rather than an instant return to non-Roman habits. This is almost certainly true if Salway is correct in his view that there was never any deliberate intention to abandon Britain, but that events on the continent so delayed a reassertion of control that ultimately there was no province left to recover.[19]

It would appear that at the time of Roman withdrawal from Wales, loyal men were appointed to posts in the area, which posts later became hereditary, so that late Roman administrators and their descendants gradually became the princes of sub-Roman times. Likewise there is considerable evidence to support the retention of a strong element of *Romanitas* in south Wales during the sub-Roman period, particularly with regard to the continued use of Roman lines of communication, the survival of the Christianity which by the time of the withdrawal was part and parcel of Roman citizenship, and the abiding influence of the Latin language.[20] Thus it was that when St. German made his missionary visit to south Wales in A.D. 429 to counter the spread of the Pelagian heresy, he found what has been described as 'a still recognizable late-Roman society, with bishops, robed officials and a tribune'.[21] Such evidence led Bowen to conclude that south-east Wales in particular was 'a thoroughly romanized area', in which a form of sub-Roman life was to continue for a century or more after the withdrawal.[22]

The survival of *Romanitas* in the church is argued in the south east of Wales by the continuance of bishops with some form of territorial or diocesan jurisdiction during the sub-Roman period.[23] Moreover, in the Celtic church as a whole during the protohistorical period, one finds the preservation of the primitive Christian custom of naming meeting places of worship after their founders or the owner of the house. This preserves the conservative continental practice of the fifth century but differs from the developments that occurred

[17] P.V. Webster, 'The Roman Period', *Glamorgan County History, II, Early Glamorgan: Prehistory and Early History* (Cardiff, 1984), 305.

[18] Ibid.

[19] Ibid., 308; Peter Salway, *Roman Britain* (Oxford, 1981), 415–45.

[20] Webster, op. cit., 308–9.

[21] J.K. Knight, 'Glamorgan A.D. 400–1100: Archaeology and History', *Glamorgan County History*, II, 316.

[22] S.S.S., x; S.C.S.W., 14–15.

[23] S.S.S., x.

in much of western Christendom in the succeeding centuries.[24] This element of conservative Romanism is also present in the manner in which the leading families of this sub-Roman society clung to the Latin language as though to a birth-right. Latin, together with what has been termed 'all the greatness that was Rome', was seen as the rightful inheritance of these chieftains, and their tombstones were invariably inscribed not in their native British tongue but in Latin.[25]

As well as being an area in which a sense of continuing Romanism was preserved in the consciousness of the people, south Wales was also a place of refuge for like-minded folk from other parts of southern Britain forced to flee during the fifth century before the Saxon invaders.[26] Their immigration could only have served to strengthen the native population's sense of forming a remnant of the great Roman people. North Wales was also not without its Roman survivals. It is now generally accepted that before their departure, the Romans settled north Wales with *foederati*, moved into the area from southern Scotland. It is this movement, it is now believed, that was to become known as the invasion of the 'Sons of Cunedda', and the descendants of these immigrants were to form a focus around which Christianity, Latin and Romanism generally were to survive in the north after the Roman withdrawal.[27]

The importance of these remnants of the Roman population to the survival of Christianity and the emergence of the Celtic church in Wales is now widely acknowledged. It also deserves to be recognized that their faith was but one aspect of their Romanism. These were people who were Roman citizens by birth, and their law was therefore Roman law. Given that they may at first have looked to the return of the Roman forces of government and defence, it is reasonable to imagine them consciously attempting to preserve their Roman lifestyle and their Roman customs. In other words, the population of Wales after the departure of the Romans bears a distinct cultural resemblance to peoples of southern France, Italy and Spain who had once known Roman rule, and who after the fall of the empire in the west continued to live according to the vulgar Roman law, the Roman customs as they remembered them.

Nor is this connection between the population of Wales and the peoples of the vulgar Roman law fanciful. The reality is that south Wales and southern Gaul had enjoyed important links during Roman times, particularly with regard to trade. This is borne out abundantly by the archaeological evidence from Roman settlements in south Wales.[28] These connections remained operational during the sub-Roman period, when they were kept alive by the use of the western sea routes. Indeed, although these sea routes were in use even before the coming of the Romans, their preservation after the fall of the western empire can be

24 S.C.S.W., 2.
25 Ibid., 99–100.
26 Ibid., 35.
27 Ibid., 70–72; S.S.S., xi.
28 Webster, op. cit., 302–3.

attributed in the main to the surviving Roman tradition in western Europe,[29] a tradition that was highly prized in Wales.

The evidence for continued connections between Wales and the Gallo-Roman population of France is again plentiful. At one end of the scale lie such items as the similarity between the liturgy of the Celtic church in Wales and that of the Gallican church, which liturgies may have been identical.[30] There is also the continued importation of Mediterranean and Gaulish pottery. As J.K. Knight has written regarding south Wales in the period A.D. 450–650, 'its cultural affinities lie not so much with the barbarian successor states as with areas like Spain, non-Frankish Gaul or parts of Italy, where a post-Roman society used similar inscriptions and pottery'.[31] During the sixth century, south Wales saw the appearance of simple forms of the chi-rho monogram above the Latin memorial inscriptions that were still adhered to, similar to those encountered on early Christian inscriptions in Gaul and Spain.[32] The Latin inscriptions on these stones is normally in the *Hic Iacet* form, which formula also occurs in Italy, France and the Rhineland. V.E. Nash-Williams in his magisterial study of *The Early Christian Monuments of Wales* argues for a French influence, and within France locates the main area of influence within the Rhine valley, around the great Roman cities of Lyon and Vienne.[33] He has demonstrated that the early Christians who are commemorated by these stones had migrated to Wales from western Gaul by means of the sea routes and settled in the north-western and south-western portions of the country, with a marked concentration in the Brecon area. These immigrants probably chose Wales as a settlement because of cultural affinities and helped reinforce the remnant of Roman culture which existed there.[34] Their inscriptions are dated by the consular year, and witness the continuation of an ordered system of government on Roman lines within Wales during the sixth century.[35]

Another feature of the continuing Romanism of the south-eastern corner of Wales, in particular, was the respect accorded to classical learning. This feature

[29] S.S.S., 79.

[30] R.W.D. Fenn, 'The Age of the Saints', *A History of the Church in Wales*, David Walker, ed. (Penarth, 1976), 19.

[31] Knight, op. cit., 318.

[32] Ibid., 345.

[33] Ibid., 335, citing Nash-Williams, op. cit.; S.C.S.W., 16–17; S.S.S., 50–53.

[34] S.C.S.W., 54–55; S.S.S., 61–62.

[35] S.C.S.W., 20–21, citing Nash-Williams, op. cit., nos. 103, 104:

> One of their memorials at Penmachno in Caernarvonshire states that it was set up 'in the time of Justinus the Consul'. Justinus was consul in A.D. 540 and the use of his name was limited on the continent to monuments in the Lyon district. He was the last consul whose name appears on inscriptions in the western world. This reference to Justinus not only dates the inscription and indicates its associations with the Lyon area but also shows that this thoroughly Roman culture was carried into Wales. Indeed, a nearby inscription mentions a *magistratus* and a *civis* indicating an ordered system of government on the Roman model in north-west Wales in sub-Roman times.

See also S.S.S., 52–53. It is also worth noting that the development of the monastic element in Celtic Christianity is associated with immigration from these parts of France: see, S.S.S., 128.

is linked with the earliest saints of this area, Dyfrig, Cadoc and Illtud. Dyfrig, or Dubricius, has many of the attributes of an ecclesiastic in the Roman provincial mould, while Cadoc is believed to have been descended from a princeling of Gwent, who as has been shown, was probably originally a Roman administrator in that area. All three are said to have been followers of St. German,[36] which description again reinforces the Gallic connection. Indeed, the influence of German is of great importance to the argument because, although born in Auxerre to noble parents, he was most probably educated at Lyon and Arles before undertaking legal studies at Rome where he was to practise most successfully. On return to Gaul, he was appointed to the office of *dux* of the area around Auxerre, and this he remained until ordained against his will. His biography is significantly recorded by Constantius of Lyons, so that there is plenty of evidence to connect the saint with Roman Gaul, and particularly with the Lyons area.[37] Constantius' *Life* therefore accords with the archaeological evidence concerning the links between Wales and the Gallo-Roman culture of the Lyons area, later to be part of the *pays de droit écrit*.

The evidence therefore points to Wales being, during the fifth and sixth centuries, a land with a conscious Roman heritage, which heritage was most closely bound to the Christian faith. This Roman inheritance was kept alive and indeed reinvigorated by immigrants from Gaul as the Frankish invasions progressed southward. The people of Wales appear to have preserved their Roman heritage by retaining a devotion to the use of Latin and by upholding Roman forms of government. They are comparable in this regard to the lands of southern France, Spain and Italy, where the memory of Roman law was also preserved in vulgar form. It is difficult not to conclude that there is a high probability that the customs of Wales at this time would have preserved this cardinal element of the Roman tradition. Such a tradition would militate against the ordeal being received into the legal order as a method of proof when the western sea routes ceased to connect Wales with Roman Gaul but with the Frankish kingdom.

Ireland, on the other hand, had no such Roman heritage. When the Gallican missionaries, Palladius and later Secundinus, Auxilius and Iserninus, arrived in the south-east, they would not have been able to appeal to the sort of common cultural values which had appertained in Wales. The Frankish method of proof may have proved more attractive than the other methods of trial which the Patrick traditions associate with the arrival of Christianity. Ireland provided fertile soil for the transplanting of the ordeal from the Frankish kingdom with which the western sea routes were to bring it into contact. Wales, however, had memories of better ways, and may therefore have felt little if any temptation to abandon them in favour of less sophisticated techniques.

36 S.S.S., 136–37; 67–69.

37 C.J. Smith, 'St. German of Auxerre', *The History of Roath St. German's*, Marmaduke Warner and A.C. Hooper, ed. (Cardiff, 1934), 17–24.

There is one question that remains to be asked. Indeed, the final purpose of this essay is to raise it, although no attempt will be made to answer it. Given the ready acceptance of Roman culture in many parts of Wales and their jealous retention of the same after the Roman departure, given the continued connections with those parts of Europe which were similarly inclined and the haven offered by Wales to peoples from certain of those lands as the territory of the empire was gradually lost, did the Welsh preserve a large, if vulgar, element of Roman law in their native customs? The difficulty posed by this question is that the Welsh law books come from a much later period, yet the weight of archaeological and cultural evidence which derives from the protohistorical period demands that it be given serious consideration.

Chapter 2

The Presentation of Cases in Medieval Chancery Bills

Timothy S. Haskett

The medieval chancery bill is a petition, an instrument by means of which a person who believes that he has no common law remedy, or that an existing remedy is ineffective, asks the chancellor of England to provide redress.[1] Such bills survive from the late fourteenth century onwards in great numbers, sufficient, in fact, to warrant their collection into a separate class in the Public Record Office as C 1, Early Chancery Proceedings. There are perhaps 90,000 cases in C 1 for the period before 1500, but problems apart from the sheer bulk of the material have limited scholarly assessment of these records, even though they constitute the main body of evidence for the activity of the medieval court of chancery. Usually, although by no means always, the bill is the only documentation for a case, there being only scattered depositions, writs and other miscellaneous related material in the C 1 bundles. And the bills themselves are for the most part not dated directly; they are addressed to a chancellor identified by his bishopric alone, and could thus be placed in a variety of periods. Notwithstanding that further work in C 1 and other fifteenth-century chancery records will surely improve both our general understanding of the medieval court of chancery and of individual cases therein, it remains that the bills themselves are legitimately the subject of a precise diplomatic analysis. As the paramount primary source for the court, they are quite eloquent, but only in certain respects. The purpose of this study is to demonstrate how an analysis of the way in which cases are presented in the chancery bills may advance our understanding of several important aspects of the court. It is based on a group of 200 chancery bills, selected because they can – unusually – be dated precisely: they were submitted between 1432 and 1443, during the tenure of Chancellor John Stafford, bishop of Bath and Wells.[2]

The medieval chancery bill displays a distinct canon of form, and this form

[1] The author would like to thank Professor J.H. Baker for several important suggestions concerning this essay. Any errors that may remain are, of course, the author's own.

[2] They are found in Bundle 9 of the Early Chancery Proceedings, hence C 1/9. For a complete description of the records that pertain to the medieval court of chancery, see T.S. Haskett, *The 'Equity' Side of the English Court of Chancery in the Late Middle Ages: A Method of Approach*, (Diss. University of Toronto, 1987), 42–82. Unlike the vast majority of medieval chancery bills, these 200 display a memorandum of surety on their faces which provides the precise day, month and regnal year that two men undertook in chancery to stand surety for the verity of the petitioner's case (see the appended texts).

is used by the composers of these petitions to present a petitioner's case to the chancellor as forcefully and as clearly as possible.[3] Each of the eleven distinct sections that constitute the chancery bill serves a particular function and the document as a whole displays a reasoned and developed line of argument. This characteristic is especially important because of the less formal nature of the process of the court of chancery in comparison with that of the common law courts. An appreciation of this documentary form is invaluable in the search for a better understanding of what the court did, of how it functioned and of what its patrons thought it could accomplish – indeed, the image that the bills provide of the chancellor and his court is rare in the history of legal institutions, for it is derived from the viewpoint of the petitioner himself.

The canon of chancery bill form in the early fifteenth century may be presented briefly.[4] The document usually begins with an *Address* to the chancellor, which is generally set apart from the main body of the bill. The bill itself commences with the *Incipit*, the first task of which is to ask the chancellor to take notice of the description of the case that is to come. This is followed by what is normally the longest and most complex part of the bill: the *Recital*, wherein the petitioner presents a description of what should have happened in his situation. In a few cases, this is replaced by a simple statement of the problem that the petitioner has encountered, especially in cases of simple attack or robbery. The *Recital* leads naturally to a presentation of the specific *Problem* which has prompted the bill; here the petitioner usually describes the manner in which the matter described in the *Recital* has miscarried or been subverted. In most bills this is followed by an explicit *Conclusion*, describing the effects, either present or expected, caused by the *Problem*. It consists of two parts: first, the petitioner sets forth the particular hardship he now suffers, or fears he will soon experience, as a result of his problem; secondly, he elucidates the form of redress that he seeks. These four sections of the document (*Incipit; Recital; Problem; Conclusion*) together constitute the description of the case; once this has been presented to the chancellor, the petitioner makes his prayer, itself divided into six sections.

It is introduced by the *Supplication*, wherein the petitioner addresses the chancellor for the second time, asking him to take note of his particular appeal. Following this, the petitioner presents a description of the mechanism through which he hopes to receive the redress he seeks. First, he asks the chancellor for *Consideration* of his case as he has just presented it, or of both the case and an additional element or two. Secondly, he presents a *Request for Process*, asking the chancellor for a subpoena direct to the respondent, which will require the latter's appearance before the chancellor, often specifically in the

[3] Haskett, 84–244, contains a detailed discussion of the form of the chancery bill. It should be noted, however, that the terminology employed to describe the distinct sections of the bill has been modified since the time of that study, and the newer form is used herein.

[4] See the appended text Case One: *Gye* v. *Luffyng; Gye* v. *Luffyng*, for an example of the following elements of form.

chancery. The chancellor is also asked to provide for this appearance on a certain day, and this under a certain penalty should the respondent fail to appear. Once the respondent is before the chancellor, the petitioner asks thirdly for his *Examination*, usually specifically on the matter which has been described earlier in the bill. Fourthly and finally, some form of *Remedy* is requested by the petitioner, usually in an unspecified form. It is here, in the *Remedy*, that is found the guiding principle of the redress that the petitioner seeks, for appeal is often made to conscience as that which is to rule the activity of the court of chancery. The prayer is completed and the bill closed with an *Explicit*, which normally invokes right conduct toward God and charitable action between men.

As is evident from the foregoing description, the bills do not provide direct insight into the way in which the chancellor and his staff saw the operation of their court – they present neither judgement nor legal opinion. What they do allow is an appreciation of how chancery was viewed by those who approached it seeking resolutions of their problems. These bills, in fact, describe a broad range of perceptions on the part of petitioners: there are definite qualities that are seen to reside in the chancellor whose help is sought; there is a very precise mechanism of redress hoped for and expected; there is a clear vision that the principle of conscience motivates – or should motivate – the entire activity of the court. The detail and creativity in the presentation of these elements, and their consistent appearance in the bills, is such that they must reflect the manner in which the court of chancery did, in fact, function. Further, the written English of these bills shows their provenance to be outside the chancery, indicating the activity in the country of men – very probably lawyers – who knew well the proper form with which to approach the court of chancery, and who used it skilfully to present cases in a clear and forceful manner.[5]

The level of precision striven for in presenting a case, and the deftness with which the canon of chancery bill form was manipulated by composers in order to achieve this skilful presentation, can be seen most clearly in cases wherein more than one bill pertaining to the same matter survives. There are only twelve such examples found among the 200 surveyed, making them rare and valuable records indeed. The two discussed here demonstrate the nuances of presentation that were thought to ensure the greatest chance of success for a case in chancery.[6]

[5] The hands, style and idiom, and the language employed in the drawing of these instruments identify them as occupying a middle ground in the development of chancery standard English, displaying some influence by this new form, but retaining many local and regional characteristics. See, Haskett, 245–70.

[6] The other cases are: *Frauncey*s v. *Gayrstang* (C 1/9 nos.285, 286); *Dawe* v. *Tanner, Monke, Balhorn, Ede* (C 1/9 nos.270, 269); *Godfray* v. *Middelton, Shippe, London* (C 1/9 nos.103, 102); *Abraham* v. *Abraham* (C 1/9 nos.193, 192); *Stowell, Stowell* v. *Colcok, Sturmyn* (C 1/9 nos.139a, 139b); *Furse* v. *Strepe, Lechelond* (C 1/9 nos.3a, 3b); *Besyles* v. *Somerton* (C 1/9 nos.128, 127); *Somerset* v. *Sharp* (C 1/9 nos.124b, 124a); *Bydon* v. *Frollebury* (C 1/9 nos.262a, 262b); *Ilberd* v. *Kayleway, Jonys, Parker* (C 1/9 nos.201a, 201b). They are discussed in Haskett, 271–355, and eight are described briefly below, at nn. 16–23.

The first case is unique in that the two bills pertaining to the matter come not from a single petitioner or group of petitioners, but were drawn for two different petitioners concerned with the same problem.[7] Isabell, the widow of John Gye of Salisbury, and Gye's nephew and heir, also named John Gye, bring separate bills against the priest Thomas Luffyng, claiming that he embezzled the elder Gye's testament and forged another to replace it. Both petitioners describe in the *Recital* that certain parts of a holding were bequeathed by Gye, with Isabell to have one messuage, one cottage and one garden, while John was to receive two tenements. In addition, Isabell claims that she was also bequeathed all the utensils of her husband's hall, all his beds, and all the vessels belonging to his kitchen and pantry. The problem that the two petitioners face is the same: their legacies are, under the terms of the testament forged by Luffyng, to be sold by William Hore, an executor of Gye who is in fact in collusion with Luffyng regarding the embezzlement and forgery. Ironically, Isabell herself remains an executrix of the false will, and is thus to assist in the selling of what was to have been hers.

As is clear from the memoranda of surety, these bills were entered in chancery within two days of each other (16 and 18 June 1439), and the same two men, John Wykeham and Thomas Pakyn, stood surety for both petitioners.[8] In both documents the *Address* and the bill are in one hand and the memorandum in another, but the *Address* and bill hand is the same for both documents – they were drawn by the same scribe. And if this scribe was not himself the composer of the bills, then he was working under the guidance of one man who was responsible for both instruments. This is indicated by the overall structure and style of the bills, for the sections which describe aspects of the cases that are common to both are virtually the same, with only stylistic changes. The central point of the *Recital*, the description of the writing of Gye's will by Luffyng (ll. 44–47), is the same in the bills save for a few orthographical changes. This is also true of the description of the main problem encountered: the embezzlement of the testament and forgery of another (ll. 53–58).[9] The description of the probate of the forgery in the Court of Arches on 6 March 1435 in order to avoid the reading of the document in the presence of those who had any interest in it, and presumably knowledge of it, too, is the same (ll. 74–80).[10]

[7] *Gye* v. *Luffyng*, *Gye* v. *Luffyng* (Public Record Office, C 1/9 nos.119, 120). See appended text, Case One.

[8] There is, however, some variance as to Pakyn's domicile.

[9] In addition to orthographical variants, there is in C 1/9, no.120 the addition of Gye's abode (l. 57) and in C 1/9, no.119 the expanded description of the document as a 'writyng and wille' (l. 53). Word order is slightly altered at ll. 57–58.

[10] There is but one variant: in this description (l. 79) C 1/9 no.119 describes the testament as 'true', whereas in C 1/9 no.120 this emphasis is not found. In two phrases (ll. 75–76, 79–80) the word order is slightly altered.

Although the order of the wording of the description of the 'approval' of the forgery at Salisbury is different in the two bills (ll. 82–91), the fact that the provisions of this document were contrary to the true will is clear.

Around these consistent elements in the two bills, the variant aspects of each case are clearly set forth. The holding of which Gye was seised and from which his bequests to the two petitioners came is described in both bills, but not in exactly the same way: Isabell states that it comprised five messuages, one cottage and three gardens, with appurtenances, while John notes that it was simply five messuages with appurtenances. They do agree that it was in New Salisbury and held in demesne as in fee. Because there are two distinct petitioners in these bills, it is to be expected that the sections of each document that reflect upon them personally would be distinct. In the *Incipit*, Isabell describes herself as a poor and continual orator, while John presents himself as simply the chancellor's continual orator. In the *Conclusion* Isabell notes her great hurt, hindrance and undoing as the widow of the testator, while John, as befits his position with respect to Gye, refers to his disinheritance.

The various sections that comprise the plea follow the same order in both documents, but there are stylistic variants in each. Isabell in her *Supplication* looks to the 'right myghty' qualities of the chancellor, while John invokes his graciousness; Isabell asks consideration of the premises, John of the fact that he is poor and fatherless. A request for a subpoena is present in the *Request for Process* of both bills, as is a description of its effect in the appearance of Luffyng before the chancellor and his examination, in Isabell's bill on the matter and in John's on the premises. Regardless of the difference between the bequests to each petitioner from Gye's holding, the same type of specific remedy is asked for initially: Luffyng is to pay damages to the petitioners amounting to the value of the part of the holding that they should each have had, for the period since Gye's death. Because of the untruth and deceit of the approbation of the forgery at Salisbury, Luffyng is also to pay the full value of the two messuages that John should have had, and Isabell is to be paid the value of the utensils and household furniture that should have been hers. To these requests it is added that such penalties are appropriate because Luffyng disturbed the possession of Isabell and caused the disinheritance of John.

What these two bills present, then, is the activity of a single composer drafting two separate bills relative to the same general case, and the documents show clearly a person working within a variety of the canon of chancery bill form that is his own. The overall order and structure of the documents is the same, as are many of the phrases and much of the vocabulary. There is a distinguishable and consistent style to the bills. As to the writing itself, differences in orthography and morphology between the two documents show clearly just how variable a single writer's language could be, even between bills as closely related as these.[11] The composer worked within an established form, developing a particular style and idiom which he adapted to the varying circumstances of the case and the petitioner. Within this style, variation in language on the part of the writer was, if not extreme, then at least considerable. The level of precision with which a bill was crafted is clear from the way that the individual aspects of each of these two cases are carefully built around their common central problem of embezzlement and forgery.

For all the care in the composition of the bill, neither of these examples was free from error or without need of modification once it was initially drawn. Both display an erasure and filler in the description of the *Recital*, in exactly the same place (l. 46), and it would appear that a name originally inserted as one of the witnesses to the writing of the true will was removed upon assessment of the completed bill. Of greater interest are the interlinear modifications, three of which occur in C 1/9 no. 119 and one in C 1/9 no. 120. All are in the same hand, which is distinct from that in which the bills were initially written, and this clearly indicates a close assessment of the documents some time after they were written. Whether this was undertaken by the petitioners, the composer, or some other adviser, is not determinable from the evidence of the bills, but at some stage the documents were altered by the same person.

The changes involve most importantly the insertion in both documents of the crucial fact that along with Hore, Luffyng embezzled the true testament (ll. 54–55), and also in C 1/9 no. 119 the clarification that the witnesses to this testament were present when it was rehearsed (l. 48), as well as a statement of the value of the vessels and household furniture that Isabell claims (ll. 39–40). The presence of the first of these modifications in both documents shows that the two bills were assessed and altered at the same time, that one was not written and modified first and the other copied from it; had this been the case the bill that was drawn second would have incorporated the change. Further, there is no reason to assume that these alterations might have been made in the chancery. In addition to the necessity of having to account for the precision of the substance of the changes – a precision that indicates a close familiarity with the case, such as would be had by the petitioners or the composer – this would require the presumption that bills submitted into chancery on different days could have been altered by the same scribe during process of the cases in the court. The hands of the scribes who entered the memoranda of surety are quite different, and neither is that of the interlineations, so these changes

[11] The ubiquitous final *e* appears in both bills in instances where it is absent in the same word in the same place in the other; the plural inflection *ez* is present twice in C 1/9 no.119 where the word in C 1/9 no.120 displays *es*, but there is also an example of the use of *ez* in this latter bill; the double *e* ('deeth') and double *d* ('bedde') of 119 are not found in 120; in 120 *y* is substituted for *i* and *i* for *e*, but the substitution *y* for *e* is present in both documents. The non-chancery standard 'seid' appears in place of 'said' in 120, but so does 'said' in place of 'seid'; 'which' replaces 'wich', 'on' replaces 'oon', and 'beseker' 'besecher' in 119, though 'bisecher' is also present in this bill. For a discussion of the major characteristics of chancery standard English, see John H. Fisher, 'Chancery and the Emergence of Standard Written English in the Fifteenth Century', *Speculum*, lii (1982), 830–99.

could not have been made at the time the bill was submitted. As has been demonstrated elsewhere, the scribe who entered the memorandum of surety did occasionally make changes to the bill, but such instances can be clearly determined.[12] In addition, as will be suggested at the conclusion of this essay, there is no evidence to suggest that alteration of the bill, let alone of such significant elements of the case it presents, was allowed once the court had taken cognizance of the matter. A high level of vigilance is suggested by these changes, and may be indicative of the regular assessment of chancery bills upon their completion. The single correcting hand implies the supervision of an adviser to the petitioners, and is demonstrative of the expertise that underlies the production of the chancery bills, production which takes place away from the chancery itself.

The significance of this particular pair of bills is that they demonstrate three things: first, there is the identifiable canon of chancery bill form, whose requirements are fully respected; second, within these constraints, the details of each case are nonetheless precisely described, the writer tailoring his recitation to the particular difficulties of both Isabell and John; and, third, the striving for precision in the presentation of a case is very high indeed, resulting in the assessment and modification of the instruments after they were initially drawn.

The second case has been selected from nine examples wherein a petitioner, or group of petitioners, presented at different times two bills pursuant to a single case. The documents allow the progress of the case to be followed for a period of just over nine months.[13] John Ardale and his wife Joan, daughter of Richard Brill, presented their first bill in chancery on 24 January 1439, with Robert Wade and Thomas Ardale standing surety for them (C 1/9 no. 216). Their case concerns a use with the condition specified by a declared intention. The petitioners describe how Joan's father, Richard Brill, enfeoffed the clerk Simon Alcock, and others, in a holding and declared his intention: that these feoffees after his death should enfeoff Joan in the holding, to have and hold to her and her bodily heirs. If Joan were to die without issue, the holding was to be sold by the feoffees. These feoffees themselves enfeoffed Robert Wright, now dead, John Stodey and Thomas Boydon in the holding, to perform this intention. The problem has now arisen that these secondary feoffees have alienated the holding to strangers.

The preservation of a document relating to process on the case – a rare occurrence for the early chancery records – shows that the petitioners were successful in eliciting their subpoenas, for Stodey and Boydon appeared in the chancery on 10 February, only seventeen days after the bill was presented. The record of their examination is preserved as C 1/9, no. 217. This deposition presents a considerably different account of the conditions upon the

[12] A detailed discussion of modifications and alterations on the bills may be found in Haskett, 356–417.

[13] *Ardale, Ardale* v. *Stodey, Boydon* (Public Record Office, C 1/9, nos.216–18). See appended text, Case Two.

enfeoffment to use made by Brill. According to the respondents, the intention declared by the feoffor to his feoffees was that they were to make estate, not to Joan Ardale his daughter, but to Joan the daughter of John Cabron and to her bodily heirs. If this woman died without issue, reversion of the holding was to be sold with the money to be disposed for Brill's soul. Stodey and Boydon support their contention by reference to the written last will of Brill which, they assert, contains this intention. To add even more force to their claim, they note that this will was proved before the ordinary of the diocese of London, and thus bears his seal. But this must already have been clear to the court, for the will, we are told, was present in chancery and had been opened and read. Finally, the respondents address the possibility of subsequent revision of this provision by Brill, stating that he declared to them no last will other than that described, and this they offer to prove as the court will.[14]

It seems to have taken John and Joan Ardale some time to recover from the reply made by Stodey and Boydon. But within nine months they had another bill in chancery concerning the matter (C 1/9 no. 218). It is a rare example wherein the hand of the *Address* is not the same as the bill hand – nor, indeed, is it that of the memorandum. Further, the *Address* is written in English, while the bill, like its precursor, is in French, indicating that it was added some time after the original drawing of the instrument, although not in the chancery. This new bill is written in a hand different from that of the earlier one, but was clearly copied from it. Changes in morphology and orthography are evident throughout C 1/9 no. 218, but are not extreme, indicating differences in the personal preferences of the two scribes who wrote the bills.[15] The most significant change in the later bill does not, however, involve language but substance. In response to

[14] One other important aspect of this examination deserves attention: the explicit mention that the feoffor declared orally to his feoffees the provision in his written last will that concerned their obligations with respect to the use he had established. This might be taken to indicate that enfeoffments to use were regularly governed by a written statement of the intention of the feoffor, and not simply an oral agreement. But if there were regularly made a written record of such conditions it would be expected that petitioners whose claims rested upon them would be eager to put forward such documents in support of their cases. This is only very rarely the case, and it must be generally assumed that in cases concerning conditions upon enfeoffments to use, any mention of the feoffor declaring his will with respect to such a condition, and where a written record of this condition is not expressly mentioned, must be taken as a reference to an expression of intention and not construed as a reference to a written will. See, Haskett, 453–56.

[15] Many of the changes involve substitutions in the plural inflections of *es* for *ez*, or vice-versa. The writer who copied from the earlier bill tends to substitute *ez* for *es* more than the reverse, for it appears in five and two instances respectively. There are also examples of the substitution in C 1/9 no.218 of 'vouz' for 'vous', and 'redressez' for 'redresses', which also indicate the preference of the later scribe for *ez* forms. Other changes involve the addition of a final *e*, the removal of a *u* and alterations from *ei* to *ai*, *e* to *o*, *ou* to *o*, *e* to *ea* and *y* to *i*. More substantial is the change in the description of the place requested for the appearance of the respondents, 'Chauncellerie' becoming 'Chauncerye' (l. 74). There are also alterations in the presentation of names: 'Bryll' becomes 'Brill', 'Stodey' becomes 'Stodeye' and the names of the towns in which the holding in question is located change from 'Westylbery' and 'Estylbery' to 'Westilbery' and 'Estilbery'.

One change indicates that the copying scribe in a single instance mistranscribed the earlier bill. Rather than naming Thomas Boydon as a respondent, he has written 'Thomas Roydon'. Compared with the evidence of the earlier bill and the examination, it seems likely that this is a simple error, rather than an intentional change.

the statements made by the respondents in their examination, a brief new section has been inserted into the description of the earlier bill (ll. 26–29). The petitioners now recognize the position of Joan, daughter of John Cabron, in the provisions of the intention by which Richard Brill governed his enfeoffment to use. The description in the *Recital* now states that Brill declared his intention to the original feoffees – Alcock and others – that after his death they enfeoff in tail Joan, daughter of John Cabron, when she came of full age. In the case of default of her issue, the holding was to go to Brill's daughter Joan. From this point onwards the new bill is identical in substance to the earlier one.

Such a position taken by the petitioners in their second attempt ignores or, more likely, implicitly denies some major elements of the respondents' claims as presented in their chancery examination, especially their contention that in default of issue from Joan Cabron the reversion of the holding was to be sold for alms. In claiming that Cabron is to hold in tail only, it also attacks the respondents' assumption that she is to have simple estate. Mention of the sale of the holding is present in the new bill, as in the old, to the effect that sale is to take place only if Joan Ardale fails to have issue. Further, although the rights of Joan Cabron have now been admitted, no other alteration is made in the bill to indicate whether she is dead (either with or without issue), under age, or peaceably holding in tail. Finally, the appeal for remedy remains general, indicating that the petitioners see no need to alter their request in order to address the new elements of their case. Thus it seems most likely that the petitioners are still directing their complaint against the improper alienation by the secondary feoffees, regardless of who should presently have estate. If the petitioners succeed in securing the right of Cabron's daughter to the holding, and if their contention of her estate in tail is found valid, Joan Ardale can still look forward to gaining estate for herself in due course – that is, as remainderman when the now-recognized *cestui que use* dies without issue, or her issue dies. Why did the error appear in the Ardales' initial bill? Deliberate obfuscation cannot be ruled out – ignoring the right of Joan Cabron would certainly bring them the holding more directly and quickly. Nor can we rule out simple ignorance of Brill's written and declared intention concerning the use; but it is perhaps less credible to suppose that his daughter and her husband were so uninformed about a significant part of her inheritance. An intriguing question remains, of course, as to the validity and content of the written last will that the respondents presented in chancery to support their claim. Stodey and Boydon may indeed have misinterpreted the provision regarding the condition incumbent upon the use, for it is hard to imagine that in the face of damning documentary evidence the Ardales would try another bill upon basically the same grounds, unless there were such flaws in the respondents' understanding of the condition on the use.

What this series of documents demonstrates, then, is care and precision in the pursuit of the case. The change introduced in the second bill indicates a considerable degree of analysis and expertise in assessing the evidence put forth by the respondents, and precision in adapting the claims of the first bill to deal with the new, or perhaps ignored or overlooked, information pertinent to the case. Initial failure was clearly the result of inaccuracy in presentation, and the degree of error was too significant for the court to either overlook, or modify during process – that is, the case could not go forward on the original bill.

The necessity of presenting an accurate case to the court of chancery is confirmed by eight other bill-pairs in which a failed bill is altered and re-submitted. The nature of the errors they contain of course varies with their substance. While it is not possible to ascertain precisely what degree of error would lead the court of chancery to dismiss a bill – for there was certainly no set rule to guide such a determination – these cases do give us some understanding of the type of inaccuracy that was required before this would happen.

Inaccuracy concerning a will governing the devolution of certain goods and chattels caused failure in the first of these eight examples. The petitioner initially described the central document as a last will sealed with the seal of the testator, and complained of the subsequent forgery of a new will, the removal of the seal and its affixation to the forgery. Unfortunately for him, although the specific document in question was indeed a last will, it was in fact sewn to the testator's testament and the two were sealed not with the testator's seal, but with that of the archdeacon of Norwich. It is this seal that the respondents had removed and placed on the forgery. Thus while the petitioner may have been correct about a forgery having been made and a seal having been misused, his errors with regard to the details of the matter caused his case to fail.[16]

Several bills concerning enfeoffments to use failed on substantive grounds for a number of reasons. In one example the cause was a mistake as to whether the feoffor had been seised alone, or with another person, for this significantly affected the subsequent claim of failure to re-enfeoff.[17] Another bill concerning a use failed not only because of a number of simple errors, such as describing feoffees as feoffors, but also because of outright contradiction with respect to the petitioner's role in selling the property in question.[18] A third case involving a use also failed upon error in the description of a sale. This time, the petitioner presented himself initially as the preferred buyer, whereas the correct provisions governing the use allowed him the property as of right and for a sum such as might be accorded with the executors. So again, we see here a petitioner who was apparently well and truly in the right in terms of the crucial issue at stake, but who mis-stated the facts of his position.[19]

In a category of its own, outright error in the identification of the respondent was in one case clearly sufficient for dismissal.[20] More complex reasons may, however, be discerned for cases concerning copyhold and coparcenery. In the copyhold case, the error lay in presenting the lord as having seized the holding permanently, and in asking for his summons as respondent. This was rectified

[16] *Fraunceys* v. *Gayrstang* (C 1/9 nos.285, 286).
[17] *Dawe* v. *Tanner, Monke, Balhorn, Ede* (C 1/9 nos.270, 269).
[18] *Godfray* v. *Middelton, Shippe, London* (C 1/9 nos.103, 102).
[19] *Besyles* v. *Somerton* (C 1/9 nos.128, 127).
[20] *Abraham* v. *Abraham* (C 1/9 nos.193, 192).

by making his legitimate interim seisin clear, and by directing the complaint properly against an intruder claiming a right to the holding.[21] In the coparcenery case, failure to mention the petitioner's curtesy right, omission of a number of coparceners, and especially not specifying a common law bar that existed due to the undivided nature of the coparcenery, were clearly sufficient to induce the court to dismiss the original bill.[22]

The final example concerns a case involving the seizure and detention of goods, and two main errors appear to have caused the necessity of redrafting the bill before it entered the court. One was the implicit admission of the respondent's premises for seizure, and the other the failure to mention that the petitioner lacked common law remedy because of the power of the respondent.[23]

It may be concluded that despite the less formal nature of process by bill in comparison with common law procedure, the court of chancery did not offer an opportunity for success upon slipshod or uninformed petitions – bills could and did fail. That a complaint be cast according to the established canon of chancery bill form was clearly an initial requirement. Further, the striving after precise and forceful presentation demonstrated in the bills discussed here was a response to a demand made by the court in its refusal either to entertain, or to allow significant modification of, substantively inaccurate presentations. It should be remembered that the 200 bills from which these examples are drawn all display a memorandum of surety, added in the chancery, which states that it is the matter as specified in that particular bill – '*materiam in hac supplicacione specificatam*' – that the petitioner must prove to be true, not a significant variant of that matter which might finally be made clear after a number of significant in-court changes to the case. Just as a common law case would fail if an inappropriate writ were purchased, a chancery petition would not succeed if the bill that was drawn to initiate process was faulty in substance. Composers, scribes and assessors worked hard to ensure correctness, in order to give the petitioner his best chance of success, and this work is seen most clearly in these bill-pairs.

21 *Stowell, Stowell* v. *Colcok, Sturmyn* (C 1/9 nos.139a, 139b).

22 *Furse* v. *Strepe, Lechelond* (C 1/9 nos.3a, 3b).

23 *Somerset* v. *Sharp* (C 1/9 nos.124b, 124a).

Appendix

CASE ONE

Gye v. *Luffyng*; *Gye* v. *Luffyng*

Public Record Office, Early Chancery Proceedings
C 1/9, nos. 119, 120

C 1/9, no. 119	C 1/9, no. 120
[*ADDRESS*]	
Vnto the honourabill gracious lord and fader yn god Bisshop of Bath and Chaunceller of Ingelond	Vnto the full honourabill lord and fader yn god Bysshop of Bath and Chaunceller of Ingelond
[*INCIPIT*]	
Mekely besechith youre pouere and contynuall Oratrice Isabell that was the wyf of John Gye of Saresbury	Mekely besechith your contynuall Oratour John Gye the yonger
[*RECITAL*]	
that where as the said John Gye	that were as John Gye of Saresbury vncle to your besecher whos heir he ys that ys to saye sone to Rauf brother to the said John Gye of Saresbury
was seisid of v mees I cotage and iij gardyns with here appurtenauncez yn Newe Saresbury yn his demesne as yn fee	was seised of v^{e} mees with the appurtenaunces yn Newe Saresbury yn his demesne as yn fee
yn his deeth bedde at Newe Sarum by his last wille diuisid to the said Isabell and to hure assignez I mees I cotage and I gardyn with here appurtenauncez of the forseid v mees Cotage and iij gardynez Also by the same wille the said John Gye bequath to the said Isaball all the	wher of the said John Gye of Saresbury yn hys deth bed of the said mees seisid at Newe Saresbury by his laste wille diuysid ij tenementz with their appurtenauncz yn his testament to your said besecher and to his heirs foreuermore

vtensill to his halle belongyng all his beddys all his vessell of lede of tynne of gold and of siluer to þe valewe of C li.[1] and all that euer longid to his kechyn and to his Pantrye,

which wille and diuise sire Thomas Luffyng [Preste wr]ote[2] John Lambard Henry Burnage and Richard Gore beyng present at þe rehersyng of[3] the seid wille and bequest of the said John Gye

which wille and diuise sir Thomas Luffyng Preste wrot[2] John Lambard Henry Burnage and Richard Gore beyng there and knowyng the said last wille and duiuse of the said John Gye of Saresbury

[*PROBLEM*]

which writyng and wille ys enbeselyd by þe seid sir Thomas and[4] William Hore on executour of the said John Gye and an other testament by hem forgid that ys to saie that the seid John Gye yaue and bequath to the said William Hore and to his heirs the said mies with his appurtenauncz, to your said suppliaunt diuisid and bequeth and the seid cotage and gardyn to your said suppliaunt bequeth to be sold by the said William Hore and Isabell executours of the said John Gye And also all the seid vtensill to the said Isabell bequeth, to the said William Hore.

wich writyng ys enbesilid by þe seid sir Thomas and[4] William Hore oon executour of the said John Gye of Sarum and by hem an other testament forgid by whiche forgid testament the seid ij mees sholde be sold by the said William Hore and Isabell late the wyf of the said John Gye of Sarum executours of the said testatour

Which forgid testament was made and provid at the Archez yn London to that purpos to putte awaie the knoulech of theym that hadde any interesse of the true testament made at Sarum

wich forgid testament was made and provid at London yn the Arches to that purpos to putte awaie the knoulech of theym that hadde any interesse of the said testament at Saresbury made

which forgid testament after the probat there of made atte London the vj day of March

wich testament forgid the said sir Thomas deceitfull approuyd at Saresbury the vj

[1] *to . . . li.* interlined, *manu alia*, but the same hand that added the subsequent two interlineations in this bill (ll. 48, 54–55) as well as that which wrote the single interlineation in no. 120 (ll. 54–55).

[2] Followed by a short erased section covered with filler.

[3] *at . . . rehersyng* interlined; *of* written over *at*, both *manu alia* (see above, n. 1).

[4] *þe . . . and* interlined, *manu alia* (see above, n. 1).

the yere of the regne of kyng Henry the vj the xiij the seid sir Thomas deceitfully approvid at Sarum aforesaid contrarie to the wille and diuise which the seid sir Thomas wrote	day of March the yere of the regne of kyng Henry the vj the xiij contrarie to the said wille and diuise wiche the same sir Thomas Luffyng wrote

[*CONCLUSION*]

to grete hurt hyndryng and anientisshement of your said suppliaunt	vnto disheritaunce of your seid besecher
withoute your gracious remedie of conscience yn this materes.	withoute youre gracious remedie of conscience yn this matere to be hadde,

[*SUPPLICATION*]

Where fore like yt to your right myghty lordship	like yt to your gracious lordship

[*CONSIDERATION*]

graciously to considre thes premissez and	to considre the pouerte of your said besecher faderles

[*REQUEST FOR PROCESS*]

to sende for the same sir Thomas by a writte sub pena	to sende for the said Thomas Luffyng by a writte sub pena
	to appere byfore you

[*EXAMINATION*]

before you to be examynyd yn the Chauncerie of this materes abouesaid	and to be examyned of this premissez

[*REMEDY*]

and thereuppon to compelle the seid sir Thomas to yelde damagez to youre said suppliaunt vnto the value of the reuenuz of the said j mes j cotage and j gardyn sitthe the deth of the said John Gye of Sarum	and thereuppon to compelle the seid sir Thomas to yelde damages to your seid besecher vnto the value of reuenuz of the said ij mees sitthe the decesse ofthe said John Gye of Sarum
and of the said vtensill and vstilmentz for the deceite and vntrouth of the approbat at Sarum of the seid forgid testament	with the vtterly value of the said ij mees for the deceite and vntrouth of the approbat at Sarum of the said forgid testament

which causith the disturbaunce of the possession of your seid suppliaunt of the londez to hure bequeth and the godes aforsaid	which causith disheritaunce of your said besecher
where of your said beseker hath no remedie at the comen lawe	for as moche as your said besecher hath no remedie at the comen lawe yn this partie

[*EXPLICIT*]

And that the loue of god and yn w[a]ye of [c]har[ite]	And that for loue of god and yn way of charite.

[*MEMORANDUM OF SURETY*]

Memorandum quod decimo octauo die Junij Anno regni Regis Henrici sexti decimo septimo [*18 June 1439*] Johannes Wykeham de London' Gentilman et Thomas Pakyn de Salisbury in Comitatu Wiltes' Gentilman coram domino Rege in Cancellaria sua personaliter constituti ma[nucep]erunt videlicet vterque eorum pro Isabella nuper vxore Johannis Gye de Saresbury quod in casu quo ipsa materiam in hac supplicacione specificatam veram probare non poterit, tunc prefato Thome Luffyng omnia dampna et expensas que ipse ea ocasione sustinebit eidem Thome satisfaciet iuxta formam statuti in hac parte editi et provisi	Memorandum quod sexto decimo die Junij Anno regni Regis Henrici sexti post conquestum decimo septimo [*16 June 1439*] Johannes Wykam de London' Gentilman et Thomas Pakyn de London' Gentilman coram ipso domino Rege in Cancellaria sua personaliter constituti manuceperunt videlicet vterque eorum pro infrascripto Johanne Gye quod in casu quo ipse materiam in hac supplicacione specificatam veram probare non poterit, tunc infrascripto Thome Luffyng omnia dampna et expensas que ipse ea ocasione sustinebit satisfaciet eidem iuxta formam statuti inde editi et provisi

CASE TWO

Ardale, Ardale v. *Stodey, Boydon*

Public Record Office, Early Chancery Proceedings C 1/9, nos. 216–218

C 1/9, no. 216	C 1/9, no. 218
[*ADDRESS*]	
A nostre tresgracious seigniour le Chaunceller Dengletere	To the full gracious lord the Chaunceller of Inglond
[*INCIPIT*]	
Supplie humblement vous pouerez oratours John Ardale et Johane sa femme file du Richard Bryll nadgairs de Westylbery en le Counte Dessex	Supplie humblement voz poueres Oratours John Ardale et Johane sa femme file du Richard Brill nadgairs de Westilbery en le Counte Dessex
[*RECITAL*]	
qe come le dit Richard nadgairs enfeffa vn Simond Alcock Clerk et autres en certeinz terres et tenementz appellez Merlowys et Clerkys in Westylbery et Estylbery et declara sa volunte cestassauoir qe mesmes lez feffes me[inte]naunt apres la mort le dit Richard enfefferent	qe come le dit Richard nadgairs enfeffa vne Simond Alcock Clerk et autres en certein terres et ten[ementz a]ppellez Merlowys et Clerkys in Westilbery et Estilbery et declara sa volunte cestassauiour qe mesmes lez feffez maigtenaunt apres la mort le dit Richard enfefferont
	Johane file de John Cabron quant ele vient a son pleyn age en le taile et pur defaut dissue le remaindre ent a
la dite Johane en toutz lez terres et tenementz auauntditz a auoir et tenir a luy et a ses heires de son corps issuauntz Et si la dite Johane morust saunz heir de son corps issuauntz qadonques mesmes lez terres et tenementz soient venduz per lez ditz feffees et lez	la dit Johane en toutz lez terrez et tenementz auauntditz a auoir et tenir a luy et a sez heires de son corps issuauntz Et si la dite Johane morust saunz heir de son corps issuauntz qe adonqes mesmes lez terres et tenementz soient venduz per lez ditz feffez et lez ditz

ditz feffees enfefferent vn Robert Wryght ore mort et vne John Stodey et Thomas Boydon ore [en] plein vie en lez terrez et tenementz auauntditz de perfourmer la dit volunte	feffez enfefferont vn Robert Wryght ore mort et vne John Stodey et Thomas Roydon ore en plein vie en lez terrez et tenementz auauntditz de performer le dit volunte
[*PROBLEM*]	
les queux feffees ount alienes as autres estraunges lez ditz terres et tenementz encountre la volunte suisdice	les qeux feffes ount alienez as auters estraunges lez ditz terres et tenementz encountre la volunte suisdice
[*CONCLUSION*]	
a disheritaunce et perpetuel destruccion lez ditz suppliantz	a disheretaunce et perpetuel distruccion lez ditz suppliantz
sils ne soient remedies per vostre tressage discrecion	sils ne soient remediez per vostre tressage discrecion
[*SUPPLICATION*]	
Que plese a vostre tresgraciouse seigniorie	Que please a vostre tresgraciouse seigniorie
[*REQUEST FOR PROCESS*]	
grauntier as ditz suppliantz seueralx briefs de sub pena directz as dits John Stodey et Thomas Boydon	grauntier as ditz suppliantz seueralx briefs de sub pena directz as ditz John Stodeye et Thomas Roydon
destre deuaunt vous en la Chauncellerie nostre seigniour le Roy	destre deuaunt vous en la Chauncerye nostre seigniour le Roy
a vn certein iour per vous alymyters	a vn certein iour per vous alimiter
[*REMEDY*]	
pur y estre redresses come bone foy et conscience demaundent	pur y estre redressez come bone foye et conscience demaundent
[*EXPLICIT*]	
et ceo pur dieu et en ouere de charite	et ceo pur dieu et ouere de charite
[*MEMORANDUM OF SURETY*]	
Memorandum quod vicesimo quarto Januarij Anno regni Regis Henrici sexti decimo septimo [*24 January 1439*]	Memorandum quod vj die Nouembris Anno regni Regis Henrici sexti xviij [*6 November 1439*] Robertus Wade

Robertus Wade de Comitatu Essex' Gentilman et Thomas Ardale de Comitatu Essex' Gentilman	de[5] Aweley in Comitatu Essex' Gentilman Thomas Ardall de Westhordon' in eodem Comitatu Gentilman
coram domino Rege in Cancellaria sua personaliter constituti manuceperunt pro predicto Johanne Ardale et Johanna quod in casu	coram dicto domino Rege in Cancellaria sua personaliter constituti manuceperunt pro predicto Johanne Ardall et Johanna vxore eius quod in casu
quo ipsi materiam in hac supplicacione specificatam veram probare non poterint, tunc prefatis Johanni Stodey et Thome in supplicacione predicta similiter nominatis omnia dampna et expensas que ipsi ea occasione sustinebunt satisfacient iuxta formam statuti inde editi et prouisi	quod ipsi materiam superius expressatam bonam et veram probare non possint quod tunc ipsi pro custis et expensis in materia predicta[6] per predictos Johannem Stodey et Thomam Boydon factis satisfacient etcetera

C.1/9, no. 217

Examinacio Johannis Stodey et Thome Boydon facta Anno septimodecimo Regis Henrici sexti

John Stodey and Thomas Boydon I sworn in the Chauncery in pleyn Court the .x. day of Feuerzer ye .xvij. zer of kyng Henry the sext [*10 February 1439*] of certayn articles which ben contenyd in a supplicacioun to whome yis cedull is annexed sais vppon hir othes abouesaid yat they as itt supposed to be the said peticioun that Richard Brill shuld haue declared his last will in his lyf that the said Thomas Boydon and his cofeffes shuld haue enfeffed the said Johane Ardale in ye said supplicacioun named in certayn landes and tenementz called Merlowes and Clerkes in Westilbery and Estilbery to haue to hir and to hir[7] heirs of hir body laufully begotyn The said Richard declared his last will yat the said feoffes shulde make astate vn to Johanne the doughter of John Capron of the said landes and tenementz and to ye heirs of hir body begetyn And if she died with oute[8] issue the reuersioun of ye said landes and tenementz shuld be sold and disposed for the soule of ye forsaid Richard as be his last will in yis case writen and to ye said feoffes declared. And with the Ordynary seal of the diocyse of London seled and afore the ordenay[9] of ye said diocyse proved and in ye said Chauncery opynly red and shewed itt appereth more pleynly Also ye said feffes says vppon hir said othes yat ye forsaid Richard declared to tham no othir last will than the last will abouerehersed atte no tyme And yat thei will make gude be notabill and worthy proves if ye said Court will award itt.

5 Interlined, *manu eadem*.

6 Interlined, *manu eadem*.

7 *and . . . hir* interlined, *manu eadem*.

8 This word was omitted when the document was first drawn, and as the line of writing ended originally with *with*, it was added in the right hand margin, *manu eadem*.

9 Sic.

Chapter 3

The Early Development of the Laws of the Anglo-Scottish Marches, 1249–1448

Henry Summerson

Considering that they helped to regulate the affairs of a not inconsiderable portion of Britain for several centuries, the laws of the Anglo-Scottish marches have been surprisingly neglected by legal historians.[1] Documentary evidence is fullest for the sixteenth century and good studies exist of their administration and observance in this period,[2] but less work has been done on the medieval antecedents of the march laws,[3] and so this essay will try to fill a gap by attempting to trace their development over the two centuries following their first codification in 1249.[4] As recorded in that year, the Laws of the Marches were essentially a set of regulations for the prosecution of offences committed by the inhabitants of one country inside the territory of the other, and for the recovery of property stolen or lent across their common border. In theory all acts of theft or violence committed by Scots against Englishmen in the latter's country, and vice-versa, were to be judged on the march in accordance with these laws. In practice, a Scot assaulted in London was unlikely to sue for redress on the Solway or at Reddenburn – though robberies at sea continued to be so justiciable – and the jurisdiction of the laws was effectively limited to the border lands of England and Scotland.

Some very ancient elements, going back perhaps as far as the tenth century (the prescribed sites for judicial meetings may be an example) have been identified in the code of 1249 by Professor Barrow.[5] Nevertheless, it is possible to see that that code was something more than an antiquarian rag-bag. Compurgation, of course, was ancient in both England and Scotland, though in the form prescribed in 1249 – the recovery of stolen goods was obtained

[1] Unless otherwise stated, all unpublished documents cited are in the Public Record Office, London.

[2] In D.L.W. Tough, *The Last Years of a Frontier* (Oxford, 1928) and T.I. Rae, *The Administration of the Scottish Frontier, 1513–1603* (Edinburgh, 1966).

[3] The best account, though written at the beginning of this century, remains that of G. Neilson, 'The March Laws', *Stair Society Miscellany I*, Stair Society, xxvi (Edinburgh, 1971), 12–77. See also D. Hay, 'Booty in Border Warfare', *Transactions of the Dumfriesshire and Galloway Natural History and Antiquarian Society*, Third Series, xxxi (1952–53), 145–66, and C. Neville, 'Border Law in Late Medieval England', *Jour. Legal Hist.*, ix (1988), 335–56.

[4] *A[cts of the] P[arliaments of] S[cotland], I, (A.D. 1124–1423)*, T. Thomson and C. Innes, ed. (Record Commission, 1844), 413–16.

[5] G.W.S. Barrow, *The Kingdom of the Scots* (1973), 155–60.

'by the oath of six lawful men and himself the seventh' – the oath-helpers look as much like a posse of pursuers as a means of proof. But the judicial combat which the laws allowed as an alternative to compurgation, and which was in fact the only accepted means of settling disputed issues, was unknown in either country before 1066. The fiefs in whose courts it was laid down that compurgation might take place were likewise a product of the Anglo-Norman feudalism of the twelfth century, while the burgesses who might be distrained in one country for the debts incurred by their fellows in another, though found in increasing numbers in the border shires as the twelfth century progressed, are not recorded there any earlier. Although the 1249 code was produced by the sworn oath of twelve knights of each kingdom, and on previous occasions men from the two realms had met to pronounce on disputed issues, above all on the course of the border line itself,[6] there was no role for the jury as a means of proof. Perhaps this was the result of mutual suspicion,[7] perhaps just of conservatism. The position of the sworn inquest as a means of proof in criminal cases was finally established in Scotland only in 1230;[8] in England barely ten years before that, and it would certainly take time to make it acceptable to both sides on the marches, where the duel seems to have become very well entrenched, even the clergy being obliged to take part in person.[9] But conservatism was no bar to change and the 1249 code, for all its archaisms, bears, as observed above, unmistakeable signs of development and adaptation during the not-too-distant past.

Many changes would have been self-generating, made to meet the needs of the time. But there was also the possibility of external intervention. The state of their borders and relations between their realms were naturally of close interest to the kings of England and Scots; indeed the willingness of their subjects to invoke that interest is responsible for a good deal of the source material for this essay. A petition to Edward I by one Henry Scot, who bought a horse at Carlisle fair, probably in 1279, and was later charged with being in possession of stolen goods, sheds light both on the operation of march law in the late thirteenth century and on how royal action could lead to its modification.[10] An inquest held in 1380 on Henry's petition told how a man robbed who believed his property had been taken from one kingdom to the other must himself cross the border and publicize the crime. If he found the robber within forty days, he should secure a writ from the sheriff of Cumberland to the sheriff of Dumfriesshire – that is, if the suspect had fled to England – giving notice of the duel by which the issue would be decided, and

[6] *Calendar of Documents relating to Scotland*, J. Bain, ed. 4 vols. (Edinburgh, 1881–88), i, no.1749; Barrow, op. cit., 155–56.

[7] A.A.M. Duncan, *Scotland: The Making of the Kingdom* (Edinburgh, 1978), 537–38.

[8] I.D. Willock, *The Origins and Development of the Jury in Scotland*, Stair Society, xxiii (Edinburgh, 1966), 23.

[9] *Councils and Synods II, Part I*, F.M. Powicke and C.R. Cheney, ed. (Oxford, 1964), 283–84.

[10] Bain, op. cit., ii, no.183.

which would be fought on the Scottish side of the Solway. Once proceedings had got this far, the plaintiff could claim damages at will, and the defendant must find sureties for their payment, whatever the sum named, otherwise, as Henry Scot put it, he 'must undergo judgement as though legally convicted'. If he did find sureties and was then defeated in the duel, however, he would only have to pay two thirds of the sum demanded. Cases from Cumberland and Northumberland in the 1290s point to similar proceedings in cases of homicide,[11] the damages claimed here being doubtless the manbote – wergeld – mentioned in the 1249 code. If this looks like another archaic survival, the same can surely be said of the insistence on the defendant's finding sureties and the consequence of his being unable to do so, strongly reminiscent as this is of clauses in the laws of Cnut (possibly mediated through clause 12 of the Assize of Clarendon) providing for the arrest and imprisonment, even for the outright slaughter, followed by burial in unconsecrated ground, of men with no sureties,[12] their absence being seen as a clear sign of unworthiness. But although such considerations of antiquity may be of interest in the twentieth century, they meant little in the thirteenth. Edward I was in Cumberland in 1280 and could have investigated the matter for himself if he had wanted to. Whether or not he did so, what he learned from the inquest was so little to his liking that in 1280 or 1281 he abolished the procedure described. Inevitably the Scots followed suit.[13]

At the end of a decade which produced several reports of groups of criminals crossing the border from Scotland into England,[14] such a procedure was not likely to be much help in keeping the peace in the Marches anyway. No doubt it seemed better that the existing processes of the common law should be adapted to the needs of the region. Hence the case recorded at a Newcastle gaol delivery in 1308, when, after a thief had been convicted of stealing cows at the suit of their owner – who was no less a figure than the son of the earl of Dunbar – the latter demanded the return of his cattle 'in accordance with the custom of the march between England and Scotland in use until now'.[15] The men of Northumberland, questioned about this by the justices, upheld the claim, declaring that goods stolen in Scotland and carried into England, or vice-versa, should indeed be returned to their owner if the thief had been convicted at the former's suit 'before whatever justices', in other words, in a properly constituted court. There is not likely to have been any shortage of such courts, since in the English borders there were numerous liberties with the franchise of gallows to supplement periodic visitations by gaol delivery justices, just as in Scotland the justiciars' courts were reinforced by those of

11 JUST/1/137, m 13; JUST/1/652, m 36d.

12 *English Historical Documents, I, c. 500–1042*, D. Whitelock, ed. (1955), 424.

13 What appears to be a simplified procedure at Berwick was recorded in 1293, *Documents Illustrative of the History of Scotland*, J. Stevenson, ed. (Edinburgh, 1870), i, 392–93.

14 SC1/7, no.84; SC1/13, no.156; SC8/277, no.13807.

15 JUST/3/53/2, m 4/1d.

baronial jurisdiction,[16] of which pit and gallows were an essential component. It is possible that the suit required for a successful prosecution represents a survival of the six oath-helpers of 1249, but the text does not say so, and men pursuing stolen livestock were in any case unlikely to go out unattended. The earl of Dunbar's son was said to have been accompanied by the servant from whose custody his livestock had been stolen, and it seems improbable that this was the limit of his retinue; a man of his standing would surely have had other attendants able to support his claim to his beasts, and so usually would other plaintiffs. This was certainly, for a plaintiff, a much simpler and less risky process than that described in 1280, and the only problem was that in 1308 England and Scotland were at war. At that date English arms still held the initiative, if only just, but more significant was the fact that the earls of Dunbar were then on the English side – one may doubt if such proceedings would have taken place had the prosecutor been a notorious Scottish patriot.

In the end, as one might have expected, national enmities made the procedure described in 1308 unviable. There was no chance of Englishmen or Scots being able to go crossing the border in the hope of recovering stolen goods through a court held in the opposing realm. There was no reversion to the duel, however, as an impartial means of proof. Instead there developed the use of the international jury, with equal numbers from both sides, employed in the thirteenth century for civil purposes, and as a means of settling legal points like the 1249 code, now used to decide upon the criminal cases which came to form much of the business of the march days, the assemblies arranged between representatives of both sides principally in order to secure the numerous truces which interspersed outbreaks of open hostilities by providing restitution and compensation for the acts of pillage and violence carried out in breach of those truces. It is noteworthy that the procedure of 1308 had been specifically said to apply in both realms. Changes in procedure would have had to be acceptable to both sides if they were to win acceptance. How this was contrived is unknown, though since the principle, and to some extent the practice, of the mixed jury were known already, its use in criminal cases may have been a natural development, using the only viable means of providing justice on cross-border cases once that of 1308 had become impracticable. All that can be said for certain is that in 1345 an ex-chamberlain of Berwick, in an action involving goods taken at sea which was heard in the Exchequer of Pleas, stated that 'such trespass done on the march between English and Scots should be terminated before the justices of the same march, that is, by six men of England and six of Scotland, and not elsewhere'.[17]

Such a procedure was entirely in line with that found on national boundaries elsewhere. In Gascony, for instance, cross-border robberies were amended at a *jour en marche* by the decision of *arbitri* chosen from both sides. But

[16] *An Introduction to Scottish Legal History*, Stair Society, xx (Edinburgh, 1958), 296.

[17] E 13/71, mm 41, 41d.

in Gascony such process came to be seen as pernicious: 'The innocent were frequently punished and the guilty remained unpunished, encouraged in their misdeeds'.[18] The laws and courts of the Anglo-Scottish borders were only too fallible, but nobody ever said that of them. For all their shortcomings, they suited a society within which they had to operate. There is nothing anomalous in speaking of a society; the border line was basically artificial, dividing a region united in language and in economic and social structures. If the use of the singular in the statement of 1383 that an indenture settling disputed points had been drawn up 'for the gratification and relief of the community which on each side was complaining of having been much damaged and injured' was the result of clerical error, then that error was an inadvertently revealing one.[19] Among the characteristics to be found on both sides of the border was a willingness to settle disputes by arbitration. Of Scotland Dr. Grant has written that 'most disputes and crimes did not come before formal law courts, but were settled out of court', and that 'great emphasis was laid on restitution and compensation'.[20]

In northern England, where visits by royal justices were yearly at best, arbitration seems to have been just as much used. To settle a dispute in Cumberland in 1403, for instance, it was agreed that the case should be referred to four arbitrators, two on each side. If that failed, an impartial umpire would be tried. Only if that, too, did not work would the matter at issue go before the king's justices at their next coming.[21] The point is important because march procedure aimed above all at redress, as was to be expected where breaches of truce were involved;[22] references to punishment are rare and inconsistent.[23] March days were often referred to as *jours de redresce* or *jours de reparation,* and the society of the Anglo-Scottish borders was well adapted by domestic legal experience to the bargaining and compromises entailed in the calculation of reparations. Thus when in 1371 a *solempne assise des Engles come des Escotz* condemned Sir Hugh de Dacre to pay £100 to the earl of Douglas for unspecified offences doubtless connected with the quarrel between the Dacres and the Douglases over the lordship of Liddesdale,[24] the award of this round sum would certainly have represented a compromise between conflicting claims and allegations, made possible by a realism which tempered the reluctance of Englishmen to give anything to Scots with the realization that these assemblies were also occasions for Scots to give redress to Englishmen. Treaties and truces might prescribe full restitution of plundered goods, but the reality will have been less tidy.

18 P. Chaplais, *English Medieval Diplomatic Practice, Part I*, i (1982), nos.204, 205 (365–66).

19 E 39/102, no.36.

20 A. Grant, *Independence and Nationhood: Scotland 1306–1469* (1984), 157–58.

21 Cumbria Record Office, Carlisle, D/AY, no.156.

22 M.H. Keen, *The Laws of War in the Late Middle Ages* (1965), 215–16.

23 E.g. A.P.S., i, 713–14; T. Rymer, *Foedera* (1727), viii, 17–18, 54–57; x, 330.

24 SC1/40, no.188.

Awarding redress was one thing, securing payment of it quite another. The letter in which Henry, Lord Percy notified the English chancellor of the award against Hugh de Dacre shows how it might be done, for as Percy went on to explain, he had paid the £100 to Douglas himself, in order to preserve the existing truce (*en salvacion des ditz trewes*), intending to recover his money from Dacre afterwards. His action underlines the responsibility laid upon him by his office, one of fundamental importance to the development of march law and procedure, namely that of warden of the march.[25] Having originated at the beginning of the fourteenth century as military officers responsible for the protection of the northern borders of England, they came to be entrusted with the maintenance of truces, and acquired an internal jurisdiction to enable them to fulfil this function, which was defined in 1336 as 'the power of chastising and punishing all those who have transgressed against or attempted anything against the form of the said truce or armistice or any article of the same'.[26] In 1351 the warden of the English west march – equivalent officers had by now appeared on the Scottish side of the border – was set upon while 'taking steps to punish trespassers against the peace in Gilsland *and* those who committed offences against the truce with the Scots'.[27] Percy could probably have acted directly against Dacre for breach of truce, and may indeed have done so, to ensure that his case came to a march day. As it was, it was the wardens or their deputies who organized the march sessions, and can be seen on occasion to have taken a good deal of trouble about it. For one march day, held at Gretna Hill on the Scottish west march late in the reign of Edward III, Lord Percy's deputies seem to have issued formal summonses to what was described as 'touz les bones gentz' of Cumberland, and since one of the latter was said to have attended because he had been chosen 'de passer en un assis solonc les usages marchez', they may have chosen the jurors in advance as well.[28] In the following reign Percy, now earl of Northumberland, twice sent letters to a member of the Swinburne family, ordering his attendance at march days to be held at Kershope Bridge. In the second of these Swinburne was required to be present so as 'to act and take for your people as will be ordered by our deputies there'.[29] It would thus appear that the leading men of the region were expected to answer for breaches of truces perpetrated by their tenants and retainers, just as their own infractions might initially be paid for by the march warden. In theory, at least, the redress awarded at march days should have been given by those best able to provide it.

[25] See R.R. Reid, 'The Office of Warden of the Marches: Its Origin and Early History', *Eng. Hist. Rev.*, xxxii (1917), 479–96; R.L. Storey, 'The Wardens of the Marches of England towards Scotland, 1377–1489', *Eng. Hist.Rev.*, lxxii (1957), 593–615.

[26] *Rotuli Scotie*, i (Record Commission, 1814), 397.

[27] *Calendar of Patent Rolls, 1350–1354*, 202 (my italics).

[28] SC8/62, no.3083.

[29] Northumberland Record Office, Gosforth, ZSW1, nos.101, 102.

The giving of redress was, however, to some extent dictated by issues of local rank and standing. The importance of men like Dacre and Douglas was such that their disputes could easily drag the whole border region into open conflict, and so Percy had himself paid the award against Dacre, to ensure that the truce was kept. Where lesser men were concerned, it was probably regarded as more important to ensure that cross-border antagonisms were not exacerbated by excessive awards against either side than that exact justice should always be done. A letter sent by the earl of Northumberland to his bailiffs at Alnwick in 1378, directing them to inquire into the goods of Scots taken by Englishmen since a recent truce, and asking for information as to the value of those goods, so that he knew how much to claim from the Scots at the next march day,[30] shows that in the fourteenth century, as in the sixteenth,[31] wardens tended to aim for reciprocity in their dealings with their opposite numbers by trying to make demands for reparations of equal value. Presumably their control over the personnel of the juries which awarded redress was such as to enable the wardens to ensure that jurors did not upset this particular applecart. The fact that awards (even small ones, sometimes)[32] were quite often paid by the wardens[33] must have done much to give the march laws such effectiveness as they had.

It seems unlikely that this practice was adopted solely in order to ensure that justice was done across the frontier. It is significant that Percy's letter of 1371 was addressed to the royal chancellor, for there was an important political dimension to such cases. This stemmed from the Franco-Scottish alliance which remained in force, to a greater or lesser extent, throughout the fourteenth and fifteenth centuries. For England this meant the danger of a double attack: when she was at peace with France she might be less inclined to make concessions to Scotland, but when she was at war with France, and particularly when that war was going badly, she became willing to conciliate the Scots. The importance of march days as a means of conciliation, by ensuring that truces were observed and satisfactory redress given for breaches of them, was all the greater because there existed other means of obtaining reparations which could only have exacerbated ill-feeling, based on self-help.

Several truces and treaties mention the injured party's right to pursue stolen goods. In the procedure described in 1249 and 1308 pursuit was to be closely followed by judicial proceedings, but this had then become impossible, and recovery came to be a simple matter of following, perhaps with hound and horn, within a time limit which came to be laid down as

30 SC1/43, no.86.

31 T.I. Rae, *Administration of the Scottish Frontier*, 56.

32 E.g. *Calendar of Patent Rolls, 1385–1389*, 412, the sum of £7.18s.4d.

33 E.g. *Rotuli Scotie*, ii (Record Commission, 1819), 18, 21, 37; *Calendar of Patent Rolls, 1381–1385*, 137–38; DURH3/32, m 6.

six days.[34] All too often, however, recovery became retaliation, through a reprisal or distraint taken wherever sufficient goods could be found. The laws of war allowed this – and the sanction of those laws was highly relevant because a truce was only a suspension of war, not a peaceful alternative to it,[35] and England and Scotland were not in fact at peace at any time in the fourteenth and fifteenth centuries – with the proviso that it was only permissible when all other means of obtaining redress were exhausted. The Anglo-Scottish borderers accepted the lawfulness of such retaliation (they usually referred to such acts as distraints, showing that for them, as for the Italian jurist Baldus, reprisal and distraint were synonymous)[36] but ignored the proviso. Reprisals could be taken on a large scale. In an indenture of 1385 the earls of Northumberland and Douglas undertook to prevent the 'gretter' men of either side from raiding the the other with an 'oste'.[37] Just what might happen when one of those 'gretter' men set out in pursuit of reprisals is shown by a petition to parliament in 1387–88 by William Heron (as lord of Ford castle a very important man on the English east march), in which he told how, after he had suffered losses estimated at £600 to Scottish raids, he had retaliated by taking a distraint for which the earl of Northumberland, as warden, had later made him give his victims 320 oxen and cows, 1600 sheep and £100 in cash.[38] There was a real risk that raiding and counter-raiding on this scale might develop into open war. In 1386 and 1387 – the likely years, that is, of the attack upon Heron and his retaliation – there was a truce in force between Scotland and England, but the latter stood in serious danger of invasion from France. It was a matter of some importance, therefore, that the Scots should be dissuaded from military collaboration with their traditional allies, and consequently essential that reprisals for breaches of truce should be preempted by full and speedy redress given under process of law.

March days, and the law administered at them, were primarily concerned with redress – in the words of one fourteenth-century petition 'to amend damages done on both sides and to establish the said peace'.[39] This was hardly the case with the courts held by the wardens of the marches for the maintenance of truces, courts which, as already observed, were in existence by the middle of the fourteenth century. The latter were, indeed, increasingly directed to punishing truce-breakers in accordance with march law, but since punishment under the latter varied, being sometimes capital and sometimes only financial, this may only represent an instruction to the wardens to keep

[34] Rymer, *Foedera,* vii, 526–27; viii, 54–57; x, 330.
[35] Keen, *Laws of War*, 104.
[36] Keen, op. cit., 218–30.
[37] A.P.S., i, 713–14.
[38] *Rotuli Parliamentorum*, iii (1783), 255–56.
[39] SC8/62, no.3083.

their penalties in step with those imposed at days of truce. It should be stressed that march days and what came to be known as warden courts possessed distinct though complementary jurisdictions. The former dealt with allegations of truce-breaking and claims for damages brought by Scots and English, and vice-versa, the latter with breaches of truce which were apparently presented by a jury – as early as 1348 inquiries as to thieves and truce-breakers were to be made 'by the oath of honest and lawful men of those parts' – naming only the jurors' compatriots as responsible.[40] The former was an international assembly, but in England, at least, the warden court was a royal court, able to impose financial penalties and expected to account for them to the exchequer.[41]

An apparent exception to the rule that proceedings in the two courts were usually initiated in different ways, those at march days originating in personal accusations, whereas warden courts were able to receive presentments on oath as well as individual complaints, is provided by the case of one John Prince, described in 1394 as having been 'indicted in accordance with the law of the marches for homicide committed on the said marches in breach of the truce . . .' He had fled to Yorkshire, where he was arrested for other felonies, but he was nevertheless to be handed over to the earl of Northumberland 'to stand to right for that homicide according to march law at the next march day to be held there . . .'[42] It is not clear, however, how such an indictment could have been made except in a warden court, and it is possible that it had first been made in a warden court but was to be tried at a march day, perhaps because a private accusation had followed the public charge. There must in fact have been a good deal of duplication of accusation at the two courts, even though in 1384 the warden court acquired a more distinctive character when its authority was widened to give it cognizance of military cases involving the spoils of war and of treasonable contacts with the Scots.[43] 1384 was also the year in which open warfare was resumed after a truce lasting since 1357. Pillaging over the border became lawful, but it was a practice always liable to give rise to disputes among those engaged in it. Contacts with the Scots, as the king of England's enemies, could always be construed as treasonable, but such prosecutions as have been recorded, usually for collaboration in crime, were heard before justices of gaol delivery.[44] The latter, however, generally steered clear of the northern counties in times of war or the threat of it – there were no gaol deliveries recorded in Cumberland between 1384 and 1390, for instance – and the wardens, with their newly-extended jurisdiction, took over. That

40 *Rotuli Scotie*, i, 718–19. By the 1430s the warden appears to have been able to act as a sort of public prosecutor by bringing accusations of truce-breaking in his own court, DURH3/37, m 8d.

41 Cf. E 101/53/17.

42 C 54/235, m 5.

43 *Rotuli Scotie*, ii, 81.

44 H. Summerson, 'Crime and Society in Medieval Cumberland', *Transactions of the Cumberland and Westmorland Antiquarian and Archaeological Society*, Second Series, lxxxii (1982), 114–15.

jurisdiction was not exclusive, and a few cases of cross-border cooperation in evil-doing were heard at gaol deliveries in the fifteenth century (all of them in Northumberland), but to an increasing extent the wardens seem to have established an effective monopoly. Indeed they were as likely to encroach on the jurisdiction of gaol delivery justices as the other way round. The earliest surviving records of presentments made to a warden court, from the English east march in the years on either side of 1500, show it receiving accusations of felonies indistinguishable from those made at gaol deliveries, as well as charges of criminal cooperation with Scots.[45] By then the ban on any dealings between Englishmen and Scots which might give material aid or comfort to the enemy had proliferated into a whole range of offences, all coming under the general heading of march treason.

Treason, of course, was a capital offence. In 1401 the earl of Northumberland was paid £200 for holding two march days and £30 'for the arrest of six traitors of the marches of Scotland put to death because of their treason'.[46] Military offences, however, could be settled by march law. March days were used to make arrangements over prisoners and ransoms,[47] and the fact that combats were fought between English and Scottish knights in the 1380s and 1390s, sometimes at places where march days were held and sometimes to the death,[48] suggests that at the very least the laws of war and march process were not incompatible. (It should be said that such combats cannot be regarded as descended from the duels prescribed in the code of 1249, but were fought between knights jealous of their status in carefully prepared lists – five of them were made at Berwick in 1396 for 'five combats touching treason').[49] March law and the law of arms could, indeed, be openly linked. In 1386 order was given that English borderers who had ransomed prisoners without the assent of their lords, to whom a third of such ransoms was due, should be punished 'according to the courts of arms and the customs of the said marches'.[50] The curious practice of 'baughling', involving 'the bearing of a glove or picture (by the offended party) of one who had broken his bond concerning ransom, entry of prisoners, or any other just cause, and the giving out by blast of a horn, or cry, to the whole assembly that such a person was untrue', is nothing other than the procedure of dishonour of the law of arms, and march days, with their large attendances, were so well suited for it that in 1553 it was banned there, because of the disorder it commonly provoked.[51]

It is possible that the extension of the authority of the warden's court to enable it to act as a court of arms – which could have cognizance of charges of

45 SC6/Elizabeth I/3368.

46 E 404/16, no.695.

47 E.g. *Rotuli Scotie*, i, 835; ii, 79.

48 G. Neilson, *Trial by Combat* (Glasgow, 1890), 219, 220–21, 223–24.

49 E 28/26, no.153.

50 *Rotuli Scotie*, ii, 79.

51 Tough, *Last Years of a Frontier*, 104–5; Keen, *Laws of War*, 173.

treason as well as of military disputes – was intended to bring its jurisdiction, within its own limitations, into line with that of the march day courts, or perhaps even to supersede the latter, since march law went into abeyance in times of open war. It is also possible that the procedure used in a court of arms had an effect on that employed at march sessions. A mutilated document of about 1343 refers to protocols drawn up by notaries public, possibly to record breaches of truce.[52] But although by the late fourteenth century the use of written bills to initiate personal actions had long been customary in English and Scottish common law courts, and it may be assumed that the borderers were familiar with their use, there is nothing that can be construed as even suggesting their employment at march days before 1380, and no certain reference before 1397.[53] In October of that year, however, as part of the arrangements made for a day of truce to be held by the duke of Lancaster and the earl of Carrick in the following March, it was agreed that before Christmas Scottish plaintiffs should send 'thair Billes indented of thair Playntes' to Roxburgh castle (then in English hands), while aggrieved Englishmen should send their bills to Kelso abbey. These written plaints would then be sent on to the keepers of the truce – officials sometimes identical with and sometimes complementary to the wardens of the marches – who would take pledges from those accused in them, to ensure their appearance at the forthcoming march day.[54]

The fact that this measure should have been adopted 'for cause of mar playn and hastie Redresse' may indicate that it was a novelty, intended to improve march-day procedure at a time when the kings of England and Scots were both anxious to keep peace on their borders. That the innovation took the form it did may nonetheless have been at least partly due to the influence of the court of arms, which undoubtedly used such bills. In the case of *Lovell* v. *Morley* in 1395 the defendant objected to answering when no written plea was submitted, 'for by the custom of the court every plaintiff ought to set down his cause in writing'. Five years later, a charge of treason before the constable and marshal at Newcastle was made by a '*bille ou libelle*', and so, judging by its formulaic character, was the defendant's response.[55] Be that as it may, the precedent of 1397 was to be built on. In 1425 plaintiffs at march days were invited to produce 'proofs and informations' to support their claims and demands,[56] and regulations made in July 1429 indicate that such 'profes' could take the form of authenticated documents.[57] Indeed on the latter occasion they were specifically required for maritime cases. The principle recorded in 1249 that cross-border offences were justiciable only on the march had survived, and

52 SC1/42, no.19 – calendared in Bain, *Calendar of Documents relating to Scotland*, iii, no.1033, and again in *Calendar of Documents relating to Scotland*, G.G. Simpson and J.D. Galbraith, ed., v (Edinburgh, 1986), no.798.

53 Rymer, *Foedera*, vii, 276–78.

54 Rymer, *Foedera*, viii, 17–18.

55 British Library, Add. MS 9021, fos. 101, 101v, 124–25.

56 *Rotuli Scotie*, ii, 253.

57 Rymer, *Foedera*, x, 431.

it continued to be applied to misdeeds at sea as well as on land; in 1385, for instance, men of King's Lynn charged with breaking the truce by robbing a ship from Dundee were required to answer for it on the march.[58] Such a case posed obvious problems, in that piracy might be committed well away from the border, to say nothing of the coast. The use of documentary proofs met the resulting need for authentication of claims for damages and restitution.

Although the growing use of documentation at march days may have owed something to the example of the warden's chivalric jurisdiction, it must be said that the principal motive force behind this innovation was political, the determination on both sides in the last decade of the fourteenth century to make march sessions work. Bills were presented in advance so that defendants could be got into court at future sessions, and attempts were made to see that those sessions were held regularly. In 1398 it was ordered that they should be held monthly.[59] This may have been too ambitious, but there are examples from these years of march days being arranged for or held in December, January and March;[60] the king's gaol delivery justices, by contrast, came north at the most once a year in August. A similar concern for effectiveness can be discerned in the order of 1429 that march sessions should continue until all the complaints made to them had been concluded, and in an apparently new care for record-keeping, it being laid down that at every march day each side should have a 'sufficient clerk to indent all things on parchment'.[61] Since the warden's court, too, had by now come to keep written records, judging by the order of 1434 to a retiring English warden to surrender to his successor 'all the bookes of the wardein courtes',[62] it would appear that jurisdiction and procedure in both courts were by now sufficiently well established to make reference to precedent worthwhile.

The value which was placed on precedent and tradition is discernible in the preamble to the Scottish code of 1448, gathering together 'the statutis ordinancis and use of merchis' of the days of Archibald the Grim, who died in 1400.[63] March law came to have its own expertise, with experts to match, men skilled in the *fait de marche*.[64] Such was the proficiency at 'days of redresse' of Sir Robert Umfraville, a man of great experience in border affairs who died as lord of Redesdale in 1436, that Scots from 'by yonde the Scottyshe See' were said to have travelled to Berwick to have the benefit of his 'reule and regymentes'.[65] A warden who was an outsider to the region, like Henry IV's son the duke of Bedford, was well advised to hearken to 'the wisest of my council in those parts', Sir Robert Umfraville among them, before taking

58 *Calendar of Patent Rolls, 1385–1389*, 89.

59 Rymer, *Foedera*, viii, 54–57.

60 *Rotuli Scotie*, ii, 3, 145; Rymer, *Foedera*, viii, 17–18; SC8/218, no.10867; E 372/239, m 5.

61 Bain, *Calendar of Documents*, iv, appendix, no.21.

62 *Proceedings and Ordinances of the Privy Council*, iv, 271.

63 A.P.S., i, 714–16.

64 British Library, Vespasian F vii, no.119.

65 British Library, Lansdowne MS 204, fo. 220v.

action on such an issue as the adjournment of a march day.[66] Yet an awareness of movement away from even the fairly recent past may be seen in a reference of 1411 to obscure words and expressions – *diverses paroles et termes obscures* – in truces of the late fourteenth century,[67] while although the earl of Douglas consulted his 'eldest borderers' in 1448, he was frank about his innovations in matters of treason. His whole code, especially when taken together with the 'poyntis belangand to the wardane court' of the following decade, shows the extent to which new procedures could be taken on board.[68] It also shows how the development of the English warden court in matters relating to treason and the law of arms was matched in Scotland. There was nothing novel about the Scottish warden court as such, or about its cognizance of such offences as dealing with Englishmen in wartime, but it now also had jurisdiction over a whole range of military issues, like the possession of prisoners and the disciplining of men who left the army without the consent of its chief. In 1456 a man was indicted in the court of the wardenry of the Scottish middle marches for offences which included 'treasonable inbringing of Englishmen . . . and resetting of traitors and being a traitor'.[69] Indeed, the effectiveness of the warden courts on both sides of the border became such that steps had to be taken in the 1450s to ensure that the Scottish courts did not encroach upon the jurisdiction of the justice ayre, and that the English courts did not extend their jurisdiction beyond the border shires.[70]

The procedure of both warden courts and march sessions grew in sophistication during the two centuries covered by this essay, as they came to have not only their own records but also their own functionaries, at least in England, where the warden had both a bailiff for his court, employed to make arrests and keep his prison, and also – an apparently different official – a serjeant-at-arms, to attend him at march days.[71] The two courts complemented each other in the task of keeping the peace on and across the border. There can be no doubt, however, that in the administration of march law the problems arising from the march day's function of providing redress across a frontier of national hostility made it easily the less effective of the two. The development of the warden court from the last quarter of the fourteenth century may have owed something to a realization on the part of the agents of central and local government, in both realms, that it might be easier to keep the peace behind the border line than across it. Certainly the international cooperation embodied in a day of truce was not something to be relied upon. March officials might themselves be cattle thieves; it was not surprising that in 1357 William Lord Douglas should have applied to Edward III rather than to the warden of the English

66 E 28/18 (unnumbered).

67 British Library, Vespasian F vii, no.105.

68 A.P.S., i, 714.

69 W. Fraser, *The Douglas Book* (Edinburgh, 1885), iii, 433.

70 Rae, *Adminstration of the Scottish Frontier*, 60–61; *Rotuli Parliamentorum*, v, 267.

71 C 47/22/7, no.67; *Calendar of Patent Rolls, 1446–1452*, 58.

west march for redress for raids into Eskdale by Sir Robert de Tilliol and Sir Thomas de Lucy, since the relevant warden was that very same Sir Thomas de Lucy of whom Lord Douglas was complaining.[72] And march procedure simply would not work if the will to make it do so was absent. In 1398 it was laid down that bills should be dealt with alternately, first a Scots one, then an English.[73] In 1426 the Scots brought proceedings to a standstill by demanding unrealistically high compensation for the theft of six oxen and refusing to go on to the next case until it was paid.[74] Yet the fact that Anglo-Scottish march procedure did not go the way of that of Gascony, and in spite of the survival of some archaic elements managed to adapt itself to changing circumstances, often marred but sometimes made effective by politics, indicates that it was something better than useless. Even if the tone employed be that of faint praise, it may still be suggested that the laws of the marches are worth study and respect, for their achievement as well as for the aspirations they embodied.

72 E 36/190, fo. 1.

73 Rymer, *Foedera*, viii, 54–57.

74 E 28/47 (unnumbered).

Chapter 4

Forethocht Felony, Malice Aforethought and the Classification of Homicide

W. David H. Sellar

Lord Morton of Shuna: There seems to be a reluctance on the part of English legal minds to engage in a moral judgement so to speak, and bring in wickedness and evil intent. Does that in your view represent an essential element in the crime of murder?
Lord Emslie (Lord Justice General): I think it does certainly in murder. We have not, for centuries, found it difficult to invite juries to make what people call a moral judgement.

(House of Lords Select Committee Report, 1989)[1]

The mental element in the crime of murder, and the meaning to be attached to the term 'malice aforethought', is a topical issue in modern English law. A succession of controversial cases, notably *D.P.P.* v. *Smith*[2], *R.* v. *Hyam*[3], *R.* v. *Moloney*[4], and *R.* v. *Hancock and Shankland*[5] have given rise to prolonged debate on the proper definition of murder. In 1988 Lord Goff set out an eloquent plea for law reform in an article entitled 'The Mental Element in the Crime of Murder' in the *Law Quarterly Review* in which he considered Scots as well as English law.[6] This prompted the appointment of a House of Lords Select Committee which heard evidence from both jurisdictions before reporting in 1989.

A parallel debate regarding the medieval English law of homicide, which might equally be entitled 'The Mental Element in the Crime of Murder', has also taken place over the last twenty years or so, leading contributors being J.M. Kaye in the *Law Quarterly Review* for 1967,[7] and Thomas Green in the *Michigan Law Review* for 1975–76.[8] This debate has revolved around

1 *Report of the House of Lords Select Committee on Murder and Life Imprisonment* (HMSO, 1989), iii, 470.

2 [1961] A.C. 290.

3 [1975] A.C. 55.

4 [1985] A.C. 905.

5 [1986] A.C. 455.

6 *Law Quart. Rev.*, civ (1988), 30–59; and see also Glanville Williams, 'The Mens Rea of Murder: Leave it Alone', *Law Quart. Rev.*, cv (1989), 387–97.

7 J.M. Kaye, 'The Early History of Murder and Manslaughter', *Law Quart. Rev.*, lxxxiii (1967), 365–95 and 569–601.

8 T.A. Green, 'The Jury and the English Law of Homicide', *Michigan Law Rev.*, lxxiv (1975–76), 414–99; a revised version appears as chapter 3, 'Judge, Jury, and the Evolution of the Criminal Law in Medieval England' in T.A. Green, *Verdict According to Conscience* (Chicago and London, 1985, 1988).

the exact meaning to be attached to the words 'malice prepense', or 'malice aforethought' in the leading statute of 1390 and the century following. In simple terms the question has been in what circumstances, if any, did 'malice aforethought' carry its obvious and literal meaning of premeditation, and when did it merely signal a deliberate and intentional killing – one committed, it may be, on the spur of the moment without premeditation. The answer to this question affects an understanding of the later development of the law of homicide in England, and in particular the rise of the distinction between murder and manslaughter, and the relationship between both these terms and the concept of 'chance medley'.

It would be both impertinent and unwise for a Scots lawyer to intervene in the English debate, medieval or modern. So far as the modern law is concerned the Scottish witnesses who gave evidence to the Select Committee declared, virtually without exception, that they were satisfied with the existing position under Scottish common law, and were against the drafting of a new statutory definition of the crime of murder for Scotland. Sheriff Gordon, indeed, the author of the leading modern work on Scots criminal law, professed himself puzzled at the need to consider the Scottish definition of murder at all. It was 'almost impossible for a Scottish judge to go astray when directing a jury on the mens rea of murder'.[9] All he had to do was to quote the classic definition of murder in Macdonald's *Criminal Law*, 'Murder is constituted by any wilful act causing the destruction of life, whether intended to kill, or displaying such wicked recklessness as to imply a disposition depraved enough to be regardless of the consequences'.[10] The Select Committee recommended a new statutory definition of the crime of murder for England but, noting the strength of the Scottish evidence in favour of the existing common law, concluded that however desirable uniformity of definition might be in theory they 'could not justify the imposition on Scotland of changes which would be so unwelcome'.[11] They also noted that statutory definition of 'the elusive concept of "wicked recklessness"' would be very difficult, and considered that 'that very flexibility of "wicked recklessness" which is seen as its virtue in Scotland precludes the use of precise and definite language which is normally and rightly expected in a statute defining a criminal offence'.[12]

This essay considers the historical development of the classification of homicide in Scotland, with particular reference to the use of the term 'forethocht felony', the native Scottish equivalent of the English lawyer's

9 *Select Committee Report*, iii, 553.

10 J.H.A. Macdonald, *A Practical Treatise on the Criminal Law of Scotland*, 5th ed. (Edinburgh, 1948), 89. Macdonald, who subsequently became Lord Justice-Clerk, was thirty years old when he first framed this definition in 1866.

11 *Select Committee Report*, i, para. 42.

12 Ibid., para. 43.

'malice aforethought'. As the Scottish evidence has occasionally been brought into play in the medieval English debate, I hope that this study will provide further ammunition for English legal historians. I believe, too, that the study of the historical development of the law of homicide in these islands and, in particular, the changing meanings attached to the term 'murder' prompts reflection on the modern debate as to how far it is desirable or even possible to frame a watertight statutory definition of the crime. Many Scots lawyers will be surprised, incidentally, to learn that the notion of malice aforethought or 'forethocht felony' was part and parcel of their law for over 500 years, as it plays no part in Scots law today.

To return briefly to the history of homicide in England, Maitland believed that '*malice prepense*' in the statute of 1390 did indeed signify premeditation, and that this constituted the essential ingredient in the crime of murder. During the fifteenth century, he argued, premeditated killing or murder could be contrasted with killing in the heat of the moment, deliberately perhaps, but without premeditation. Maitland, like Stephen before him, argued for a continuous development in the law from the statute of 1390, through the fifteenth century, to the distinction made in the sixteenth century between murder and manslaughter. He used Scottish evidence from the fourteenth and fifteenth centuries as a link in the chain of his argument. He also pointed back to the English case of *John de Warenne* v. *Alan de la Zouche* in 1270, in which actings *ex praecogitata malitia* were contrasted with those *ex motu iracundiae* in apparent anticipation of the later distinction between malice aforethought and chance medley or *chaudemellee*.[13]

Maitland's view was generally accepted until the publication in 1967 of Kaye's articles. Kaye set out to prove that *malice prepense* in the statute of 1390 denoted a killing done 'wickedly' or 'wilfully' or 'without lawful excuse', but not necessarily with premeditation. He saw no line of continuous development between the statute of 1390 and the emergence of the distinction between murder and manslaughter in the sixteenth century. In Kaye's view the courts redefined murder and manslaughter in the middle of the sixteenth century 'making the distinction between them depend on the presence or absence of premeditation: thus manslaughter, or chance medley, came to mean a deliberate killing "upon a sudden occasion"'. Manslaughter or chance medley, argued Kaye, had previously described not a deliberate, but 'an accidental killing which took place in the course or furtherance of an act of violence not directed at the person slain or any member of his company'.[14] He also argued that 'chance medley' was distinct, not only etymologically but also conceptually, from '*chaudemellee*' – actings in hot blood.[15] Kaye

[13] F.W. Maitland, 'The Early History of Malice Aforethought' (1883), *Collected Papers* (Cambridge, 1911), i, 304–28. See also Pollock and Maitland, *History of English Law*, 2nd ed. (Cambridge, 1898; rptd. 1968, with an introduction by S.F.C. Milsom), ii, 468–69 and 485–88.

[14] Ubi supra n.7, 369–70.

[15] Ibid., 376.

was unimpressed by the relevance of the Scottish evidence, and regarded *De Warenne* v. *De la Zouche* as an isolated case from which no safe conclusion could be drawn.[16]

Kaye's view became the new orthodoxy. Reservations have been expressed, however, by both Thomas Green and John Baker. Green writes that 'the weight of the evidence suggests that by 1390 *malitia precogitata* had come at least temporarily and in one significant context' – that of homicide – to have the meaning of true malice aforethought.[17] He notes that in a charge to a grand jury in 1403 homicide 'of those who lie in wait *par malice devant pourpense*' was distinguished from homicide *chaude melle*.[18] Green further points out that the term 'chance medley' (*chance melle*) appears as early as 1388, and believes that in the late fourteenth and early fifteenth centuries 'the two terms *chaude melle* (literally "hot medley") and *chance melle* (literally "chance medley") appear to have been interchangeable'.[19] However, he believes that the distinction drawn by the statute of 1390 was relatively shortlived. Baker comments that 'the notion of malice aforethought was not much discussed [in the fifteenth century], and it is uncertain whether it denoted actual premeditation'. 'At least by the end of the fifteenth century', he writes, 'lawyers recognised a second kind of felonious homicide which they called chance-medley'.[20]

Compared with the richness of the English record, the sources for the history of homicide in Scotland in the middle ages are sparse indeed. The most we can hope to discern is the bare outline of the law as set forth in treatises, formularies and statute. We have no record of coroners' indictments, no trial rolls to guide us. The detailed research into the workings of the jury which has proved so fruitful in England, and the distinction which it has been possible to draw even in medieval times between societal and purely legal concepts of crime, including murder, are quite impossible to parallel in Scotland. Thomas Green has exposed the workings of the 'nullifying' jury in medieval English practice, reaching its own decisions in spite of, rather than in accordance with strict law.[21] We may suspect – in view of Green's work we must suspect – that the nullifying jury was at work in Scotland, as in England, but we cannot demonstrate the proposition. More surprising perhaps, at least to an English legal historian, than the poverty of the Scottish record, for that is well known, is the lack of comment on what little does exist. Apart from some able studies on assythment (that is, compensation payable to the kin for mutilation or slaughter), and the blood feud so closely associated with it, little has been written about the development of the law of homicide in Scotland to

16 Ibid., 374–75.

17 Ubi supra n.8, 463 and n.182.

18 Ibid., 467 and n.200.

19 Ibid., 467 and n.200.

20 J.H. Baker, *Reports of Sir John Spelman*, ii, Selden Society, cxiv (1978), Introduction, *304*.

21 T.A. Green, *Verdict According to Conscience*, especially chapter two, 'Societal Concepts of Criminal Liability and Jury Nullification of the Law in the Thirteenth and Fourteenth Centuries'.

set against the veritable torrent of research and writing recently in England.[22] This essay should, therefore, be regarded as tentative.

The prominence of assythment and the blood feud in the Scottish record points to a significant difference between the operation of the law of homicide in Scotland and in England in the later middle ages. Although much in the early Scots law of homicide was clearly borrowed from Anglo-Norman England, including trial by jury and the process of indictment, in Scotland the crown's right to prosecute for homicide was circumscribed for centuries by the right of the kin of the victim to seek vengeance or, alternatively, to accept assythment. Even after the crown's right to proceed, regardless of the wishes of the kin, was clearly recognized towards the end of the sixteenth century, the right to assythment – known also, significantly, as 'kinboot' – remained in cases where the death penalty had not been exacted; and a full pardon, or remission, from the crown remained conditional on satisfying the just demands of the kin of the deceased for compensation.[23] Examples of assythment occur with some regularity until the middle of the eighteenth century, and it was only in 1976, after a belated attempt at revival in the case of *M'Kendrick* v. *Sinclair*,[24] which was argued up to the House of Lords, that the action of assythment was finally abolished in Scots law.[25] The operation of the law of homicide in Scotland, therefore, involved a delicate counterpoint between public and private right long after private considerations ceased to play any part in English law.

As is well known, the word 'murder' is cognate with Germanic 'mord' and Scandinavian 'morð' signifying a secret killing; and there can be little doubt that 'murder' was first used in Scotland as in England in this sense. In Celtic law too, to judge from the Irish evidence, a secret killing was regarded as a particularly heinous form of homicide.[26] This early meaning of 'murder' is to be understood against the background of the blood feud and private vengeance. It antedates public justice. All killing potentially gave rise to a blood feud or claim for compensation. A secret killing was particularly reprehensible because – among other reasons – the kin of the murdered man would not know against whom to seek redress. This early definition of murder as a secret killing long survived the growth of the king's peace and the recognition of 'pleas of the crown' in both Scotland and England.

The term *murdrum* first appears on record in Scotland in the reign of William

[22] See particularly J. Wormald, 'Bloodfeud, Kindred and Government in Early Modern Scotland', *Past and Present*, lxxxvii (1980), 54–97; and also R. Black, 'Historical Survey of Delictual Liability in Scotland for Personal Injuries and Death – Part I, Early History', *Comp. and Int. Law Jour. of Southern Africa*, viii (1975), 46–70; C.H.W. Gane, 'The Effect of a Pardon in Scots Law', *Jurid. Rev., N.S.*, xxv (1980), 18–46; and K. Brown, *Bloodfeud in Scotland, 1573–1625* (Edinburgh, 1986).

[23] See, in addition to the authorities cited in n.22, J. Irvine Smith and Ian Macdonald, 'Criminal Law', *Introduction to Scottish Legal History*, Stair Society, xx (Edinburgh, 1958), 280–301; and J. Irvine Smith, *Justiciary Cases 1624–1650*, ii, Stair Society, xxvii (Edinburgh, 1972), Introduction.

[24] 1972 S.C. (H.L.) 25.

[25] Damages (Scotland) Act 1976, s. 6.

[26] Fergus Kelly, *Guide to Early Irish Law* (Dublin, 1988), 128.

I (1165–1214) when it appears as one of the pleas of the crown, excepted from the grant of Annandale to Robert de Brus: 'Exceptis regalibus que ad regalitatem meam spectant Scilicet . . . Causa de murdra'.[27] At this time it presumably bore its original meaning of a secret killing. The earliest known classification of homicide in Scots law occurs in the treatise known as *Regiam Majestatem*, once thought to date from the first half of the thirteenth century, but now dated later, probably to the years shortly after 1318. This section of the *Regiam* is lifted almost verbatim from 'Glanvill's' *De Legibus*, compiled over a century previously, and reflects the ancient use of the term 'murder' to denote a secret killing:

> Duo autem genera sunt homicidii: unum quod dicitur murdrum quod nullo vidente vel sciente clam perpetratur . . . secundum genus homicidii est illud quod dicitur simplex homicidium.[28]

'Murder', therefore, is contrasted in the *Regiam* with 'simple' homicide.

The next evidence for the classification of homicide in Scotland comes from two well known statutes of 1369/70 and 1371/72. The 1370 statute of David II enacted that the king should not grant a remission for homicide until an inquest had determined whether the killing had been committed *per murthyr vel per praecogitatam malitiam*.[29] The statute of Robert II, two years later – perhaps rather statutes, as there are a number of separate provisions – follows the same classification, and enacts that when homicide has been committed an inquest or assize should determine whether the killing was committed *ex certo et deliberato proposito vel per forthouchfelony sive murthir vel ex calore iracundiae viz chaudemellee*.[30] The 1372 statute also uses the shorter formulation of *per forthouchfelony vel per murthir* in contrast to *per chaudemellee*: if the assize finds forethocht felony or murder then sentence is to be carried out without delay; if, on the other hand, it finds *chaudmellee* the accused is to have the exceptions and defences already permitted by law and custom – 'habebit dilaciones et defensiones legitimas et debitas per leges Regni et consuetudines hactenus approbatas'. The statute continues that in the case of a killer seeking sanctuary an assize should determine whether the deed was *per murthir sive per forthouchfelony* or whether it was *per chaudemelle*. Only in the latter case should benefit of sanctuary be allowed.

Two near contemporary formularies, the Bute manuscript and Formulary E, show that these statutes were no dead letter. Each contains a style directing the holding of an inquest to determine whether someone had killed another by

[27] *Regesta Regum Scottorum II: The Acts of William I*, G.W.S. Barrow, ed. (Edinburgh, 1971), 179.

[28] *Regiam Majestatem*, Lord Cooper, ed., Stair Society, xi (Edinburgh, 1947), iv, 5; (iv, 4 in the A[cts of the] P[arliaments of] S[cotland], T. Thomson and Cosmo Innes, ed. (Record Commission, 1814–75), 633. And see *Glanvill*, G.D.H. Hall, ed. (1965), xiv, 3.

[29] A.P.S., i, 509.

[30] A.P.S., i, 547–48.

forethocht felony or not. The texts are nearly identical and mirror the words of the statute of 1372:

> Inquisitio si talis interfecit talem per forthought felony vel non. Jacobus dei gratia vicecomiti et balliuis suis salutem. Mandamus etc. quatinus per probos et fideles homines patrie per quos rei veritas melius sciri poterit magno sacramento interveniente diligentem et fidelem inquisitionem fieri faciatis si talis lator presencium talem *ex iracundie inconsulto calore nec per murthir nec per forthocht felony interfecit. Et si et in quantum rei alias dedicit* [sic] *occasionem et causam sue mortis ex predicto inconsulto iracundie calore vel aliter*. Et que et quales circumstancie intervenerunt in morte et causa mortis dicti R. Et quid per dictam inquisitionem diligenter et fideliter factam esse inveneritis sub sigillo vestro vicecomitis et sub sigillis eorum qui dictam inquisicionem intererunt faciendum ad capellam nostram mittatis et hoc breve.[31]

The wording of the rubric, incidentally, clearly incorporating the category of 'murder' within forethocht felony, shows that the *vel* and *sive* occurring in David II's statute between murthyr and *praecogitatam malitiam*, and in Robert II's statute between *ex certo et deliberato proposito, forthouchfelony* and *murthir* are conjunctive.

At least two fifteenth century Scottish statutes also mention forethocht felony and contrast it with actions on a 'suddante' or *chaudemellee*. The first, an Act of James I in 1425, is concerned not so much with homicide specifically but more generally with breaches of the king's peace.[32] Should anyone complain that the king's peace has been broken upon him, it runs, the appropriate officer of the law is to summon both parties and inquire diligently and without favour whether the deed was done upon forethocht felony or 'throw suddande chaudemellay'. 'Ande gif it be fundyn forthocht

[31] Inquest [to determine] whether one killed another through forethocht felony or not.

James by the grace of God to his sheriff and bailies greeting. We command etc. that you cause a diligent and faithful inquest to be held, under application of the great oath, by good and faithful men of the country by whom the truth of the matter can be better known to determine whether the bearer of these presents [i.e. the petitioner] killed another *in anger in the heat of the moment and not through murder or forethocht felony; and whether and in what respect he [the deceased] gave him occasion and cause for his death arising out of anger in the heat of the moment foresaid or otherwise*; and what were the general circumstances of the death and the cause of the death of the said R. And send whatever you find transacted diligently and faithfully by the said inquest along with this brieve to our chapel under your own seal as sheriff and under the seals of those who served on the said inquest.

(In translating I have utilized Bute's 'et si et in quantum ipse ei alias dederit', which is clearly preferable to the 'et si et in quantum rei alias dedicit' of Formulary E).

The text is taken from *Formulary E: Scottish Letters and Brieves, 1286–1424*, A.A.M. Duncan, ed. (Univ. of Glasgow, Scottish History Dept. Occasional Papers, 1976), no.14. The italics are mine. Formulary E is Edinburgh University Library MS Borland no.207. Professor Duncan describes this late fifteenth century manuscript 'as evidently a copy of an earlier MS, the date of which is indicated by inclusion of legislation of 1424 and the absence of any later material'. This earlier material was itself composite. Compare Bute MS – *Register of Brieves*, Lord Cooper, ed., Stair Society, x (Edinburgh, 1946), no.68. Duncan dates Bute to *c.* 1400.

[32] A.P.S., ii, 9.

felony', the statute continues, 'the party salbe chalangyt incontinent of the kingis pece breking be the officiaris of the lawe the quhilkis sall ger the party hurte be fullely assythit [compensated] efter the quantite of the skaithe [harm] that he has sustenyt'. Thereafter the malefactor is to be in the king's mercy as regards life and limb. If, on the other hand, 'the trespass be done of suddande chauldemelly the party scathit sall folowe [pursue the action] and the party trespassande sall defende eftir the coursis of the auld lawis of the realme'. This last sentence is in line with the provision in the 1372 statute that if the inquest finds *chaudemellee* the defender is to have the exceptions and defences allowed by law and custom.

The second statute dates from 1469 in James III's reign.[33] The preamble complains of 'gret slachteris quhilkis has bene Richt commone ymang the kingis liegiis now and of late baith of forethocht felony and of suddante'. Many of those who have committed slaughter hope to be granted sanctuary, but the law does not permit those who have committed 'forthocht felony *tanquam Incediator viarum et per Industriam*' to enjoy sanctuary. An assise is therefore to determine whether there has been forethocht felony or not, and only if it finds 'suddante' is sanctuary to be granted. As Lord Cooper pointed out, the statute's *tanquam Incediator viarum et per Industriam* follows the Vulgate's rendering of Exodus xxi, 14 which speaks of a manslayer coming *tanquam insidiator et per industriam*.[34] This passage would have been familiar to all canon lawyers as it heads the treatment of homicide in *Decretals* V, xii. According to the rubric there, the incorrigible manslayer (*homicida incorrigibilis*) is to be handed over to the secular arm to be put to death – *ut moriatur* – Exodus xxi, 14 being cited as authority for this proposition.

It is clear then that from the last third of the fourteenth century at latest a new classification of homicide was beginning to replace the division between murder and simple homicide found in *Regiam Majestatem*. Or rather, the new classification came to exist alongside the old; it did not entirely supersede it. The term 'murder' began to extend its ambit and move from its older and more restricted meaning of a secret killing to cover all killing done with forethocht felony. Killing by forethocht felony was contrasted with killing in the heat of the moment, *chaudemellee*, killing which – or so it would appear – was not premeditated. This second type of killing, although clearly culpable, was not viewed with such outright disfavour as murder: unlike murderers, killers by *chaudemellee* were not excluded from benefit of sanctuary, nor necessarily from a royal pardon. This new classification has moved away from the world of the blood feud towards a public criminal law. The king's peace extends over all the land. All killing becomes technically criminal. The mental element in homicide – never entirely disregarded – becomes more important. Which killers are to be allowed to claim sanctuary? To whom shall the king extend his pardon? Cases of pure misadventure and self-defence certainly, but what else besides?

33 A.P.S., ii, 95–96.

34 Cooper, op. cit., 255; see also Maitland, 'Malice Aforethought', 326–27.

There is a further example of the use of the term forethocht felony in fifteenth century Scots which is very instructive. It occurs in Sir Gilbert of the Haye's translation into Scots (*c.* 1456) of Honoré Bonet's *Arbre des Batailles*.[35] Bonet lived *c.* 1340–1410 and his *Arbre des Batailles* is a celebrated early work on what would now be termed public international law. In c. 3 Bonet discusses the morality of a challenge to combat as a means of settling a dispute. He aims to show that such a challenge is expressly forbidden by all laws, God's and man's. First, he says, it is against the law of nature. Here he is in Haye's rather free translation:

> And first and formast, I preve it be resoun naturale. For gage of bataill cummys ay [comes always] of *forethocht felouny*. Bot naturaly all maner of creature naturale has a passioun of nature that is callit the first movement; that is, quhen a man or beste is *sudaynly* sterte, thair naturale inclinacioun gevis thame of thair complexioun to a brethe, and a *sudayn hete of ire of vengeance* quhilk efterwart stanchis efter that hete. *Bot bataill taking cumis of lang forset and forethocht purpos of malice that is nocht naturale to man.*[36]

This is a most valuable passage, for not only does it duplicate the terms of art used in the law, but it gives an insight into the mentality, the way of thinking, which distinguished between slaughter 'on a suddanty', or *chaudemellee*, and forethocht felony.

At this point it is worth noting in parenthesis that Lord Cooper, in the notes to his edition of *Regiam Majestatem*, interpreted the development of the law of homicide in Scotland rather differently.[37] Partly, it would seem, through misdating the style which appears in the Bute formulary, Cooper placed the first appearance of the distinction between murder and forethocht felony, on the one hand, and homicide *ex iracundiae inconsulto calore* on the other, in the thirteenth century – a hundred years or more too early. He then continued, 'It is likely enough that these humane distinctions tended to become blunted and obscured during the Wars [of Independence with England], and it may be on this account that the matter had to be taken up afresh under French influence two generations later'. He then pointed to the French *Ordonnance* of 1356 which classified the more serious forms of homicide as those *perpetrés de mauvaiz agait, par mauvaise volonté et par deliberacion*,[38] and suggested that David II brought back from France the ideas which prompted the Scottish legislation of 1370 and 1372. Even if one lays aside the misdating of the Bute style, this scenario is quite speculative and would need considerable further supporting evidence to be rendered credible. In fact, it is the close correspondence between Scots and English law which

[35] *Gilbert of the Haye's Prose Manuscript*, i, *The Buke of the Law of Armys*, J.H. Stevenson, ed., Scottish Text Society, xliv (Edinburgh, 1901).

[36] Ibid., c. cx, 256 (my italics).

[37] Cooper, op. cit., 255.

[38] *Ordonnances des Rois de France* (Paris, 1723–1849), iii, 129.

is really remarkable.[39] The parallels with France are best understood in the context of a wider European background.

The distinction drawn in the law of homicide between forethocht felony and *chaudemellee* had a very long run in Scots law, and was only finally laid to rest by Baron Hume's great work on the criminal law at the end of the eighteenth century. It can be traced in legal writings and, from the early sixteenth century onwards, in actual cases.

Sir James Balfour, writing towards the end of the sixteenth century, notes (here following *Regiam Majestatem*):

> Thai ar twa kindis of man-slauchter, the ane is callit murther, and the uther callit simple slauchter. Murther is done privatlie, na man seand nor knawand the samin bot allanerlie [only] the slayer and his complices, swa that the cry of the people followis not suddenlie thairupon, as is usit in the law of slauchter.

But he also writes that 'na slauchter done be chance or chaud-melle, sould be callit murther; for all murther is committit be foirthocht felonie'.[40]

In his *De Verborum Significatione*, published in 1597,[41] Sir John Skene notes under 'FORTHOCHT':

> FORTHOCHT fellony, *praecogitata malitia*, quhilk is don and committed wittinglie and willinglie, after deliberation and set purpose, and is different from *chaudemelle*;

and under 'CHAUD-MELLE':

> In latin Rixa, an hoat suddaine tuilzie or debaite, quhilk is opponed as contrar to forthoucht fellonie, vide *Melletum*;

and under 'MELLETUM':

> Ane French word *Melle*, dissension, strife, debate . . . And in the actes of Parliament, and practique of this realme, *Chaud-mella* is ane faulte or trespasse, quhilk is committed be ane hoate suddaintie, and nocht of set purpose or *praecogitata malitia*.

Skene printed an interesting but almost entirely neglected tract 'Of Crimes and Judges in Criminall Causes' along with his English translation of *Regiam Majestatem* in 1609. Here we find 'Of Slauchter – Manslauchter, committed voluntarlie be forethought-felonie or casually be chaudemelle, generally is punished be death . . .'.[42] The juxtaposition of 'voluntary' and 'casual' in this passage is of particular interest. It points forward, as will be seen, to the Act of 1649 and to Hume, but also back to the civilians and the canon law.

39 For a reassessment which builds on the work of several scholars see W.D.H. Sellar, 'The Common Law of Scotland and the Common Law of England', *The British Isles 1100–1500: Comparisons, Contrasts and Connections*, R.R. Davies, ed. (Edinburgh, 1988), 82–99.

40 *Balfour's Practicks*, ii, P.G.B. McNeill, ed., Stair Society, xxii (Edinburgh, 1963), 512.

41 Sir John Skene, *De Verborum Sigificatione: The Exposition of the Terms and Difficil Wordes, conteined in the Foure Buikes of Regiam Majestatem etc.* (Edinburgh, 1597).

42 *Of Crime, and Judges in Criminall Causes conform to the Lawes of this Realme*, 2.6.1.

Irvings v. *Bell* in 1646 illustrates the use of the various terms in practice.[43] The case concerned the scope of a royal remission from 'suddane slauchter and killing'. There was much discussion of *Regiam Majestatem* and the old statutes on homicide; and the contrast was made between 'murthour quod factum fuit per precogitatam malitiam' and 'naikit slauchter be chaudmella per rixam vel per infortuniam'.[44] The term 'naikit slauchter' is, of course, an echo of the *Regiam's 'simplex homicidium'*. The two classifications – the older distinction between murder and simple homicide, and the later contrast between forethocht felony and *chaudemellee* – seemed to co-exist side by side reasonably well in practice, the term 'murder' being increasingly equated with forethocht felony, although its original meaning of a secret killing was long remembered. It would have been quite logical had Scots law developed a further classification in the sixteenth century, based on provocation, corresponding to the division between 'murder' and 'manslaughter' in contemporary England, but this did not happen. Instead, all was thrown into confusion by a further statute, passed initially in 1649, and re-enacted in 1661.[45]

The main purpose of this statute was to detail the types of homicide which should not carry the death penalty. It introduced to the statute book the term 'casual homicide', already encountered in the tract printed by Skene in 1609:

> *Act anent severall Degrees of Casuall homicide*
>
> The Estats of parliament etc for removeall of all questiounes and doubts that may arise heereafter in Criminall persuits for slaughter Statuts and ordaines that the cases of homicide after following viz Casuall homicide Homicide in laufull defence and Homicide committed upon theives and robbers breaking hous in the night or incase of masterfull Depredatioun or in the persute of Denounced or Declared rebellis for Criminall causes or of such who assist and Defend the rebellis by armes and by force opposes the persute and apprehending of thame whilk shall happin to fall out in tyme comeing nor any of thame shall not be punished by death And that notwithstanding of any Lawis or acts of parliament or any practik made heiretofore or observed in punishing of slaughter Bot that the Manslayer in any of the cases aforesaid shall be assoilzied [absolved] from any Criminall persute pursued against him for his lyfe for the said slaughter before any Judge Criminall within this kingdome . . .

Unfortunately, the statute omitted to define what was meant by 'casual homicide'. Standing the previous legislation, which still remained in force, save where specifically altered by the statute, a number of different interpretations were clearly possible. A killing *chaudemellee* might be said to be a killing by chance, *casu*, in so far as there had been no premeditation or forethocht felony.

[43] *Justiciary Cases 1624–1650*, iii, J. Irvine Smith, ed., Stair Society, xxviii (Edinburgh, 1974), 583–88.

[44] Ibid., 585–86.

[45] A.P.S., vi (2), 173, c. 96: an Act of Charles II, passed on 13 February 1649 (King's Printer's edition 1649 c. 19); re-enacted in 1661 after the Restoration (A.P.S., vii, 203, c. 217; Glendook c. 22).

Was such a killing, therefore, 'casual homicide'? If so, *chaudemellee* would not carry the death penalty. Alternatively, did casual homicide refer only to killing by chance in the quite different sense of mere accident, or pure misadventure? If so, killing *chaudemellee* was a capital offence. And what about a death caused by culpable negligence? These and other points of interpretation were raised in case after case, and the relevant passages in *Regiam Majestatem* and the fourteenth century statutes trotted out again and again.

In *Dalmahoy or Ralstoun* v. *Mason*, for example, in 1674 the deceased, Ralstoun, had apparently been drunk and had provoked and assaulted the pannel [accused], Mason.[46] Mason retaliated and beat Ralstoun who fell and cut open his head on the edge of a bunker or chest. Ralstoun, who in addition to being drunk was said to have been aged and infirm and recently recovered from sickness, took no proper care of the wound but stayed 'in frosty weather for three hours after'. He died some time later from 'defluxion and swelling' rather than directly from the wound. A number of possible defences were clearly available to the pannel on the facts, but the case reveals considerable uncertainty about terminology. The pannel denied 'precogitate malice' and forethocht felony. If the wound was his fault he pleaded either casual homicide or self-defence. The widow insisted on 'simple slauchter' and said that casual homicide was only relevant where the effect was not and could not have been foreseen. The Lord Advocate, acting with the widow and children of the deceased, argued that the defence of casual homicide did not apply in that *culpa casui precedens* the pannel *causam rixae dedit* to the defunct, and after giving him the wound pursued him further.[47] The pannel then denied *culpa precedens* and maintained that the killing was 'clearly casual being neither intended not expected to be repute deliberate and resolved'.[48] The court found the libel [indictment] relevant only to *poenam extraordinariam* – that is, they excluded the death penalty – and remitted the case and defences to an assize. The assize found self-defence 'all in one voice except one' [!].[49]

In the course of time the balance tilted towards interpreting casual homicide to exclude *chaudemellee*. Thus Sir George Mackenzie in his *Matters Criminal*, published in 1678, defines casual homicide in these terms: '*Homicidium casuale* is when a Man is killed casually, without either the Fault or Design of the Killer', and 'Casual Slaughter, or Homicide, then, is which is occasioned by Mistake and just Ignorance'.[50] He notes, however, that 'Slaughter and Murder did of old differ': murder, properly so called, was committed upon

[46] *Justiciary Records, 1661–1678*, ii, W.G. Scott-Moncrieff, ed., Scottish History Society, First Series, xlix (Edinburgh, 1905), 287–94.

[47] Ibid., 292.

[48] Ibid., 293.

[49] Ibid., 294.

[50] Sir George Mackenzie, *Laws and Customs of Scotland in Matters Criminal*, (1678), I, xi, 6 in *Collected Works*, ii (Edinburgh, 1722), 98.

forethocht felony, in contrast with '*Chaudmella*, or Slaughter committed upon Suddenty'. 'All casual Slaughter', he writes, 'was of old comprehended under the Word *Chaudmella*'.[51] Mackenzie then discusses the wording of the 1649 Act and points out that the definition of casual homicide there is ambiguous and inadequate in that its relationship to *chaudmellee*, and generally to '*homicidium culposum*', is not clear. However, he writes that William Douglas's case determined 'that in our Law, though Murder was not at first designed, yet if it was designed the Time the Stroke was given, the Killer is guilty of Murder: That Premeditation is requisite to make Murder capital, being only such as *antecedit actum, licet non congressum*'.[52] In other words, killing *chaudemellee* should not fall under the protection of the Act.

Mackenzie contrasts 'murder' and 'slaughter', but it is clear that the unqualified term 'slauchter', or 'manslauchter', was used in a general way – as for example by Balfour and Skene in the passages quoted above – to cover the entire field of homicide. Lord Kames, too, uses 'manslaughter' in a general sense in 1757 in his *Statute Law of Scotland* where he writes of 'murder, which is manslaughter upon forethought felony'.[53] In English law, of course, the term 'manslaughter' came to be used in the sixteenth century in a narrower sense and was distinguished from 'murder'; yet it is interesting to note Baker's comment, 'It might have been more logical if the English word had been retained for the genus, and "murder" and "chance-medley" used for the species'.[54]

Chaudemellee was referred to in 1752 in one of the most notorious murder trials in eighteenth century Scotland: the 'Appin murder', immortalized by Robert Louis Stevenson in *Kidnapped*, in which James Stewart of the Glens was charged with the murder of 'the Red Fox', Colin Campbell of Glenure. In the course of the trial, Stewart's counsel, Thomas Millar, said 'And, first, it will be observed, that the murder is not said to have been committed from sudden passion, or *chaudmelle*, as the law expresses it, but to have been premeditated and resolved upon for some days before it was committed. Now, to render malice of so high a nature probable, some very strong ground or cause ought to have been assigned for it'.[55] He went on to refer to *Regiam Majestatem* and the various statutes.

The old classification was finally consigned to well-deserved oblivion by Baron David Hume in his magisterial *Commentaries on Crime* (1797). Hume distinguished four categories of homicide 'though perhaps not fully distinguished in our practice by appropriated names': aggravated murder, murder, culpable homicide, and homicide 'free of all blame', this last

[51] Ibid., I, xi, 11.

[52] Ibid., I, xi, 12.

[53] Henry Home, Lord Kames, *Statute Law of Scotland* (Edinburgh, 1757), 204.

[54] Baker, op. cit. n.20, *305*.

[55] *Scots Magazine* (1752), 231.

comprising casual homicide and justifiable homicide.[56] With the exception of the first, these categories are, broadly speaking, still in use today. Hume noted that 'casual homicide' had sometimes been taken to include *chaudemellee* in the past, but considered that it was more appropriate to restrict the term to 'pure misadventure without any act of the killer's will'.[57] Of murder he said, 'The characteristic of this sort of homicide is that it is done wilfully and out of malice aforethought'.[58] Note that in Hume the polite English 'malice aforethought' has taken over from the native forethocht felony. After Hume the familiar question arose again as to whether 'malice aforethought' necessarily involved premeditation, or whether it merely signified a deliberate and wilful killing. The point was finally settled in favour of the latter in the case of *Charles MacDonald* in 1867.[59] After that the term 'malice aforethought' was otiose and gradually passed out of Scots law after a life of 500 years or more.

The Scottish evidence may be sparse but it seems clear enough. It points to the consistent and uninterrupted use of the term malice aforethought to describe a premeditated, rather than a merely deliberate homicide, from at least the later fourteenth until the eighteenth century. The actual legal term of art changes from the Latin *praecogitata malitia* of the statute of 1370, through the Scots 'forethocht felony', to the more familiar 'malice aforethought'. Maitland thought the Scottish evidence was relevant to an understanding of the development of the English law of homicide. Kaye was not convinced. He wrote that the evidence of the statutes of David II and Robert II should not be pushed too far in view of the generally accepted belief that Scots law at this period owed more to France and the civil law than to England.[60] Here Kaye relies too much on Lord Cooper's distinctly speculative account of the development of homicide noted above. There is, *per contra*, good reason to believe that the impact of the Anglo-Norman law on most areas of Scots law, including the criminal law, was a lasting one – or, at any rate that it lasted until long after the Wars of Independence put an end to amicable relations between Scotland and England. For my part, I am at least as impressed by the English as by the French connection, and, like Maitland, would be inclined to view the English case of *De Warenne* v. *De la Zouche* in 1270, dismissed by Kaye, with its reference to *praecogitata malitia*, as part of the jigsaw.[61]

Kaye points to the dearth of early recorded cases in Scotland. From the standpoint of the richer English record this is undoubtedly true; yet the burden of the Scottish evidence is clear. Kaye also believed there to be a danger of

[56] Baron David Hume, *Commentaries on the Law of Scotland respecting Crimes* (Edinburgh, 1797), i, 282.

[57] Hume discusses the 1649 Act and *chaudemellee* at i, 369–76. The quotation is from p.283.

[58] Ibid., 390.

[59] (1867) 5 Irv. 525.

[60] Op. cit. n.7, 376.

[61] In fact, the wording of the French *Ordonnance* of 1356 (*perpetrés de mauvaiz agait, par mauvaise volonté et par deliberacion*) seems closer to the 1390 statute's *par agait, assaut ou malice prepense* than to any Scottish parallel.

making a false analogy in the later middle ages between the 'chaudemellee' of Scots law and the English 'chance medley'.[62] Since Kaye wrote, however, as already noted, Green has pointed to the use of '*chance melle*' in England as early as 1388, and suggested that the terms *chaudemelle* and *chance melle* (or *medley*) were at that stage interchangeable.[63] It is curious, certainly, that *chaudmellee* should appear on the Scottish record in 1372, sixteen years before the first recorded English use of *chance melle*. I doubt, however, if Kaye is right to suggest that the term 'chance medley' would have been 'meaningless' to the judges of Edward III.[64]

The correspondence between Scots law, where the distinction between forethocht felony and *chaudemellee* appears already in 1370, and English law can hardly be accidental; and the borrowing is more likely to have been from English law to Scots rather than vice-versa.[65] The meaning to be attached to 'malice aforethought' or 'malice prepense' in the English law of homicide in the late fourteenth and fifteenth centuries should surely be re-examined, the more so given the light which Bonet's *Arbre des Batailles* throws on contemporary patterns of thought about homicide.

Be that as it may, the divergence between the later Scots and English law of homicide is instructive. The widening of the meaning of 'murder' to extend from a secret killing to all cases of forethocht felony or malice aforethought was related in both jurisdictions to a strengthening of public justice and an increasing emphasis on the mental element in the crime of murder. In the sixteenth century the English courts advanced a stage further by developing the defence of provocation and distinguishing between 'murder' and 'manslaughter'. The Scottish courts did not follow suit; nor indeed did Scots law develop the exception of 'benefit of clergy' to temper the strict severity of the law and further develop the classification of homicide, as happened in England. The Scottish debate on the place of the doctrines of provocation and self-defence and their relationship to the mental element in homicide did not gather momentum until the later seventeenth century. By then the Act of 1649 and increasing civilian influence determined that Scots law would follow a different course from England.

The term 'casual homicide', already present in Skene's tract of 1609, and sanctioned by the statute of 1649, has been in regular use in Scots law ever since. Sir George Mackenzie, and later Hume, devote some space to its proper definition. Hume divided homicide into murder, culpable homicide, casual homicide and justifiable homicide. Gerald Gordon classifies homicide in modern Scots law as criminal or non-criminal: criminal homicide

[62] Above, at n.15. It is perhaps worth noting that Sir James Balfour in Scotland equated chance medley and *chaudemellee* (above at n.40) just as did Sir Edward Coke in England.

[63] Above, at nn.17–19.

[64] Op. cit. n.7, 583.

[65] A closer examination of the various terms of art used in England and Scotland in connection with homicide than has been possible in this paper might help to settle the issue.

comprises 'murder' and 'culpable homicide', the latter being either 'voluntary' or 'involuntary'; non-criminal homicide is either 'casual' or 'justifiable'.[66] What is the source of these terms of art: 'casual' and 'voluntary', 'culpable' and 'justifiable'? The answer again will surprise modern Scots lawyers. These terms all derive, at one remove or another, from the medieval canon law; more particularly from Book V, chapter xii of the *Decretals*, compiled by St. Raymund of Peñafort for Pope Gregory IX and promulgated in 1234. This chapter has already been mentioned as the likely source of the quotation from Exodus xxi in the Scots Act of 1469.[67] It is entitled *De Homicidio Voluntario vel Casuali* and is full of decisions on the nature of 'casual homicide' and the role played by fault or *culpa*. Earlier still the canonist Bernard of Pavia (d. 1213) had already divided homicide into four categories – *iustitia, necessitate, casu et voluntate* – discussing each at some length.[68] The same St. Raymund who compiled the *Decretals* also compiled the *Summa de Casibus Poenitentiae*, which has been identified as a key source for Bracton's treatment of homicide in thirteenth century English law.[69] And so the wheel turns full circle.[70]

Although I have argued that the expression 'forethocht felony', or 'malice aforethought', has quite definite overtones of premeditation in the medieval law, the final word must be one of caution. It would be a mistake to attach too strict or precise a meaning to the various terms discussed: terms such as 'casual', 'deliberate' and 'malice aforethought'. These terms all have several shades of meaning, some of which overlap. Which precise nuance is to be attached will depend on circumstance, and the circumstances of homicide are infinitely varied. The perception of what constitutes the most heinous form of homicide, to which the name 'murder' can properly be applied, varies from generation to generation. If a study of the historical background suggests anything, it is that there is little merit in attempting too precise a definition of murder, particularly where a jury is concerned. Gerald Gordon has noted for modern Scots law that there is 'no academically satisfactory definition of murder', nothing to delimit murder clearly from culpable homicide.[71] The same, apparently, might be said of modern English law. There the *mens rea* of murder is 'malice aforethought'; this, of course, being now a technical term which need no longer infer either real malice or premeditation. Murder is an unlawful killing with malice aforethought. Manslaughter is an unlawful killing

66 G.H. Gordon, *Criminal Law of Scotland*, 2nd ed. (Edinburgh, 1978), para. 23–09.

67 Above, at n.34.

68 For Bernard of Pavia, see appendix ii to *Bracton and Azo*, F.W. Maitland, ed., Selden Society, viii (1894).

69 F. Schulz, 'Bracton and Raymond of Penafort', *Law Quart. Rev.*, lxi (1945), 286–92.

70 The main channel of influence so far as later Scots law was concerned was undoubtedly civilian. Sir George Mackenzie (*Matters Criminal*, I, xi, 1), for example, notes that the civilians divide homicide into four categories: homicide committed casually; in defence; culpably; and 'wilfully' [i.e. 'voluntarily']. English law was heavily influenced at the outset by the canon law. The topic is a large one and is clearly worth further study.

71 Gordon, para. 23–19.

without malice aforethought.[72] There is no reason to believe that medieval definitions were any more clear cut than that. It is as well that the jury should have considerable scope. The rise in convictions for murder as against culpable homicide or manslaughter after the the abolition of capital punishment in 1965 tells its own story.

[72] See, for example, J.C. Smith and B. Hogan, *Criminal Law*, 6th ed. (1988), 327–28.

Chapter 5

The Structure of English Common Law in the Seventeenth Century*

David J. Seipp

By the year 1600, English common lawyers had carried on for more than three centuries without a comprehensive, systematic treatise describing the whole of their law.[1] By 1600, many of them had begun to see the need for such a work. At this time lawyers were producing a greater volume of legal writing than before, introducing new forms of legal literature, and devoting more of their attention to problems they saw affecting the common law as a whole:[2] problems of defining the common law, of setting it apart from other bodies of law, of describing the legitimate sources of the common law, of explaining the foundations of its authority, of articulating the general principles that underlay its specific applications, and of discerning an orderly classification of the subject matter of law. In short lawyers and scholars joined in the call for a 'method', what now would be called a 'structure' for the common law 'method', the acquisition of knowledge through classification.[3]

* The John M. Olin Foundation generously supported the research and writing of this paper. Spelling, capitalization and punctuation of quotations in the text are altered to modern form.

[1] The classic treatises of the late twelfth and thirteenth centuries – *Glanvill*, *Bracton*, *Britton* and *Fleta* – though long out of date, were being published and cited by common lawyers. Editions of *Britton* appeared in (or shortly before) 1540 and in 1640, *Glanvill* in 1554, 1557 and 1604, *Bracton*, the work most directly modelled on Justinian's *Institutes*, in 1569 and 1640, and *Fleta* in 1647. P.H. Winfield, *The Chief Sources of English Legal History* (Cambridge, Mass., 1925), 258–68; D.E.C. Yale, '"Of No Mean Authority": Some Later Uses of Bracton', *On the Laws and Customs of England: Essays in Honor of Samuel E. Thorne*, M.S. Arnold et al., ed. (Chapel Hill, 1981), 285; L.A. Knafla, *Law and Politics in Jacobean England: The Tracts of Lord Chancellor Ellesmere* (Cambridge, 1977), 45, 49, 217–18, 248–49, 326.

[2] On this increase in 'self-conscious' writing about the common law, see, e.g., W.S. Holdsworth, 'The Reception of Roman Law in the Sixteenth Century', *Law Quart. Rev.*, xxvii (1912), 239; P. Stein, 'Continental Influences on English Legal Thought, 1600–1900', *La formazione storica del diritto moderno in Europa* (Florence, 1977), iii, 1107; W.R. Prest, 'The Art of Law and the Law of God: Sir Henry Finch (1558–1625)', *Puritans and Revolutionaries: Essays in Seventeenth-Century History Presented to Christopher Hill*, D. Pennington and K. Thomas, ed. (Oxford, 1978), 115–16.

[3] W.R. Prest, 'The Dialectical Origins of Finch's *Law*', *Cambridge Law Jour.*, xxxvi (1977), 348; L.A. Knafla, 'Ramism and the English Renaissance', *Science, Technology, and Culture in Historical Perspective*, L.A. Knafla, M.S. Staum and T.H.E. Travers, ed. (Calgary, 1976), 34; A.W.B. Simpson, 'The Rise and Fall of the Legal Treatise: Legal Principles and the Forms of Legal Literature', *Univ. Chicago Law Rev.*, xlviii (1981), 649; B.J. Shapiro, 'Law and Science in Seventeenth-Century England', *Stanford Law Rev.*, xxi (1969), 740, 761. On the importance of 'method' in sixteenth century continental thought, see, e.g., D.R. Kelley, 'Gaius Noster: Substructures of Western Social Thought', *Amer. Hist. Rev.*, lxxxiv (1979), 629–30; N.W. Gilbert, *Renaissance Concepts of Method* (New York, 1960), 95–96; W.J. Ong, *Ramus, Method, and the Decay of Dialogue* (Cambridge, Mass., 1958), 226–28.

Several factors help explain this heightened concern about the character and sources of the common law. In the period around 1600, politically charged jurisdictional conflicts with other courts in England fed the lawyers' chauvinism about the superiority, antiquity, stability and certainty of their common law.[4] Lawyers in 1600 also confronted the prospect that James VI of Scotland would succeed Elizabeth and, on taking the throne, would seek to integrate English law with Scottish law, a law they saw as 'civil', hence 'foreign', hence undesirable.[5] Broader intellectual changes were at work as well. More and more of these lawyers had come to the Inns of Court from the universities, where they were exposed to new educational methods aimed at reducing complex wholes to their simplest elements.[6] The common law itself had been changing: written pleading slowly replaced oral pleading, post-trial motions made it possible for courts to resolve more doctrinal issues, and lawyers looked to their volumes of reported cases for settled points of law rather than for models of clever pleading.[7] In legal education an oral tradition was giving way to a mass of disorderly legal texts.

The lawyers' evident concern about giving order, 'method', or structure to the common law leads us toward some of their assumptions about what the common law was. For students and practitioners at the Inns of Court in 1600, the common law was a body of knowledge, not a process. It was something one could know, not something one did.[8] The problem was that this knowledge could not be acquired easily. The common law was not written down in any single text, nor was it simply the sum of all the written records and reports of what the courts had decided.[9] It was, as John Baker has shown, the 'common erudition' of the justices, serjeants, benchers and apprentices, an unwritten understanding reflected only imperfectly in the many volumes of lawyers'

4 See, e.g., J.G.A. Pocock, 'A Retrospect from 1986', *The Ancient Constitution and the Feudal Law: A Study of English Historical Thought in the Seventeenth Century* (Cambridge, 1987), 261–80; D.R. Kelley, 'A Rejoinder', *Past and Present*, lxxii (1976), 144; J.H. Baker, Introduction to *The Reports of Sir John Spelman*, Selden Society, xciv (1978), *33*; W.R. Prest, 'The Art of Law', 115–16; C.P. Rodgers, 'Humanism, History and the Common Law', *Jour. Legal Hist.*, vi (1985), 138–39.

5 B.P. Levack, 'The Proposed Union of English and Scots Law in the Seventeenth Century', *Jurid. Rev., N.S.*, xx (1975), 99–100.

6 L.A. Knafla, 'The Matriculation Revolution and Education at the Inns of Court in Renaissance England', *Tudor Men and Institutions: Studies in English Law and Government*, A.J. Slavin, ed. (Baton Rouge, 1972), 247; W.R. Prest, *The Rise of the Barristers* (Oxford, 1986), 110–13.

7 G.J. Turner, Introduction to *The Year Books of 4 Edward II*, Selden Society, xxvi (1914), xxix; P. Stein, 'The Procedural Models of the Sixteenth Century', *Jurid. Rev., N.S.*, xxvii (1982), 192–93; J.H. Baker, 'English Law and the Renaissance', *Camb. Law Jour.*, xliv (1985), 57; G. de C. Parmiter, *Edmund Plowden: An Elizabethan Recusant Lawyer* (1987), 114. Compare F.L. Boersma, *An Introduction to Fitzherbert's Abridgement* (1981), 21 with J.H. Baker, Selden Society, xciv (1978), *96*.

8 E.W. Ives, 'The Common Lawyers', *Profession, Vocation and Culture in Later Medieval England*, C.H. Clough, ed. (Liverpool, 1982), 192.

9 Francis Bacon proposed the drastic remedy of codification in order to reduce the 'body of law' to the texts of statutes and reported judgments, *De Augmentis Scientiarum*, bk. 8, Aph. 77, 1st ed. (1623); *The Works of Francis Bacon*, J. Spedding, R.E. Ellis and D.D. Heath, ed., i (1872), 821.

writings.[10] Mastery of this legal knowledge was said to come only after decades of diligent apprenticeship.[11] To one who had studied long enough, the rational structure of the common law finally became apparent.[12]

By 1600, more lawyers were looking for a quicker and surer way to acquire this common erudition. Perhaps the number of lawyers or would-be lawyers had grown too large to perpetuate an oral tradition of such complexity. Whatever the cause, students at the Inns of Court relied more on private reading of printed books and of manuscripts than on the old learning exercises, based as they were on oral transmission of legal knowledge and skill.[13] Students used any sort of books they could find. Much of the legal literature at the time treated the common law, the body of legal knowledge, as consisting principally of propositions that could be set forth in brief sentences. The writers referred to such propositions variously as 'principles', 'maxims', 'grounds' or 'rules'. These principles were very narrow and detailed, however, and there seemed to be no end of them. Some beginners must have despaired of finding out all these bits of legal knowledge, or of making sense of them as parts of a working system, or of putting them into some ordered framework in which they could be found again.[14] If the common law did indeed have a rational structure, might not one of the learned elders of the profession set out that structure in writing, so that students could gain some view of the whole of their intended discipline?

In the books that law students used in 1600, one could find several competing schemes for organizing the content of the common law – the writs, the tenures, the alphabet and the chronological order of the kings' reigns – but very little consistency in the use of any of these methods. These elementary works, however, all seemed to hint at the existence of a single structure into which the principles would fit. The books all made mention of a number of 'categories' that appeared to encompass all actions, all possessions, all persons or all law, but rarely explained what these categories contained or

[10] Baker, Selden Society, xciv (1978), *123–24*, *161*; Baker, 'English Law and the Renaissance', 57.

[11] See, e.g., J. Fortescue, *De Natura Legis Naturae*, pt. 1, ch. 43, *The Works of Sir John Fortescue*, T. (Fortescue), Lord Clermont, ed. (1869), 102 (twenty years study); W. Staunford, *An Exposicion of the Kinges Prerogatiue* (1657), fo. iiii ('the knowledge of the said laws is placed so farre of, the iourney thereunto so exceeding long and paineful'); E. Coke, *The First Part of the Institutes of the Lawes of England, or, A Commentarie upon Littleton* (1628), 97b; E. Coke, Preface to *The Third Part of the Reports*, new ed. (1826), xxxv; W.R. Prest, *The Inns of Court under Elizabeth I and the Early Stuarts, 1590–1640* (1972), 141–42.

[12] Simpson, 'Rise and Fall of the Legal Treatise', 638; H. Wheeler, 'The Invention of Modern Empiricism: Juridical Foundations of Francis Bacon's Philosophy of Science', *Law Lib. Jour.*, lxxvi (1983), 107.

[13] See, e.g., Prest, *Inns of Court*, 132, 140–41; cf. Baker, Selden Society, xciv (1978), 131 (early sixteenth century). On the older oral tradition see E.G. Henderson, 'Legal Literature and the Impact of Printing on the English Legal Profession', *Law Lib. Jour.*, lxviii (1975), 291.

[14] Prest, *Inns of Court*, 142; Prest, 'Dialectical Origins', 327; Simpson, 'Rise and Fall of the Legal Treatise', 638; Ives, 'Common Lawyers', 197; Rodgers, 'Humanism, History, and the Common Law', 153–54; C. Hill, *Intellectual Origins of the English Revolution* (Oxford, 1965), 227–31.

how they might be distinguished. One could find in the common law literature of 1600 the fragments of a structure that was already a thousand years old when the *Bracton* treatise first applied it to English law in the mid thirteenth century.[15] These fragments came mainly from the *Institutes* of Justinian, the introductory text of every university student of civil or canon law.

After 1600, a few remarkable lawyers attempted to set forth all of the common law as an organized body of knowledge. The first to publish his efforts was not a common lawyer at all, but England's leading civilian, John Cowell. He cited *Bracton* to the common lawyers as authority for the wholesale adoption of Justinian's *Institutes* as a structure for compiling the law of England and comparing it with other laws. Soon after, Henry Finch produced a classification of the common law in which he adapted the general order of the *Institutes* in light of his experience as a common lawyer, his university training in formal logic and his devout religious convictions. Finch's work was the more popular of the two, certainly among common lawyers.

By the mid seventeenth century, both works were overshadowed by Edward Coke's massive, authoritative and unstructured *Institutes of the Laws of England*. Coke was not a devotee of 'method', and his *Institutes* resembled Justinian's not at all. Nevertheless, the conception remained among English common lawyers that the substance of Coke's *Institutes* could be combined with a structural framework like Finch's or Cowell's. Late in the century, Matthew Hale satisfied himself of the soundness of this vision of the common law. The image was of a vast unwritten 'text' of the common law, ordered by the basic categories upon which all lawyers could agree, and from which general notions of property, contract, criminal liability and constitutional rights could emerge.

I. The Structure of Cowell's Institutiones

In 1605 students at the Inns of Court at last could find an 'Institutes' that surveyed the 'whole' of English common law, systematically, in a single volume. It was in Latin, entitled *Institutiones Iuris Anglicani*, and was published in Cambridge. The author, John Cowell, announced that he had 'composed and digested the laws of England' in a structure that reproduced all the book and title headings of Justinian's *Institutes* in order, verbatim.[16] The text that Cowell put in his first title began with three of the first four passages in the first title of the Roman *Institutes*. He gave as citations,

[15] Bracton, *On the Laws and Customs of England*, G.E. Woodbine, ed., S.E. Thorne, tr. (Cambridge, Mass., 1968–77).

[16] J. Cowell, *Institutiones Juris Anglicani* (1605), includes a title, 3.7, on consanguinity of slaves that is not divided from 3.6 in modern editions, see *Justinian's Institutes*, P. Krueger, ed., P. Birks and G. McLeod, tr. (1987), but was present in standard editions of the time, e.g., *Corpus Iuris Civilis*, D. Gothofredus, ed. (1610).

however, not the references a civilian would expect, but the book, chapter and paragraph in the *Bracton* treatise where each of these passages could be found.[17] Thereafter Cowell cited *Bracton*, alone or with other early treatises, in all the passages that explained the main classifications of subject-matter: such as the division of the English law into public and private law; of private law into persons, things and actions; of persons into free and unfree, independent and dependent; of things into corporeal and incorporeal; of obligations into contractual and delictual; of actions into personal and real.[18]

But for its title page and headings, Cowell's *Institutiones* would appear less a domestication of Justinian's *Institutes* than an updating of *Bracton*. Cowell filled the margins of every page with English citations: references to the old treatises, to newer works on tenures and pleas of the crown, to abridgements, statutes and reports. No effort was spared to support each proposition of English law with good English authority from works the common lawyers would have known and respected.

Of course Cowell's use of Justinian's title headings produced some ill fits and odd comparisons. The common law had no special provision for soldiers' wills, no Tertullian or Orphitian decree – here Cowell printed the titles and merely said there was nothing to say.[19] On the other hand, he found common law counterparts for Atilian tutorship, the *lex Falcidia* and the Claudian decree, but lawyers at the Inns of Court would be unlikely to head straight for those titles in order to learn about wards of court, debts due from executors and bankruptcies.[20] He used the format of the *Institutes* to better advantage in order to make some broad and helpful generalizations about 'property' as a whole, about 'contract' generally, and, even (though this was much more difficult) about the general principles of 'trespass' liability.[21] Christopher St. German had preceded Cowell here, in marking out a distinct 'law of property' and 'law of contract' for England,[22] but Cowell showed how it all fitted in.

17 Cowell, *Institutiones*, 1, citing Bracton, fo. 2b-3b (ii, 23, 25–26), all from Azo, *Summa Institutionum*, 1.1, nos. 1, 6, 9, 11. The texts are J. Inst. 1.1*pr*, 1, 3 and Azo's expanded version of J. Inst., 1.1.4. See D.R. Coquillette, 'Legal Ideology and Incorporation, I, The English Civilian Writers, 1523–1607', *Boston Univ. Law Rev.*, lxvi (1981), 74–75, rptd. *The Civilian Writers of Doctors' Commons, London* (1988), 82–83. Cowell preceded these with a *proemium* drawn from Bracton's rendering of Justinian.

18 E.g., Cowell, *Institutiones*, 1.1.3–4, 1.2.9, 1.3*pr*, 1.8*pr*, 2.2*pr*, 4.6.4.

19 Cowell, *Institutiones*, 2.11, 3.3, 3.4. See A. Watson, 'Justinian's Institutes and Some English Counterparts', *Studies in Justinian's Institutes in Memory of J.A.C. Thomas*, P.G. Stein and A.D.E. Lewis, ed. (1983), 182–83.

20 Cowell, *Institutiones*, 1.20, 2.22, 3.13.

21 The grand division of obligations required Cowell to bring together the learning on 'contract' considered generally, and to contrast it with a broad category of 'wrongs'. What united all contracts was the requirement of consent; what differentiated oral from written contracts was the requirement of consideration; what distinguished an exchange of goods from a loan for use was the element of mutuality. Ibid., 3.23.1, 3.16.4, 3.15*pr* and 2.

22 C. St. German, *Doctor and Student*, T.F.T. Plucknett and J.L. Barton, ed., Selden Society, xci (1974), 18–19, 28–29, 32–35, 56–57, 132–35, 183, 228.

Jocelyn Simon's assessment of the structure of Cowell's *Institutiones* is memorable and none too complimentary: fitting English common law into the titles and heads of Justinian's *Institutes*, he said, 'was rather like crushing an Ugly Sister's foot, bunions and all, into Cinderella's glass slipper'.[23] One might turn that remark on its head, however, and point to a different moral. What Simon said should remind us that the English lawyers' conceptions of their whole common law were not, after all, completely different from the ways civilians imagined their *Corpus Iuris*. For Cowell even to conceive the idea of compressing the mass of common law into Justinian's framework, he and his readers had to recognize that the common lawyers' learning and the *Corpus Iuris Civilis* were more or less the same sort of thing: a body of knowledge, not a process, not a sentiment. The lesson is, to keep Simon's metaphor, not that English law fitted awkwardly into the Roman slipper, but that English law was itself a foot, not a nose or a tree or a sea voyage – that Cowell could sensibly have made the effort to try it on for size.

Who was John Cowell? When he published his *Institutiones Iuris Anglicani*, Cowell was Regius Professor of Civil Law at Cambridge and Master of Trinity Hall.[24] Alongside his academic career, he maintained an active civilian practice in London.[25] Cowell was no common lawyer,[26] yet he showed considerable mastery of the common law sources and common law learning, and a willingness to provide what many students of the common law said they wanted, a single elementary work that sketched the whole of the law within a comprehensible structure.

Not only was Cowell an outsider in 1605, but he was beginning to make a reputation for himself as an opponent of the common law. In the same year that his *Institutiones* appeared, Cowell helped draft the *Articuli Cleri*, a major salvo from the church courts in their battle against the common law judges' writs of prohibition.[27] The common lawyers' antagonism focused on Cowell himself in 1610, when his second work, *The Interpreter*, came under fire for its overly 'absolutist' definitions of the terms 'King', 'Parliament', 'Prerogative' and 'Subsidy', and for a quotation of the French civilian François Hotman's jibe at the common lawyers' revered text, Littleton's *Tenures*.[28] In that year,

23 J. Simon, 'Dr. Cowell', *Camb. Law Jour.*, xxvi (1968), 263.

24 Coquillette, 'Legal Ideology and Incorporation', 71 and *Civilian Writers*, 79–80.

25 B.P. Levack, *The Civil Lawyers in England, 1603–1642: A Political Study* (Oxford, 1973), 21, 221.

26 Cowell would certainly have encountered common lawyers in his legal and governmental activities in London, but there is no evidence that he had ever studied at any of the Inns of Court or even received an honorary membership in one, as several other prominent civilians did, ibid., 129.

27 Ibid., 139. Archbishop Richard Bancroft presented this list of twenty-five complaints to the Privy Council, and the common law judges prepared a formal, point-by-point defence of their prohibitions, found in E. Coke, *Second Part of the Institutes* (1642), 601–18.

28 J. Cowell, *The Interpreter* (1607), s.v. Littleton, sig. [Ss2v], quoting F. Hotman, *De feudis commentatio tripertita* (1573), rptd. *De verbis feudalibus commentarius* (1587) s.v. Foedum, col. 18.

Cowell's law dictionary was officially (though ineffectually) suppressed by royal proclamation.[29]

Thus it was a civilian and critic of the common law who wrote what has been called the 'first' attempt 'to arrange English law in a truly rational, systematic, and scientific way'.[30] Though this might seem calculated to offend the common lawyers, from Cowell's perspective his choice of subject-matter is understandable. The first of his predecessors in the Regius Chair, Thomas Smith, had written a brief comparison of English and civil law, first published in 1583, and a younger contemporary, William Fulbecke, had published a dialogue on the civil, canon and common law in 1601.[31]

Cowell had *Bracton* as a model, to be sure, for using Justinian's *Institutes* to frame the material of English law. But Cowell the civilian would also have known about recent comparable efforts by civilians and canonists on the continent. Beginning in the 1540s, several jurists compiled texts from other parts of the *Corpus Iuris Civilis* into the structure of the *Institutes*.[32] In 1550 Eguinaire Baron produced a 'bipartite commentary' comparing Roman and French law in the order of the *Institutes*.[33] In 1563 Giovanni Paolo Lancellotti published his influential *Institutiones Iuris Canonici*, cleverly adapting Justinian's basic framework for a systematic overview of canon law.[34] Cowell's was the first of a steady stream of 'Institutes' on the laws of the European nations, followed very soon by Guy Coquille's *Institution au droict des françois* and Antoine Loisel's *Institutes coutumières*, both published in 1607.[35]

Cowell distinguished himself from most of his contemporaries across the Channel by his absolute fidelity to the precise order of Justinian's *Institutes*.

[29] See generally S.B. Chrimes, 'The Constitutional Ideas of Dr. John Cowell', *Eng. Hist. Rev.*, lxvi (1949), 199.

[30] Rodgers, 'Humanism, History, and the Common Law', 136. Cowell's was, at any rate, the first such work in the seventeenth century.

[31] T. Smith, *De Republica Anglorum*, M. Dewar, ed. (Cambridge, 1982), 145–48; Coquillette, 'Legal Ideology and Incorporation', 49–50 and *Civilian Writers*, 58. W. Fulbecke, *A Parallele or Conference of the Civill Law, the Canon Law, and the Common Law of this realm of England* (1601–02); P. Birks, Introduction to W. Fulbecke, *A Direction or Preparative to the Study of the Law*, T.H. Stirling, ed. (rptd. Godstone, 1987), xvii; Birks and McLeod, Introduction to *Justinian's Institutes*, 25; Levack, *Civil Lawyers*, 137.

[32] R. Orestano, *Introduzione allo Studio Storico del Diritto Romano*, 2nd ed. (Turin, 1961), 61 (on François Baudouin, François Hotman, Johann Schneidewin, Matthaeus Wesembecius and Joachim Mynsinger).

[33] E. Baron, *Institutionum civilium ab Iustiniano* (1550); A.L. Fell, *Origins of Legislative Sovereignty and the Legislative State*, iii (Boston, Mass., 1987), 45; Kelley, 'Gaius Noster', 632.

[34] G.P. Lancellotti, *Institutiones iuris canonici* (1563) and appended thereafter to standard editions of the *Corpus Iuris Canonici*.

[35] G. Coquille, *Institution au droict des françois* (1607); A. Loisel, *Institutes coutumières* (1607); see K. Luig, 'The Institutes of National Law in the Seventeenth and Eighteenth Centuries', *Jurid. Rev.*, *N.S.*, xvii (1972), 204. Coquille put his chapter-length essays in an order that departed considerably from Justinian's, while Loisel used a much closer adaptation of the structure of the *Institutes*, but used the framework merely to string together short proverbs. Around this time as well Etienne Pasquier dictated his discursive, scholarly *L'Interprétation des Institutes de Justinian*, incorporating French customary, statutory and case law, a work that remained in manuscript until the nineteenth century, C. Giraud ed. (Paris, 1847); D. Thickett, *Étienne Pasquier (1529–1615): The Versatile Barrister of Sixteenth-Century France* (1979), 50; Kelley, 'Gaius Noster', 634.

From the 1530s onward, many jurists in the Humanist camp criticized one or another detail in the scheme of the *Institutes* and proposed their own 'improvements' on that structure – one jettisoned 'persons', another traded 'actions' for extra-judicial 'acts', a third put 'things' ahead of 'persons' to reflect the order in which God created them.[36] The most influential of the new systematizers, Hugues Doneau, retained the basic terminology but reshuffled the topics and reinterpreted the structure of the *Institutes* as a way of dividing subjective 'rights': first our rights to our own 'persons' and limitations on those rights; next rights in regard to things, distinguishing between what is properly ours and what is merely owed to us; finally actions, the means of obtaining our rights.[37] He did not hesitate to shuffle the topics of Justinian's *Institutes* slightly to fit his new view of the relation of 'persons', 'things' and 'actions'.

Cowell took no notice of any criticisms, adaptations or reinterpretations of Justinian's order when he composed his *Institutiones*, though in several titles he found too little English law or too much. The reason for Cowell's conservatism in this regard is probably that he regarded himself as a 'Bartolist' of the old school, opposed to the Humanist camp.[38] He found the Humanists helpful in their comparative researches, and quoted them freely, but ultimately, like Bartolus in the fourteenth century, he followed the 'legal order' ordained by Justinian.[39]

It is likely that Cowell planned his *Institutiones* as part of a larger effort to improve the learning and practice of English law. He followed it two years later with his English law dictionary, *The Interpreter*, subtitled 'The

[36] Johann Apel did not see the need for a separate category of 'persons' any more than of 'times' or 'places'. He brought the whole of the law under the heads *dominium* and *obligatio*, the former subsuming actions *in rem* and the latter actions *in personam*. H.F. Jolowicz, 'Obligatio and Actio', *Law Quart. Rev.*, lxviii (1952), 472; P. Stein, 'The Fate of the Institutional System', *Huldigungsbundel Paul van Warmelo* (Pretoria, 1984), 220. François Connan kept 'persons' and 'things', but replaced 'actions' with human 'acts', including contracts, marriage and testaments, but excluding any separate treatment of judicial proceedings, Fell, *Origins of Legislative Sovereignty*, ii (Boston, Mass., 1983), 6; V. Piano Mortari, 'La sistematica come ideale umanistico dell'opera di Francesco Connano', *La storia del diritto nel quadro delle scienze storiche* (Florence, 1966), 527–28 and n. 13; C. Bergfeld, *Franciscus Connanus (1508–1551)* (Cologne, 1968), 45–46. Pierre Grégoire of Toulouse considered that 'things' should come before 'persons' as they had at the creation, and joined Connan (and Nicolas Vigelius) in expanding 'actions' to human 'acts', P. Grégoire, *Syntagma iuris universi* (1582); N. Vigelius, *Digesta juris civilis* (1568); A.P.T. Eyssel, *Doneau: sa vie et ses ouvrages* (Dijon, 1860), 200–1 and n. 143; Kelley, 'Gaius Noster', 636; A. Campbell, *The Structure of Stair's Institutions* (Glasgow, 1954), 18–19.

[37] H. Doneau, *Commentarii de iure civili* (1595–97); Eyssel, *Doneau*, 218–60; Stein, 'Fate of the Institutional System', 221; E. Andersen, *The Renaissance of Legal Science after the Middle Ages: The German Historical School no Bird Phoenix* (Copenhagen, 1974), 115–19. Doneau's rights to 'persons' included life, bodily integrity, liberty and reputation.

[38] Levack, *Civil Lawyers*, 134, 138.

[39] Andersen, *Renaissance of Legal Science*. Cowell also followed the older tradition in allocating obligations to the third part of Justinian's *Institutes*, the actions. See, e.g., H.F. Jolowicz, *Roman Foundations of Modern Law* (Oxford, 1957), 63.

Signification of Words', and announced in the preface to that work a further tract he was preparing on legal rules (*de regulis iuris*).[40] These three works, in the order Cowell planned to complete them, would have matched the three-part introductory textbooks that were popular for students of civil law: Justinian's *Institutes* followed by the two last titles of the Digest, *de verborum significatione* and *de diversis regulis iuris antiqui*.[41] This glimpse of Cowell's overall plan raises the further question – for whom did he compose his *Institutiones Juris Anglicani*?

Though the preface to the *Institutiones*, like the dedication of *The Interpreter*, addressed both civilians and common lawyers, it is now often supposed that Cowell directed his work primarily to students of civil law at Cambridge and Oxford, to teach them the laws of their own country.[42] There had been some very basic instruction on common law in or around the universities since at least the fifteenth century, and Cambridge officials in 1570 sought to require that recipients of the D.C.L. study the laws of England.[43] Cowell's work not only served this need, but gave civilians, already intimately familiar with the content of Justinian's *Institutes*, the means to draw ready lessons about the 'universal principles of justice' that underlay English and Roman law.[44]

The *Institutiones* surely provided useful knowledge to students of civil law in a most palatable form, but Cowell (or his publisher) probably had in mind a readership among students of the common law as well. The number of civilians in England was tiny, twelve or fifteen practising in London at any one time.[45] It is impossible to know how many common lawyers bought the 1605 edition

40 Cowell, *Interpreter*, preface, sig. *3v. Cowell left the final tract unfinished at his death in 1611.

41 Francis Bacon recommended to James VI and I that three such works be prepared to supplement a digest of English law, 'A Proposition to His Majesty . . . Touching the Compiling and Amendment of the Laws of England' in *Works of Francis Bacon*, xiii, 61, 70.

42 C.P. Rodgers, 'Legal Humanism and English Law – The Contribution of the English Civilians', *Irish Jur., N.S.*, xix (1984), 127–28; Stein, 'Continental Influences', 1108; Levack, *Civil Lawyers*, 137.

43 An Oxford statute of 1432 sought to regularize some (probably extramural) teaching of the 'English mode of pleading', *Statuta Antiqua Universitatis Oxoniensis*, S. Gibson, ed. (Oxford, 1931), 240–41; H. Rashdall, *The Universities of Europe in the Middle Ages*, 2nd ed. (Oxford, 1936), iii, 162; A. Giuliani, 'The Influence of Rhetoric on the Law of Evidence and Pleading', *L'Educazione Giuridica* (Perugia, 1979), ii, 228; J. Fortescue, *De Laudibus Legum Angliae*, S.B. Chrimes ed. and tr. (Cambridge, 1949), 195–96. Dr. Whitgift's reformed set of statutes for Cambridge University, promulgated in 1570 but successfully resisted by the Puritan faction within the university, had required that a doctor of laws study the laws of England soon after taking the doctorate, so that he not be ignorant of the laws of his own country, *De legum doctoribus*, ch. 14, *Cambridge University Transactions during the Puritan Controversies of the Sixteenth and Seventeenth Centuries*, J. Heywood and T. Wright, ed., i (1854), 10, ix; Levack, *Civil Lawyers*, 128. James Whitelocke reported studying the common law from a civilian's manuscript when he accepted an Oxford fellowship in civil law, M.H. Curtis, *Oxford and Cambridge in Transition, 1558–1642* (Oxford, 1959), 159–60.

44 Stein, 'Continental Influences', 1108; Watson, 'Justinian's Institutes and Some English Counterparts', 183; Levack, *Civil Lawyers*, 137.

45 Levack, *Civil Lawyers*, 3, 21–22; Coquillette, 'Legal Ideology and Incorporation', 21, n. 66 and *Civilian Writers*, 31 and n. 66. Levack counted about 200 in all the civilian callings between 1603 and 1641 and cited estimates of perhaps 2,000 barristers in the comparable period.

of the *Institutiones*, but it is reasonable to suppose that some were expected to do so. Cowell's copious citations certainly indicated a great deal of effort to make the work useful for practising common lawyers. As Cowell knew from looking over the works he was citing, students of the common law were already encountering most of the *Institutes*' major categories, suffused through the rest of their professional literature. His text was more accessible and useful than the editions of *Bracton* and *Glanvill* they were acquiring.

Historians differ in their estimates of the impact of Cowell's *Institutiones*. One writes of its 'evident popularity', another calls it a 'spectacular failure'.[46] Both estimates derive from the same evidence. Latin editions of the *Institutiones Iuris Anglicani* were published in Cambridge in 1605, in Oxford in 1630 and 1664 and in Frankfurt in 1630. An English translation appeared in London in 1651 and was reprinted in 1676. Cowell's book thus had more printings than did, for example, Francis Bacon's *Elements of the Common Laws*, though of course many fewer than Coke's *Institutes*.[47]

Some historians have accounted for the 'failure' of the *Institutiones*, if that is what it was, by pointing to Cowell's decision to use Justinian's *Institutes* as his plan. Holdsworth, in particular, thought the form of the book 'exotic', unsuitable and forced.[48] This estimate goes too far. Cowell's idea to base his compilation on the *Institutes* was probably quite sound, given the familiarity of much of the basic terminology. But his decision to make absolutely no changes in the title headings he took from Justinian no doubt reduced the book's impact for students of the common law. Though he cited *Bracton* wherever possible for the classifications and much of the content of his book, Cowell's title page made no effort to hide the civil law origin of his format. The language, title and headings of the book all made it appear less a rational ordering of English law than an effort to show how much (or little) English law had in common with Roman law.[49]

In 1651, forty years after his death, Cowell's *Institutes of the Laws of England* gained a new readership in an English translation. The title page advertized that the book was translated 'according to Act of Parliament, for

[46] Compare Watson, 'Justinian's Institutes and Some English Counterparts', 184 ('evident popularity') and Levack, *Civil Lawyers*, 138 ('partially successful') with Coquillette, 'Legal Ideology and Incorporation', 73 and *Civilian Writers*, 80–81 ('spectacular failure') and Simon, 'Dr. Cowell', 263 ('unsuccessful').

[47] Bacon's *Elements* was printed in 1630, 1636 and 1639. R.W. Gibson, *Francis Bacon: A Bibliography of His Works and of Baconiana to the Year 1750* (Oxford, 1950), xvi. Such a comparison is suggested by Bacon's own hope to surpass Coke in the estimation of future generations of lawyers, *Works of Francis Bacon*, xiii, 70.

[48] W.S. Holdsworth, *A History of English Law*, v, 3rd ed. (1945), 21, 23; Stein, 'Continental Influences', 1108; Rodgers, 'Legal Humanism', 128. See also Coquillette, 'Legal Ideology and Incorporation', 321, *Civilian Writers*, 101.

[49] B.P. Levack, *The Formation of the British State: England, Scotland, and the Union, 1603–1707* (Oxford, 1987), 138, reports discovering notes in the Inner Temple Library, of unknown authorship, recommending that one 'read Mr. Doctor Cowell's little book of Institutes for the matters of every chapter in the 4 books of Institutes, where it is shown how little of those Institutes is now our law'.

the benefit of all'. No statute or resolution singling out the *Institutiones* has come to light, however, and it is safe to assume that the publisher referred merely to the general Act of 1650 ordering all 'books of the Law of England' to be translated into English.[50] The early 1650s were a time of strident attacks on the common law generally, from many perspectives, and of some real efforts at law reform. Many sought to reduce the common law to good order, or to replace it entirely.[51]

Cowell's 1651 edition can be counted among the efforts to support and strengthen the common law. In a new preface, the anonymous translator, one 'W.G.', proclaimed Cowell a good 'Commonwealth's man' and praised his use of 'so choice a method of our English laws'.[52] 'W.G.' exposed his own common law sympathies occasionally in the text, for example, by disparaging 'Tribonianus [Justinian's compiler] in that long and wearisome work of his in digesting the law'.[53] The suspicion remains, however, that for readers in the 1650s, as in 1605, Cowell was 'not one of us' and, largely because of who he was, his *Institutes* seemed the work of an outsider looking in on the common law. By the time this English translation appeared, Cowell's work competed with the massive volumes of Coke's *Institutes* and two versions of the introductory survey by Henry Finch. Both authors had better claim to represent in their works the structure of the common law as seen from within.

Cowell had, after all, earned his place in common law lore. Edward Coke, leader of the common lawyers, seems never to have forgiven Cowell for repeating in his law dictionary what Hotman had written about Littleton. Coke himself repeated and rebutted Hotman's statement in the preface to a volume of his *Reports* in 1614, then warned that it was a 'desperate and dangerous matter for civilians and canonists . . . to write either of the common laws of England which they profess not, or against them which they know not'.[54] Common lawyers in general, it was said, took offence at Cowell's *Interpreter* on two counts, first 'that a civilian should walk in a profession several to themselves; secondly that he should pluck up the pales of the hard terms wherewith it was enclosed, and lay it open and obvious to common capacities'.[55] It may well be that Coke himself had it in mind to redress any

50 An Act for turning the Books of the Law, and all Proces and Proceedings in Courts of Justice, into English (22 November 1650), *Acts and Ordinances of the Interregnum, 1642–1660*, C.H. Firth and R.S. Rait, ed. (1911), ii, 455; Coquillette, 'Legal Ideology and Incorporation', 73, n. 376 and *Civilian Writers*, 82, n. 376.

51 D. Veall, *The Popular Movement for Law Reform, 1640–1660* (Oxford, 1970), 77–78, 87–88, 104, 107, 119–20; S.E. Prall, *The Agitation for Law Reform during the Puritan Revolution, 1640–1660* (The Hague, 1966), 66, 71, 90–93.

52 W.G., Preface to J. Cowell, *The Institutes of the Lawes of England* (1651), sig. A2v.

53 Ibid., 1.10.3, 20. The Latin original had *Tribonianus longo illo iuris digerendi opere fatigatus*, Cowell, *Institutiones*, 1.10.2, 19.

54 Coke, Preface to *The Tenth Part of the Reports*, xxix–xxx.

55 T. Fuller, *The History of the Worthies of England*, P.A. Nuttall, ed. (1840), i, 420 (1st ed. 1662); Chrimes, 'Constitutional Ideas of Dr. John Cowell', 465–66.

lingering effect of Cowell's earlier trespass onto his turf when he chose the overall title, *The Institutes of the Lawes of England*, for the four separate (and very differently organized) treatises that he began to publish in 1628.

Ironically the tribal animosity of the common lawyers toward Cowell and what he represented, while it did reduce the influence of his *Institutiones*, did not stop the common lawyers from adopting his law dictionary as their own. *The Interpreter* remained quite popular through several editions between 1637 and 1727.[56] In part, this was because it had very little competition. Cowell's was the most comprehensive and scholarly dictionary of English legal terms before Thomas Blount's *Nomolexicon* of 1670.[57] Common law lexicographers after Cowell borrowed his definitions freely, and some of these, such as his 'absolutist' formulation of the term 'property', eventually became common law orthodoxy.[58] A good bit of civilian thinking seeped in by such means. The chief value of the *Institutiones*, on the other hand, was its framework, and in this regard Cowell, despite all his citations to *Bracton*, was too faithful to his Roman model. The common lawyers saw much in it that they recognized, but they could not accept Justinian as their own.

Even so, it is fitting that the first author to repeat *Bracton's* attempt to put the whole of English common law into a complete, systematic structure would rely so heavily on *Bracton* and turn directly to the same model the thirteenth-century writer used, the *Institutes* of Justinian. In the three centuries between *Bracton's* last imitators and Cowell's *Institutiones*, common lawyers did not stop using the Roman categories through which *Glanvill* and *Bracton* had made sense of English practice.[59] They did, however, forsake the treatise tradition in favour of forms of legal writing that merely supplemented their primary reliance on an oral tradition to preserve and transmit legal knowledge. In the sixteenth century, that oral tradition grew progressively more difficult to maintain, and at the same time common lawyers made increasing use of the terminology of Justinian's *Institutes*. Many called for what might be termed a 'new *Bracton*', a treatise explaining how the whole of English law fitted together. Cowell gave a civilian's response; he injected the original structure of the *Institutes* once again into the stream of common law discourse, and thereby brought common law and civilian understanding of that structure into direct and fruitful juxtaposition.

[56] Coquillette, 'Legal Ideology and Incorporation', 76 and n. 400 and *Civilian Writers*, 84 and n. 400.

[57] D.S. Bland, 'Some Notes on the Evolution of the Legal Dictionary', *Jour. Leg. Hist.*, i (1980), 76–78.

[58] Ibid., 76–77; G.E. Aylmer, 'The Meaning and Definition of "Property" in Seventeenth-Century England', *Past and Present*, lxxxvi (1980), 97.

[59] D.J. Seipp, 'Roman Legal Categories in the Early Common Law', *Legal Record and Historical Reality*, T.G. Watkin, ed. (London and Ronceverte, 1989), 9–36.

II. The Structure of Finch's Nomotexnia and Law

In 1613, eight years after Cowell's *Institutiones* appeared, Henry Finch published his own 'description' of the whole of English common law under the title *Nomotexnia*, the 'art' of law.[60] Finch put this work in law French, but in 1627, two years after his death, an English version appeared with the title *Law, or a Discourse thereof*.[61] Wilfrid Prest has shown that *Nomotexnia* was in fact Finch's final version and the later published *Law* represents an earlier draft.[62] As it happened, the English draft sold much better than the French version Finch meant us to have, and will be the primary focus of this analysis.

What students at the Inns of Court encountered was more diagram than description, an extremely elaborate web of divisions and distinctions extending from the most abstract concepts of divine and human law down to the level of individual crimes, estates, writs and procedures. In both versions, Finch expanded the brief opening discussion of natural and civil law, found in Justinian's *Institutes* and similar works, into an entire Book I. Before taking up English 'positive' law, he set forth more than a hundred consecutively numbered maxims of 'native' law, universal principles of natural law and the law of reason, including those made known through other disciplines and those proper to the law itself. In Book II Finch gave only a brief opening chapter to the realm and 'persons' of England. He then proceeded through what he called the two 'parts' of the law: the rest of Book II on 'possessions' and Book III on 'punishments'. Book IV, fully half the work, concerned 'actions'. Finch's *Law* thus approximated the Roman order: persons (here in vestigial form); things; some obligations (of the non-contractual sort); and lastly, actions.[63]

When set alongside Justinian's *Institutes*, Cowell's *Institutiones* and *Bracton*, Finch's departures seem more a matter of terminology and orientation than of basic structure. In his view, persons, things and human conduct were not, strictly speaking, 'parts' of the law; they existed in the world apart from the law. Persons thus were treated first, as part of the commonwealth whose law it was, not part of the law itself. Again, the law was not composed of 'things', but concerned the 'possession' of things.[64] It was not composed of offences or wrongs, but of their 'punishment'. Finch set out to 'describe law', and

[60] H. Finch, *Nomotexnia: cestascavoir, Un Description del Common Leys Dangleterre solonque les Rules del Art* (1613).

[61] H. Finch, *Law, Or, a Discourse thereof* (1627, rptd. 1759).

[62] Prest, 'Dialectical Origins', 341–43.

[63] Watson, 'Justinian's Institutes and Some English Counterparts', 184–85, does not follow Prest's chronology, and finds greater differences among the two versions, but agrees that *Law* resembled Justinian's *Institutes* more closely.

[64] The distinction cannot be pressed too far. To Finch's ear, 'things' in English may have sounded inelegant, and *choses* in French not clearly applicable to land. 'Possessions', as a name for the aggregate that a contemporary civilian called 'things' and a later lawyer 'property', had good common law precedent: it was the topmost category in the chart appended to many sixteenth-century editions of Littleton's *Tenures*.

understood the difference between his limited task and the ambition of other jurists to describe the whole world of persons, things and human conduct from their legal perspective.

Consistent with this approach, Finch's treatment of 'persons' in both versions was very short. Cowell's *Institutiones*, by contrast, dwelt quite a bit on the Year Book learning about villein status, bastardy, marriage and wardship, all under the general rubric of 'persons'. The principal distinctions, according to Justinian and Cowell, were between the free and the unfree, between independent and dependent persons. Finch treated the few remaining rights of lords over their villeins and wards under the category of 'hereditaments' within his treatment of possessions. He kept a law of persons as the first category, but for him the two chief distinctions among persons in English law were first the division between the king and his subjects, and second that between natural persons and bodies politic or corporations. Neither distinction figured in Justinian's *Institutes*.[65]

Of Finch's two ways of classifying persons, the first – sovereign and subject – was clearly central to his conception of the shape of English law. In nearly every part of his *Nomotexnia* and *Law*, Finch distinguished the special rules that applied to the king, 'prerogative', from the statutes and case law that pertained to everyone else. This division substituted, in a way, for a public-private distinction, which is almost wholly absent in Finch's scheme. On the continent jurists had been criticizing the *Institutes*' treatment of persons for its failure to emphasize the differences between men and women, clergy and laity, Christians and non-Christians and noblemen and commoners.[66] Finch took a very different approach, in which all such differences in the conditions of persons diminished in significance when compared to the vast gulf between the sovereign and the subject. Finch left the impression that, given the sheer number of exceptions and special rules devised for the king's prerogative, everyone else was, comparatively speaking, equal before the law.[67]

In treating possessions Finch kept the major distinctions drawn by Littleton. Contracts did not stand out as the major category they had been in Cowell's *Institutiones*, but were made subsidiary to the types of personal chattels. He defined a contract restrictively, as 'a mutual agreement for the very property of

[65] In classical Roman law, a 'person' was a human being. Beginning in the twelfth century, canonists and civilians treated corporations first as fictive persons and finally as a special type of legal 'person'. See, e.g., P.W. Duff, *Personality in Roman Private Law* (Cambridge, 1938), 48–50; J. Canning, *The Political Thought of Baldus de Ubaldis* (Cambridge, 1987), 186; J.P. Canning, 'The Corporation in the Political Thought of the Italian Jurists of the Thirteenth and Fourteenth Centuries', *Hist. Pol. Thought*, i (1980), 15.

[66] Jolowicz, *Roman Foundations of Modern Law*, 69; Kelley, 'Gaius Noster', 628, 632 (Alberigo, Eguinaire Baron).

[67] Finch's earlier religious writing similarly rejected Old Testament laws based on personal distinction between free and slave, citizen and alien, clergy and laity, etc., such 'respect of persons being extinguished with us'. H. Finch, 'A Conference or Reformation', quoted in Prest, 'The Art of Law', 99.

personal things'.[68] Contract and succession, 'things' themselves in the Roman scheme, were for Finch merely among the acts having to do with possessions.

Finch's category of 'punishments' combined what later common lawyers would learn to keep separate: torts and crimes. The terminology of the common law had long lumped treason, felony and other 'trespasses' together, and was now applying the term 'criminal' to this broad range of offences. Yet trespass was a 'civil' wrong as well, and the boundary between civil and criminal proceedings was difficult to discern. Cowell had encountered a similar confusion in distinguishing the obligations arising from 'private crimes' from the material for his final chapter on 'public judgements'.

Perhaps symptomatic of this confusion, Finch consistently treated rape as a trespass with violence rather than a felony. Whether he meant thereby to advocate a change in the treatment of that offence is not clear.[69] Finch also added to the ordinary categories of petty treason against husbands and masters another classification, petty treason 'against God'. He devised this category for the crime of 'sodomitry', along with heresy and sorcery, in order to attract for the sexual offence a punishment better according with Old Testament rigour.[70] Like the rest of the classifications Finch employed, his downgrading of rape and upgrading of 'sodomitry' were not explained or justified, they were merely presented to the reader as insights into the nature of the common law.

Finally, one comes to the book on 'actions' or 'suits'. For Finch these were not a 'part' of the law but a separate dimension, a 'general and common affection scattered throughout the whole law' like blood through the body.[71] With this notion, Finch came close to a strong substance-procedure distinction. On the continent many civilian jurists reached the same conclusion that actions were wholly apart from the rest of the law, that pairing actions with persons and things was 'like comparing an architect not to a shoemaker, but to a shoe'.[72]

The principal feature of Finch's section on actions, and the aspect he developed to an extreme degree in his law French version of 1613, was the elaboration of deeper and deeper nests of categories, preferably dichotomies, from the topmost generality to the lowest particular. By way of illustration, here is how a reader ventured down Finch's pathways to reach the writ of

68 Finch, *Law*, bk.2, ch.18, 180.

69 Finch's first known draft and an annexed table, reproduced in Prest, 'Dialectical Origins', 333, 337, 349, both appear to allocate rape to the felony category (as a felony of 'carnal copulation', the 'natural' variety). Later drafts take it out of that category, ibid., 350–51, as do all published versions. Cf. H. Finch, 'A Conference and Reformation of the Same Law by the Law of God', Bodleian MS Rawl. C. 43, 24. Finch was clearly not writing about 'rape' in the more limited (and trespassory) sense of abduction, enticement or elopement of a woman, but about sexual intercourse ('carnal abusing') against her will.

70 Compare Finch, *Law*, bk.3, ch.23, 24, 218–19 with Coke, *The Third Part of the Institutes* (1644), ch.10, 58–59.

71 Finch, *Law*, bk.4, ch.1, 225.

72 Jolowicz, 'Obligatio and Actio', 472, on Apel's criticism of the pairing of actions and obligations, J. Apel, *Dialogus de studio juris recte instituendo exercendoque* (1540).

entry for reclaiming land when a leasehold tenant held over. It is, first, part of human law, not divine; positive, not natural law; common law, not civil or canon; suits at law, not 'parts' of the law; at the courts of Westminster, not county or lower courts; to draw some new thing in suit, not to defeat a prior suit; a common plea, not a plea of the crown; a real action, not personal; purely real, not mixed; a plea of land, not 'in the realty' for hereditaments or real choses; a *praecipe quod reddat*, not mort d'ancestor or *nuper obiit*; in the right, not ancestral possessory; but mixed in the right, not demanding the right; a writ of entry without tort, not from tort; on determination of an estate, not disability in making a grant; for an estate ended, not a condition broken; and finally, seventeen layers deep, it is a writ *ad terminum qui praeteriit,* not *ad communem legem*.

Here was classification! Finch put nearly all of his effort into devising ever more elaborate distinctions within divisions. The patient reader who followed all the way down each maze often found very little information collected around each of the bottommost elements of law, just some snippets of statutes, blackletter rules from the reports, and exceptions, of course, for the king's prerogative. The classification itself was clearly the greater part of what Finch was trying to accomplish in his treatment of the common law.

Who was Henry Finch? By 1613, when he published *Nomotexnia*, Henry Finch had been at Gray's Inn as student, apprentice and bencher for some thirty-five years. He had an active practice and held important retainers and recorderships.[73] His work was clearly meant for students of the common law, both absolute beginners and those far enough along in study to see the need for a view of the whole.[74] Yet Finch, in his own way, brought to the common law the perspective of a university-trained scholar.

Finch had been a student at Christ's College, Cambridge, where his tutor was Laurence Chaderton, England's first and leading exponent of Ramist logic.[75] Ramus (Pierre de la Ramée) and his followers elevated 'method' above all other aspects of logic and promoted it as a new short-cut to universal knowledge.[76] It will not oversimplify matters to put the Ramist programme this way: Law, like other bodies of knowledge, was complex. What was complex was complex because it was made up of many things, but no matter how complex, it presented a few simple, obvious divisions. If one divided up what was complex into, say, two or three parts, on the basis of some simple division, each part was already less complex than

[73] Prest, 'Dialectical Origins', 329.

[74] Cf. F.H. Lawson, 'Institutes', *Festschrift für Imre Zajtay*, R.H. Graveson et al., ed. (Tübingen, 1982), 341; 'Stair from an English Standpoint', *Stair Tercentenary Studies*, D.M. Walker, ed., Stair Society, xxx (Edinburgh, 1981), 228 ('It [could] be read only by learned lawyers, and even by them not continuously').

[75] Prest, 'Dialectical Origins', 330–31; Knafla, 'Ramism and the English Renaissance', 35–36.

[76] Knafla, 'Ramism and the English Renaissance', 34; E.J. Ashworth, *Language and Logic in the Post-Medieval Period* (Dordrecht, Boston, Reidel, 1974), 15.

the whole. One kept on dividing each of the parts into less and less complex sub-parts until one reached the bottom, the individual units of knowledge. These were simple, so simple that they could be apprehended at once. And so when one knew the simplest elements, and the simple distinctions that combined them into larger and larger aggregations to make up the whole, one understood the whole complex body of law. *Voilà*![77]

Finch made no explicit mention of Ramus in the preface or body of *Nomotexnia*. He may well have thought, as Prest suggests, that 'his ambitious efforts to systematise the common law would stand a better chance of professional acceptance if they did not appear under any specific philosophical banner'. Even so his preference for dichotomies, his spatial organization of the text on the page in almost diagrammatic form, and his neglect to explain the basis for his divisions were all quite characteristic of Ramist method.[78] In his preface Finch described the methodology: 'clarifying the subject by precise definition, dividing it into categories (*partes*), distinguishing the function of these, placing each individual item correctly in its proper place' and so on.[79]

Before the publication of *Nomotexnia*, Finch was probably better known among common lawyers for his outspoken and radical religious views.[80] He advocated conforming English common law to the law of God as set forth in the Bible, particularly by increasing the punishment for sexual crimes, and spoke out in parliament on behalf of the Puritan cause.[81] As Prest reveals, Finch originally intended to publish, alongside his *Nomotexnia*, a 'conference and reformation' detailing specific remedies for the common law's departures from the law of God.[82] Finch's Puritan faction lost the battle for the English church, and by the early 1600s he outwardly moderated his stance. He included no overt religious critique of English law in the published version of *Nomotexnia*, though some of his specific reform ideas had worked their way into early drafts of his classification of law, and

[77] See, e.g., I.D. Aikenhead, 'Students of the Common Law 1590–1615: Lives and Ideas at the Inns of Court', *Univ. Toronto Law Jour.*, xxvii (1977), 254; Ong, *Ramus, Method, and the Decay of Dialogue*, 203. Some of the assumptions here are at the basis of the later, much more sophisticated methodologies of Descartes and Leibniz. See, e.g., P.A. Schouls, *The Imposition of Method: A Study of Descartes and Locke* (Oxford, 1980), 5, 23; E.H. Wolgast, *The Grammar of Justice* (Ithaca, N.Y., London, 1987), 8.

[78] Ong, *Ramus, Method, and the Decay of Dialogue*, 199, 204–5; W.J. Ong, *Interfaces of the Word: Studies in the Evolution of Consciousness and Culture* (Ithaca, N.Y., London, 1977), 174–78; Knafla, 'Ramism and the English Renaissance', 38.

[79] Finch, *Nomotexnia*, Preface, sig. [#iv], tr. in Prest, 'Dialectical Origins', 344. He also invoked the oft-heard goal 'to form into one body, in harmonious order, the damaged and fragmented parts of the law of our country' and free it from 'confusion'.

[80] Prest, 'Dialectical Origins', 344–45. Finch was a religious radical when most common lawyers at the Inns of Court were more conservative in religious matters. Aikenhead, 'Students of the Common Law', 253.

[81] Prest, 'The Art of Law', 98–104.

[82] Prest, 'Dialectical Origins', 332; Prest, 'The Art of Law', 98.

a few remained in the English version that came into print after his death.[83]

Finch's reputation among common lawyers and at court rose after he published *Nomotexnia*, and he advanced quite rapidly within the profession. In 1614 Finch attained the rank of serjeant and was returned to parliament in a crown-controlled seat. In 1616 he received a knighthood and was named king's serjeant.[84] That year Francis Bacon recommended to James VI and I that Finch be among the half dozen lawyers named to produce an official digest of the common law, and Bacon, Finch and William Noy may have begun an effort along these lines.[85] Finch went to prison briefly for a tract of his, published anonymously in 1621, that prophesied a world empire ruled from the Holy Land by a reunited nation of Israel.[86] He recovered favour quickly, however, and even became law adviser to Bishop John Williams, the last cleric to hold the office of Lord Keeper.[87]

Though Finch drew back from his extreme position that English law be conformed to scriptural commands, there remained a religious dimension in the plan of his *Nomotexnia* and *Law*. The whole idea of revealing the mysterious contours of the law, of making the common law accessible to the common mind, of revealing its rational basis instead of merely assuring others that it had one, suggests a characteristically Protestant approach to matters of interpretation, doctrine and truth.

The structure of Finch's books also bore traces of his deeply-held religious convictions. In Book I Finch not only recognized a sphere of divinely-inspired, immutable natural law governing England's positive law, he also fleshed it out by enumerating specific rules that God had made known to mankind through the faculty of reason. In the law of persons, as we have seen, he rejected the invidious distinctions found in Roman and Old Testament law, and guided his own principle of classification by the message of the Gospels that the law should be 'no respecter of persons'. Offences against God, in Finch's scheme of things were no less than treason, and he asserted the role of the common law courts to punish them, down to the most minor transgressions.[88] Finch subtitled his work a 'description' of English law, but a work of this kind could not be merely descriptive. Finch had to make choices, and he was guided by firm ideas about how the common law ought to be structured.

Finch's *Law* was the version that achieved wide popularity among students of the common law through the remainder of the seventeenth century and

83 Prest, 'Dialectical Origins', 339–40.

84 Prest, 'Dialectical Origins', 345.

85 Bacon, 'A Proposition to His Majesty . . . Touching the Compiling and Amendment of the Laws of England', *Works of Francis Bacon*, xiii, 71; Prest, 'The Art of Law', 110.

86 [H. Finch], *The Worldes Great Restauration, Or The Calling of the Jewes* (1621); see Prest, 'The Art of Law', 95, 111, 114–15.

87 Prest, 'The Art of Law', 115.

88 Finch, Law, bk.3, chs.24–26; Finch, *Nomotexnia*, bk.2, ch.[9].

beyond. *Law* went through five editions by 1700,[89] and several copies made the crossing to seventeenth century Virginia, where colonists were much in need of short and comprehensive works on the principles of common law.[90] *Law* remained in print in the eighteenth century, and one enterprising publisher in 1759 even brought out an English translation of *Nomotexnia* to compete head to head with a new edition of *Law*.[91]

Other writers imitated, adapted and borrowed freely from Finch's structure for introductory books of their own.[92] In 1654 Edmund Wingate, a mathematician and common lawyer, published *A Summary of the Common Law of England*, a set of forty-seven elaborate tables that he 'extracted' from Books II through IV of Finch's *Law*. The first table showed the common law divided into persons (the 'circumstances' of the law), 'parts' (possessions and punishment of offences), and actions (the 'common affection' running through the law).[93] A year later Wingate appended those tables to his own work, *The Body of the Common Law of England*, in which he again followed Finch's plan, with slight modifications, to sort through a collection of hundreds of short, numbered 'rules of law'.[94] Michael Hawke, another mid century writer, drew upon Finch for his *Grounds of the Lawes of England*, and praised him for 'reducing not only the body of our laws into a compendious method, but also the grounds and rules of the same into an academical order'.[95]

Any estimate of the overall influence of a book like Finch's *Law* in shaping seventeenth-century lawyers' conceptions of the whole of their common law must begin by reckoning with another, more important work, Coke's *Institutes*. In 1628 Edward Coke published the first of his *Institutes*, the famous *Commentary on Littleton*, the only part Coke published during his lifetime. His work on the next three volumes was well advanced by 1628 and complete by 1633, but the second part, a commentary on important statutes, did not appear until 1642, and the third and fourth parts, on pleas of the

89 Editions in 1636, 1661, 1671 and 1678. A.W. Pollard and G.R. Redgrave, *A Short-Title Catalogue*, W.A. Jackson et al., ed., 2nd ed. (1976), i, no.10872; D. Wing, *A Short-Title Catalogue* (New York, 1972), ii, no. F931.

90 W.M. Billings, 'English Legal Literature as a Source of Law and Legal Practice for Seventeenth-Century Virginia', *Virginia Mag.*, lxxxvii (1979), 411–12; W.H. Bryson, *Census of Law Books in Colonial Virginia* (Charlottesville, Va., 1978), 48.

91 H. Finch, *A Description of the Common Laws of England, According to the Rules of Art* (1759). The anonymous translator announced it 'the first general Institute of the Laws of England', and praised the originality and 'peculiarity' of Finch's plan, Translator's Preface, v. For the title of 'first' of the English institutional writers, Finch also got the vote of Lawson, 'Institutes', 342.

92 E.g., the first chapter of *A Treatise of the Principall Grounds and Maximes of the Lawes of this Kingdom* (1641), attributed to William Noy, a prominent lawyer and contemporary of Finch.

93 [E. Wingate], *A Summary of the Common Law of England* (1654).

94 E. Wingate, *The Body of the Common Law of England* (1655); see R. Pound, 'The Maxims of Equity – I', *Harvard Law Rev.*, xxxiv (1921), 834.

95 M. Hawke, *The Grounds of the Lawes of England* (1657), sig. a2; Simpson, 'Rise and Fall of the Legal Treatise', 650.

crown and the jurisdiction of the courts, two years later.[96] Coke's survey of English law was massive, about seven times the length of Finch's book. It was 'comprehensive', but in a sense of the word diametrically opposed to the one that fits short works like Finch's *Law* and Wingate's *Summary*.

Coke was not a devotee of 'method'. In 1604, shortly before Cowell's *Institutiones* appeared in print, he wrote that as for 'bringing the common laws into a better method, I doubt very much of the fruit of that labour'.[97] When Coke himself was a student, he kept a 'commonplace' not under the usual set of alphabetical headings, but interleaved in his copy of Littleton's *Tenures*.[98] In the 1620s, he turned again to Littleton, 'the first book that our student takes in hand', for the text on which to hang his outpourings of common law minutiae.[99] Littleton wrote only on the subject of estates, tenures, and other incidents of landholding, but Coke was somehow able to fit all the rest of the common law into his *Commentary*. Debt and contract, trespass and treason, murder and rape, even heresy and excommunication all had their places in the vast gloss. One can envisage Coke, nearly eighty, plotting ingenious word associations to bring his wide learning to bear on a narrow text. But how would a student know to look to Littleton's chapter on tenancy at will to learn Coke's definition of trespass?[100]

Coke's *Commentary on Littleton* must have given students far less of a sense that the common law had a coherent, rational structure than they would have received by reading Littleton's *Tenures* alone. When (and if) students reached the second and third volumes of his *Institutes*, they found Coke still using the form of a gloss whenever possible, taking statutes as his texts, much as he had done as a reader at the Inner Temple. His second part, proceeding statute by statute, eluded even chronological order, and in the third, his progress through criminal matters grew fitful after the opening chapters on treason and the common law felonies. The last book proceeded court by court, and thus, through his entire *Institutes*, Coke managed to avoid using any substantive categories of his own for the presentation of legal knowledge. His method was the very antithesis of 'method' as preached by Ramus and practised by Finch.

For common lawyers in the seventeenth century and afterward, Coke's *Institutes*, though notoriously ill-arranged, were nevertheless indispensable. The volumes carried the full weight of his personal authority as the pre-eminent common lawyer of his day, and this more than made up for the deficiencies in organization. Coke's *Institutes* perpetuated the older,

96 Coke, Preface to *The First Part of the Institutes*, xl; see J.H. Baker, 'Coke's Note Books and the Sources of his Reports', *Camb. Law Jour.*, xxx (1972), 163–64.

97 Coke, Preface to *The Fourth Part of the Reports*, x.

98 Baker, 'Coke's Note Books', 148. On Coke's disapproval of abridgements, see the preface to *The Fourth Part of the Reports*, x–xi; *Palmer's Case* (1612), 10 Co. Rep. 24b, 25a; *Pilfold's Case* (1612), 10 Co. Rep. 115b, 117b; *Portington's Case* (1613), 10 Co. Rep. 35b, 41a; Coke, *First Part of the Institutes*, fo. 395a.

99 Coke, Preface to *The First Part of the Institutes*, xl.

100 Ibid., fos. 57a–57b.

unstructured forms of legal writing that had been devised to accompany the oral transmission of learning. The figure of Coke looms over seventeenth-century legal education, and the *Commentary on Littleton* was probably the most important text for students of the common law. But it was not the only text.

If students and practitioners had taken their conception of the common law solely from Coke's *Institutes*, they would have found what Coke himself described: 'a deep well', dark, mysterious, bottomless, the source of more learning than any single mind, even Coke's, could fathom.[101] Using an introductory work like Finch's *Law*, on the other hand, gave students an image of the common law as a vast diagram extending from the highest generalities to the most minute details; again, no one could conceive it all at once, but its general contours, its main parts and the ways they fit together, were fixed and known.

Many of the students coming to the Inns of Court to take up study of the common law were probably predisposed to accept Finch's conception of the common law. In 1654 the anonymous preface to the *Summary of the Common Law of England*, probably by the mathematician Edmund Wingate, praised Finch for having clothed the law in a 'logical method' so exact that it rivalled the leading textbooks on theology, geometry, logic, physics, politics and mathematics, including works by such noted scholars as Ramus himself.[102] This reminds us that the primary impact of Ramist method was on school and university textbooks.[103] Many of the standard school primers that were published in vast quantities in the seventeenth century tended to use the same sort of definitions, distinctions, tables and elaborate typographical display of information that students would later encounter in Finch's work. Seventeenth-century textbooks shaped students' expectations of what it meant to know, or begin to know, a new field of learning, and prepared them better to accept a common law of nesting categories than one of disjointed particulars dredged up from a deep well of collective wisdom.

Could Finch's form and Coke's substance be combined? The advice of Thomas Wood to 'young beginners' at common law, given soon after the close of the century, suggests that some were doing just this. He told students to read Finch first, 'the most methodical book extant' by a common lawyer, then to plough through Coke's *Institutes*, which he conceded contained 'the best authorities in our law'.[104] '[W]hatever is read' in Coke, the author

[101] Ibid., fo.71a. See *Colvin's Case* (1607), 7 Co. Rep. 1a, 4a ('no man ought to take upon himself to be wiser than the law').

[102] Wingate, Preface to *Summary of the Common Law*, sig. A3.

[103] Ong, *Ramus, Method, and the Decay of Dialogue*, 9.

[104] T. Wood, *Some Thoughts Concerning the Study of the Laws of England in the Two Universities* (1708), rptd. *The Gladsome Light of Jurisprudence: Learning the Law in England and the United States in the Eighteenth and Nineteenth Centuries*, M.H. Hoeflich, ed. and comp. (Westport, Conn., 1988), 46–47. Wood, himself a civilian, gave Finch high marks for 'almost' following the method of Justinian's *Institutes*, ibid., 46.

advised, 'the student may always keep Finch's method in his mind, and upon a review reduce all to his order'.[105] Wood himself was much influenced by Finch's scheme, and used parts of it in his own *Institutes of the Lawes of England* in 1720, as did Blackstone in his famous *Commentaries on the Laws of England* in the 1760s.[106]

Finch promised more than he could deliver, however, and other voices can be heard from the mid seventeenth century onward, complaining that the common law was still the bottomless pit that Coke depicted in his *Institutes*. Whatever popularity Cowell's and Finch's works may have had, a well-meaning lawyer could still write in the late 1640s that 'no man as yet has endeavoured to set down' the necessary 'order and method' of the common law as *Bracton* had once done,[107] and another could complain in the 1720s that 'of all the professions in the world, that pretend to book-learning, none is so destitute of institution as that of the common law'.[108] The common law, no longer an oral tradition, had indeed emerged into an age of 'book-learning'. It would continue to thrive as a vast, unwritten text of legal rules, but only if common lawyers felt they had some broad consensus on what the chapters were, how they fitted together, and how many it took to fill the complete celestial volume.

Matthew Hale, the leading common lawyer in the second half of the century, provided a fitting vignette to round out this development. Hale maintained a wide circle of acquaintances within the scientific community in London.[109] In the midst of one of their discussions, according to a contemporary report, some of his friends challenged Hale on his own ground, the common law. Surely that was 'a study that could not be brought into a scheme, nor formed into a rational science, by reason of the indigestedness of it, and the multiplicity of cases in it, which rendered it very hard to be understood, or reduced into a Method'.[110] Hale said he was 'not of their mind', and at

105 Ibid., 47.

106 See Simpson, 'Rise and Fall of the Legal Treatise', 650.

107 The unknown author recommended 'methodizing' all the titles of Brooke's *Abridgment* 'into that method of Bracton' – persons, things and actions – and added that 'the method of the imperial laws may much conduce to the framing of a method of our law'. 'Directions for the orderly reading of the law of England', Bodl. MS Rawlinson C 207, fos.245, 266, 269; see Prest, *Inns of Court*, 148.

108 R. North, 'Discourse on the Study of the Laws' (*c.* 1720s), *Gladsome Light*, 15; Holdsworth, *History of English Law*, vi, 2nd ed. (1937), 489.

109 Hale's circle included John Wilkins, Warden of Wadham College, Oxford, who composed a classification of all human knowledge to fit his new 'artificial' language. Wilkins included a table of 'judicial relations' on which Hale may have assisted. Its principal divisions were persons, actions (or proceedings), crimes and punishments, J. Wilkins, *An Essay toward a Real Character, and a Philosophical Language* (1668), 270–74. See Shapiro, 'Law and Science', 748, 762; B.J. Shapiro, *John Wilkins, 1614–1672: An Intellectual Biography* (Berkeley, Los Angeles, 1969), 155, 173–76; B.J. Shapiro, *Probability and Certainty in Seventeenth-Century England* (Princeton, Guildford, 1983), 172.

110 G. Burnett, *The Life and Death of Sir Matthew Hale* (1682), 73.

once drew out for them 'a scheme of the whole order and parts of it, in a large sheet of paper, to the great satisfaction' of everyone. His friends pressed him to complete this sketch, to 'compile a body of the English law', but he was reluctant to put forward his sketch as a definitive structure, and said this should instead be the work of a committee of eminent lawyers, at the direction of the king.[111]

Hale did complete his one-page sketch of the common law, but left it unpublished at his death. One part, which he called an 'analysis of the civil part of the law', remained in short outline form. He said in a preface to the manuscript that it was not an 'exact logical method', but at least 'a tolerable method or distribution'.[112] Civil law consisted of rights, wrongs and remedies. Rights in turn, were of persons (the sovereign and his subjects) and of things (real and personal). The other part of the common law, the criminal side, Hale filled in with full detail. His treatise on the pleas of the crown, which he also never published, began with a section on the general doctrines, then proceeded through treasons and felonies in time-honoured fashion, and ended on criminal proceedings, stage by stage, from arrest and process through to the reprieve arriving, as always, too late – just after the execution.[113]

Hale's works no doubt circulated in manuscript in the last decades of the seventeenth century, but they were not published for the wider audience of law students and practitioners until long after his death and, together with the books of Wood and Blackstone, form the next chapter in this story. Cowell and Finch stand at the head of a new line of treatises comprehending the whole of the common law within a structure of substantive categories. From the seventeenth century onward, we can begin to speak of a general law of property, a general law of contract, of criminal liability and of constitutional rights, without doing violence to the words and conceptions of the lawyers whose doctrines we describe.

111 Ibid.; E. Heward, *Matthew Hale* (1972), 147–48; Shapiro, 'Law and Science', 743–46.

112 M. Hale, Preface to *An Analysis of the Civil Part of the Law* (1713), sig. A2-A2v.

113 M. Hale, *Historia Placitorum Coronae* (1736).

Chapter 6

An Introduction to Iconographical Studies of Legal History

I. England and Wales

A.H. Manchester

As historians we are constantly searching for little-used or new sources. Until quite recently legal historians had made little effective use of the numerous volumes of nineteenth-century parliamentary papers which tell us so much about legal matters, despite the work of Holdsworth some years ago and, more recently, of Radzinowicz. Outside our own field we may note the value of filmed newsreels and of documentaries to the historian of the modern period. Simon Schama has demonstrated convincingly how an excellent narrative history of an earlier period still can be enriched by the lavish use of contemporary illustrations.[1] To what extent can we legal historians make good use of such materials in our own field? Can we usefully develop an iconography of legal history? To what extent does the work of our European colleagues help us in that inquiry?

Margariet Becker describes below the work of her own Centre for the Documentation of Legal History and Legal Iconography in Amsterdam in addition to referring to the work of other European scholars. I am making a modest start in respect of England and Wales. With the help of a grant from the Economic and Social Research Council I am seeking out representations, drawn in the main from the period 1750–1900, of law courts, law suits, trials, the legal profession and judiciary and forms of punishment and the like. The representations may be in the form of paintings, prints, sculptures or photographs. They may exist in their own right or they may be illustrations in a book. I do not include portraits of individuals within my aims except in so far as they may illustrate a more general point. For example, I am interested in a judicial portrait only if it illustrates, say, judicial dress: the personal likeness of the judge is of no interest. Such a project is by no means wholly original, even in the Anglo-American tradition. Some years ago Professor John Langbein illustrated one of his learned articles on the criminal law by means of some twelve pictures. They demonstrate very well what I have in mind.

[1] S. Schama, *Citizens* (1989).

One picture shows Sir John Fielding, the blind half-brother of Henry Fielding, the novelist, presiding at a pre-trial examination in his Bow Street chambers.[2] To the extent that it may be accurate, such a picture surely offers us at the very least an insight into how pre-trial procedure actually worked in these busy London chambers. For example, we can note a certain formality in the proceedings, who was present, and so on. More recently, J.A. Sharpe, a social historian of crime, has published a volume of illustrations of the social history of crime. They are drawn from the British Museum's huge collection which was first catalogued by F.G. Stephens and M.D. George in their *Catalogue of Political and Personal Satires*. Not only do these give us a view of the facts about crime and punishment: they also offer an expression of contemporary political and social opinion about crime and punishment.[3]

European scholars who have been working in this field for some years have demonstrated a number of uses of iconographical materials, as Mrs. Becker points out below. I myself draw attention to two. First, there is the accurate representation of a place or event. Secondly, there may be a useful representation of the public opinion of the day. We can learn from both. At the same time we must be cautious. In assessing the eighteenth-century prints we need to be aware of the emblematic tradition which culminated in the publication in English in 1709 of Caesar Ripa's *Iconologia*.[4] In Ripa we have an authoritative collection of allegorical figures which explains fully their symbolic meanings. In the eighteenth century generally an 'emblem' meant any pictorial image with a fixed symbolic association. So we have Liberty, with her cap and pole. How often we can see that symbol used to good effect in, for example, the prints which dealt with the issue of John Wilkes and freedom of the press. And Justice, with sword and scales, is an ever popular figure. Not surprisingly, Justice blindfolded or Justice assailed became stock figures in the repertoire of the printmaker. Then we come to the Devil. I am sorry to have to report that, in the prints which are of interest to us as legal historians, the Devil and the Lawyer are often portrayed as being on the friendliest of terms: indeed, the one may be seen as the agent of the other. Of course, in England and Wales we developed our own national stereotypes. Britannia and John Bull became potent symbols of national pride from the mid eighteenth century. During this early period too there were other useful symbols. A dog might symbolize fidelity or open access to the building, for example, a court, in which it was located. It is clear,

2 J.H. Langbein, 'Shaping the Eighteenth Century Criminal Trial: A View from the Ryder Sources', *Univ. Chicago Law Rev.*, l (1983), 1. Cf. J.H. Langbein, 'Illustrations as Legal Historical Sources', *Law School Record*, xxix (1983), 13.

3 J.A. Sharpe, *Crime and the Law in English Satirical Prints, 1600–1832* (1986).

4 P. Tempest, *Iconologia: or Moral Emblems by Caesar Ripa . . .* (1709). For an earlier edition used in the Netherlands see n.37 below.

therefore, that there is considerable scope for interpretation in many of the older prints.[5]

In the later eighteenth century the nature of the print began to change: in the nineteenth century other art forms developed which offered equally telling representations of public opinion and also gave what seem to be accurate representations of contemporary scenes.

I now turn to three pictures which illustrate some of these points. The first picture (Illustration 1) is entitled 'Westminster Hall: The First Day of Term'. At the far end of the Hall we see the courts of Chancery and of King's Bench. Certainly they were courts in a palatial setting, in the literal sense of the phrase; they were royal courts of justice. Yet the print makes it abundantly clear that the court structures were quite makeshift, wholly lacking in any claim to grandeur. Some years later in 1800 a commentator even found the whole of the Hall's interior 'obnoxious'.[6] It does seem a fair comment. Yet clearly the Hall was a busy open place. At the sides of the Hall you can see clearly the stalls and counters of the 'Books and printsellers, Mathematical instrument makers, Seamstresses, Haberdashers and other tradespeople', who are said to have been allowed to carry on their trades there for many years. All such stall holders were expelled shortly after 1760. The busy Hall illustrates the open nature of the Hall itself. People – rich and poor, perhaps – lawyers, talk and walk about. There is a relaxed atmosphere. Access is available even to a dog, a symbolic feature of the print. Does not all this suggest that the Hall, and the courts within it, were open to all manner of people? That confirms the point which Paley stresses in his popular *Moral and Political Philosophy* (1785) when he writes:

> A fourth requisite in the constitution of a court of justice, and equivalent to many checks upon the discretion of judges, is that its proceedings be carried on in public, apertis foribus, not only before a promiscuous concourse of bystanders, but in the audience of the whole profession of the law . . . The most corrupt judge will fear to indulge his dishonest wishes in the presence of such an assembly; . . .[7]

The second picture (Illustration 2) is entitled: 'The Bosky Magistrate'. Taken at one level it indicates little more than the relaxed nature of proceedings before a magistrate. However, the imagery tells us rather more. For example, the picture on the wall shows Justice being kicked over. Presumably this symbolizes a magistracy which is inefficient and, possibly, corrupt. On the fireplace we see what appears to be a laughing Devil with an iron in the fire. So once again there is here a comment on the magistracy. Thirdly, the magistrate is lame, a common feature in such prints. Possibly this symbolizes that Justice also is

[5] H.M. Atherton, *Political Prints in the Age of Hogarth* (1974), 127.

[6] J. Mordaunt Crook and M.H. Port, *The History of the King's Works*, H.M. Colvin, gen. ed., vi (1973), 499.

[7] At 123–25. Or see the extract in A.H. Manchester, *Sources of English Legal History* (1984), 5–6.

Fig. 1. Westminster Hall, the first day of term (*Greater London Record Office*)

Fig. 2. The Bosky Magistrate (*British Museum*)

Fig. 3. Paul Pry's Peep into Chancery (*British Museum*)

Fig. 4. The Courtroom of the Court of Holland in the Seventeenth Century

Fig. 5. (*Above*) Design for Digest 30: *De legatis et fideicommissis*

Fig. 6. (*Left*) Design for Digest 40.5: *De fideicommissariis libertatibus*

lame. And, fourthly, pigeons (or are they lovebirds?) are flying away from the dovecote. Can this indicate a breach of the peace? And so one could go on. For example, are the dogs symbolic? And what do we make of the various writings on the picture above the fireplace, and on the bowl of the caption below the picture?

My third picture (Illustration 3) is entitled: 'Paul Pry's Peep into Chancery'. It too is satirical in nature. It refers in specific terms to Chancery. It was produced in 1826, the year in which a Chancery Commission virtually absolved Lord Eldon's court of Chancery of blame in respect of two powerful allegations of undue expense and delay which were constantly levelled at it. It clearly shows people seated at a table piled high with legal papers. It offers striking visual support to the written complaints. And does not the very fact that such a print should be exhibited for sale confirm that there was a considerable degree of public support for such complaints?

Here, then, we have a mixture of description and of comment. How the iconographer values the artist who portrayed accurately. Perhaps Sir George Hayter comes close to that ideal as he had expressed a wish to be 'painter of the history of his own time'. Moreover, we know that his 'Trial of Queen Caroline' was commissioned by a member of parliament and that Hayter had made a preliminary sketch. Very probably, therefore, this painting is an accurate representation of those unique proceedings. In other instances, of which my first picture is an example, it is possible to compare and contrast other contemporary descriptive pictures of the same subject. Such comparisons are useful also in relation to the picture as comment. For example, magistrates appear to be portrayed as lame as often as lawyers are portrayed as being on friendly terms with the Devil. Clearly the tasks of assessment and of interpretation of the very many prints and, I hope, paintings will be a formidable task. In undertaking to begin that task I draw comfort from the fact that I shall be able to draw upon European experience.

II. The Netherlands

M.A. Becker-Moelands

When in 1967 some legal historians in the Netherlands founded the Dutch Centre for the Documentation of Legal History,[8] the collecting of material in the field of legal iconography became one of their tasks.[9] They started what was for the Netherlands an almost new field of interest, initiated more than

[8] In 1988 the name was changed to the Dutch Centre for the Documentation of Legal History and Legal Iconography.

[9] The range of the collection is wider than that of the English project. We also collect, for example, images of Justice, pictures concerning tax law, private law, public law, illustrated title-pages of law books and pictures of juridical legends and stories.

half a century before in Germany.

In 1900 Franz Heinemann, a German professor, published a richly illustrated book in which, for the first time, some illustrations formed the basis for the text.[10] Two years later von Amira published his famous book on the gestures in the illustrations of the *Sachsenspiegel*.[11] Here for the first time in legal history the illustrations themselves were the object of investigation. But probably the first book on legal iconography is Hans Fehr's *Recht im Bilde*.[12] In this book Fehr shows by means of authentic illustrations how much law and justice formerly were incorporated into daily life. Then legal historians seemed to lose interest and it was not until the 1960s that interest was renewed.[13] The last ten years especially have been important for legal iconography as there are now some major and growing collections in Europe.[14] In the Netherlands the collection already contains over 6,000 photographs and is still growing rapidly. The data are for the greater part on computer.[15] The documentation is done at the level of iconographical description.[16] At this level the main task of the Centre ends and the challenge for the legal historian begins, that is, iconographic interpretation, looking for a deeper meaning, and iconology, the searching for cultural, social and historical backgrounds of a picture.[17] Only then can the picture be used to its utmost extent as a legal source. Only then can it clarify, complete and correct our view of law and justice in former times; show us the interaction between, for example, law and religion. Perhaps we may even detect the influence of pictures on law.[18]

Some examples may demonstrate the use that legal historians can make of pictures. My first one (Illustration 4) is an engraving dated 1631, used as the title-page of the first edition of one of the most famous Dutch law books: *Inleidinge tot de Hollandsche rechtsgeleertheyt* by Grotius. As it looks like a

10 F. Heinemann, *Der Richter und die Rechtsgelehrten in früheren Zeiten* (Leipzig, 1900; reprinted, Düsseldorf and Cologne, 1969).

11 K. von Amira, *Die Dresdener Handschrift: Die Handgebärden in den Bilderhandschriften des Sachsenspiegels* (Leipzig, 1902).

12 H. Fehr, *Das Recht im Bilde* (Zurich, Munich and Leipzig, 1923).

13 The works of Prof. G. Kocher and Prof. W. Schild especially have been very important for the growing interest in legal iconography.

14 Austria, the University of Graz; Germany, the University of Bielefeld (private collectiion); Switzerland, the University of Zurich; Sweden, the University of Lund; Denmark, the University of Copenhagen.

15 The data are: the name of the object; the name of the artist; the date of creation; composition; material; size; in case of books, engravings etc., the name of the publisher and the town of publication; the present whereabouts; object, geographical and name entries according to a controlled open entry-system.

16 For the different levels of iconographical research see R. van Straten, *Inleiding in de iconografie* (Muiderberg, 1983).

17 Because of its time-consuming nature research is done only on a small scale.

18 This may be the case especially with satirical pictures as it may have been, for example, during the time shortly before the abolition of torture.

realistic picture we first have to establish whether it is a representation of an actual courtroom and, if so, how accurate it is. Descriptions of the courtroom of the Law Court of Holland in the Hague show that the engraving is a very realistic picture of this court.[19] In 1511 the dining hall of the counts of Holland was transformed into a courtroom. It was given a new ceiling with beams and in the north wall a gigantic chimney was built with a door on either side. Its four windows had benches. With the help of a wooden fence with the statues of fifteen animals, holding the coats-of-arms of the princes, a square was formed in which the sittings of the court took place. Within this tribunal were the benches for the judges, the barristers and the solicitors. In front of the chimney was the chair for the Stadtholder in whose name the administration of justice took place.

The engraver assumes a high stance, from which we look down on the Court of Holland in session.[20] Under a canopy is a seat with the two judges who normally form the bench.[21] Opposite them sits the prosecutor. At a table in between are pictured the clerk of the court and his secretary. On the benches in the front part of the tribunal we see men with and without hats. According to the records the first three benches on entering were for barristers, the last two for solicitors.[22] That means that the men with hats are barristers and those without hats are solicitors. As only the judges, prosecutor, barristers and solicitors were allowed within the fence, the hatless figures approaching the clerk's table are solicitors. They are wearing short capes, unlike the barristers who were obliged to wear a gown.[23] On the left, however, in the benches of the barristers there is also a man without a hat: he is standing and gesturing. Art. 55 of the court's rules of procedure gives us the explanation:[24] 'Barristers . . . while pleading will stand up and respectfully uncover their heads until the president of the court allows them to wear their hats'. Up to this point it can be checked that the engraving is realistic, and a wonderful help in visualizing seventeenth century written reports of sessions of the Court of Holland.

On closer inspection, the realistic-looking part of the public attending the sitting of the court implies more. We see all kinds of people in the public part of the hall: rich and poor, male and female, some young people and even a dog. Some of the people in the foreground and along the fence are looking at us.

[19] A. Ising, *Het Binnenhof te 's Gravenhage* (The Hague, 1879); *Beschrijving van de Grafelijke Zalen op het Binnenhof te 's Gravenhage. In opdracht van den Minister van Waterstaat bewerkt door de Commissie van advies en uitgegeven door de Maatschappij tot bevordering der Bouwkunst* (The Hague, 1907); G.G. Calkoen, 'Het Binnenhof van 1247–1747 (volgens de rentmeesterrekeningen van Noord-Holland)', *Die Haghe* (1902), 36–89; J. de Riemer, *Beschrijving van 's Gravenhage* (Delft, 1730).

[20] In reality it is impossible to look at the hall from there. In this the artist is following the fashion of his time.

[21] *Groot Plakaatboek* (The Hague and Amsterdam, 1658) [G.P.B.] Pt. II, 715, art. 50.

[22] G.P.B., II, 1082.

[23] Ibid.

[24] G.P.B., II, 716.

Forming lines, their function is to support the perspective in the illustration.[25] The two parties of four in the foreground introduce the spectator to the court session. By means of deeper engraving two persons are made darker, more outstanding. We are forced to look at them more carefully and there is no doubt that they are put where they are and in this way for a reason. The man to the right, dressed in a gown, with a paper in his hand, talking to a rather poorly dressed man and woman, is a barrister in discussion with a poor couple. The young boy standing behind him, with a bag in his hand, is his assistant. He is carrying the documents for the lawsuit in a document bag. The man to the left, wearing a short cape, also with a piece of paper in his hand, is a solicitor discussing a case with a rich client. The main figures of the two groups not only introduce us, the spectators, to the court session; they also have this function in real life.

Besides the metaphorical meaning of the main figures, the groups also have a symbolic meaning: the very old idea of equality in law.[26] This illustration shows us that in the seventeenth century the idea that equality in justice is only possible with the same legal aid for rich and poor was not a dead legal letter but a living social phenomenon.[27]

Almost in the middle of the open space between the barrister and the solicitor we see a dog. As the hall connected with the courtroom was used as a market-hall,[28] it was quite possible for a dog to slip in. Yet we see dogs in almost every picture of a court in session and it is very obvious that this dog, standing apart, looking at us, is put there deliberately. A dog can have different meanings in different contexts. In combination with a judge or an image of Justice it is a symbol of fidelity and reliability. In this picture the dog is linked to the court by a visual connection with the court-clerk, with whom it forms a line of perspective. Placed almost in the middle of the public part of the courtroom it symbolizes the open court.

This scene of the Court of Holland not only gives us a vivid picture of a seventeenth-century court sitting, with all its particularities but, on close observation, also gives us a glimpse of the legal thinking of the seventeenth century concerning equality and an open court.

Illustration 5 is a design for a tile. In 1686 an advertisement in an Amsterdam newspaper announced that in Harlingen a series of 432 tiles would be produced, each representing a title of Justinian's *Corpus Juris*.[29] The tiles, intended to be attached to brick walls, were meant to help in memorizing the Pandects. Public interest was not great enough to warrant actual production but fortunately the series of designs has been preserved almost complete.

25 By looking at us they attract our attention, strengthening their function.

26 This is probably the first picture that goes beyond equality in the administration of justice, symbolized by Justice or a judge with a rich and a poor party standing before him.

27 *Instructien voor het Hof van Holland* (The Hague, n.d.), 78.

28 E.F. Kossmann, *De boekverkopers, notarissen en cramers op het Binnenhof* (The Hague, 1932).

29 *Amsterdamse Donderdaeghse Courant*, 26 September 1686.

The design for book 30, *de legatis et fideicommissis* shows us a hall, with pillars in the background. In this hall nine men are pictured, one sitting and eight standing. One of the men standing is taller than the others and he is holding a blank square in his hand with seven pendants. Next to him is a man with a cross on his clothing. His feet are not touching the ground. Behind these two men there are two more; the four of them are all wearing the same kind of hat. The group is enclosed by two men in formal clothes. The men in the front row are all pointing at the tall man. At the left there are two figures, one with the same hat as the four in the middle. He also is pointing at the tall man. The other figure is again dressed in formal clothes.

In analyzing this drawing we have to bear in mind that the design was meant to be an aid to memory at a time when people were fond of symbols, hieroglyphs and picture puzzles. The tall man is clearly the main figure. From pictures in this series and from other pictorial sources we know that he is holding a will.[30] The seven pendants are the seven seals needed for a legal will in Roman law.[31] The blank most probably means that the question is about an inheritance of a complete estate.[32] The man sitting, also holding the will, is the testator.[33] The fact that the man holding the will is taller than the others, and that everybody is pointing at him, makes it obvious that he is the heir. The testator is also holding the will; as he is holding on to the inheritance. The cross on the clothing of the man next to him symbolizes fidelity and expresses visually the word *fides* in *fideicommissum*.[34] This man's feet are not on the ground: he is not walking on this earth any longer. The form of the cross reminds us of the cross as a symbol of death. The tall man, the fideicommissary heir, gets the inheritance only after this man's death. He is the heir in trust, who will take in succession to him (and may then have to pass the inheritance on to the next generation). But the designer gives us more than a visual representation of a simple *fideicommissum*. With the group of four and the man at the left, all wearing the same kind of beret, he portrays a family *fideicommissum*, although this form of inheritance is not discussed in book 30 of the Pandects but in book 31. A family *fideicommissum* was very often used in the Netherlands in the seventeenth century. It gave the testator power to dispose of his property for four generations. The last two generations

[30] J. Buno, *Memoriale juris civilis Romani, quo tituli omnes et praecipuae leges . . . emblematis et imaginibus . . . efficta exhibentur* (Hamburg, 1673); *Ars magna et admirabilis, speciminibus variis confirmata, qua Pandectarum tituli . . .* (Leiden, 1695).

[31] In appearance, of course, the parchment will is not Roman. However, the wax tablets used by the Romans would not be recognized by the spectator.

[32] All the wills in the series have a text, the picture of an object, or the testator pointing to an object.

[33] In Buno, *Ars magna*, cited above, and on the tiles the testators are pictured sitting in a chair or lying in bed, to symbolize that they are not in good health, for example, *Ars magna*, D. 29.6: *aeger in lecto decumbit*; D. 31: *vides testatorem aegrum in sella lecto assidentem*.

[34] *Ars magna*, D. 5.6: *crux fidem denotat*.

are literally looking over the shoulders of their forefathers at what is coming to them. The pillars in the hall suggest a public room. In the series of tiles they are often used to indicate a courtroom. The group of four is enclosed by men who are dressed like lawyers in the second half of the seventeenth century. The man at the left is talking to one.

To grasp the meaning of this special setting, with the courtroom, the lawyers and group of two at the left, one has to know that a fervent discussion was carried on between prominent seventeenth-century Dutch lawyers on whether the counting of the generations ought to start with the fideicommissary heir, or with the heir in trust. In practice it caused many lawsuits. The man with the beret on the left with his lawyer symbolizes the uncertain fourth heir. Besides being an aid to memory for a family *fideicommissum*, this design is a representation of an open legal question and a warning of the troubles which the establishing of a family *fideicommissum* could cause.

The third example (Illustration 6) has a political implication in addition to its legal aspects. In 1695, less than ten years after the failure of the tile project, Romeyn de Hooghe, a well-known Dutch engraver, who studied law at the university of Leiden, published a book containing 432 etchings, depicting the titles of the Pandects, each etching accompanied by a short explanation. They serve the same mnemotechnic purpose as the tiles. The example reproduced is taken from book 40, concerning manumission. In the etching we see a man in whose hand there is a will with a picture of a hat. In front of him is a man in a loincloth with a bald head. An explanation is given: '*pileus libertatem notat*'. For both the hat and the bald head[36] we find an explanation in Ripa's *Iconologia*:[37] 'After the head of a slave who was to be freed was shaven he was made to wear a hat. And this ceremony took place in the temple of a goddess called Feronia,[38] who was the tutelary deity of slaves'. The etching shows us a master promising his slave to free him by will. Looking at the pictures of the manumission we notice that the hats of masters and of freedmen differ considerably. The text, however, gives no explanation. Literature on the history of sixteenth- and seventeenth-century fashion tells us that the hat for the freedman was called a Spanish hat, fashionable during the Dutch war of liberation against the Spaniards, some eighty years earlier.[39] It cannot be a coincidence that Romeyn de Hooghe chose this particular hat, which reminded spectators of the time that the Dutch had no political rights, as a symbol of manumission for the Roman freedman who also had no political

[36] The hat as a symbol of freedom is only rarely mentioned in the written legal sources and the shaven head not at all. I have found the *pileus* only in CJ. 7.2.10 and 7.6.1.5. In Latin literature the *pileus* is well known (for example, Livy xxiv, 16; xxx, 45.5; Petronius, *Sat.*, 41; Tertullian, *Spect.*, 21–22), and in art and on coins and medallions the hat as a symbol of freedom is very often found in the course of the centuries.

[37] C. Ripa, *Iconologia of Uijtbeeldinghe des verstants* (Amsterdam, 1644), 573–74. In the Netherlands this book was very popular among seventeenth- and eighteenth-century artists.

[38] Feronia is probably a goddess of Etruscan origin.

[39] F.W.S. van Thienen, *Studien zur Kostümgeschichte in der Blütezeit Hollands* (Berlin, 1929).

rights. Here fashion, coming from a historical political background, serves as an aid to memory.

I hope that it will be evident not only that pictures can be very useful for the legal historian but also that making good use of them is not easy. For legal iconographical interpretation and legal iconology, next to a knowledge of legal history, a certain knowledge of the history of art is indispensable. Sometimes knowledge of the Bible, mythology, history and literature and, as shown, even of the fashions of former centuries is also essential. That each period has its own questions and therefore its own difficulties will be clear. When we realize how great the influence of foreign countries was on our national art, our national history, literature and philosophy, the importance of working on similar collections in several countries of Europe will be recognized. Good scholarship in this field is only possible through interaction, interaction of available material, interaction of ideas, interaction between countries and interaction between disciplines.

Illustrations from bygone ages can tell us, if rightly understood, a great deal about law and justice in the times of our forefathers. They are the more important as they give us not the written model rules but mostly the view of non-lawyers, of the people who lived under those rules.

Chapter 7

Disputations of Scots Students Attending Universities in the Northern Netherlands

Paul Nève

The universities of the northern Netherlands are all relatively new. Leyden was founded in 1575 for the provinces of Holland and Zeeland, Franeker for Friesland in 1585 and Groningen in 1614 for the province of the same name. In 1636 the university of Utrecht grew from the municipal Illustrious School and the Illustrious School of Harderwijk was transformed in 1647–48 into the university of Guelderland.[1] For a short time there was a second university in Guelders, the academy of Nijmegen (1656–79).[2]

Before looking at the Scots who studied at these universities, we have to deal with the question: where on the Continent did Scots study before the foundation of Leyden university? As far as I can judge, the answer is at the Brabantine (southern Netherlands) university of Louvain, founded in 1425. From 1426 to 1453 fifty-four Scotsmen matriculated there (16 per cent of all foreign students), and their number rose to 119 in the period from 1453 to 1485 (25.7 per cent) and to 182 in 1486–1527 (19.5 per cent). From then it fell sharply: seventy-one Scotsmen (3.3 per cent) enrolled from 1527 to 1569.[3] Before the foundation of the Louvain *alma mater*, Scots studied in Cologne and before that in France, chiefly in Paris and Orleans. In this respect Louvain profited from the political troubles in which France was involved during the fifteenth century. When, for example, their stay in Paris became troublesome for Scots students during the period 1408–37, as a result of the Burgundian war and growing English influence, they moved initially to Cologne and later to Louvain. Even when the Parisian university became accessible to them again, they remained loyal to Louvain. As a result of the revolt that flared up in the Netherlands against the central government of Charles V and

[1] W.Th.M. Frijhoff, *La société néerlandaise et ses gradués, 1575–1814: Une recherche sérielle sur le statut des intellectuels à partir des registres universitaires avec une bibliographie, des annexes statistiques et un resumé en néerlandais* (Amsterdam, 1981), 13–18.

[2] J. van den Boom, *Voorlopige lijst van studenten van de Kwartierlijke Akademie te Nijmegen, 1655–1679* (Nijmegen, 1981).

[3] See H. de Ridder-Symoens, 'Internationalismus versus Nationalismus an Universitäten um 1500 nach zumeist südniederländischen Quellen', *Europa 1500: Integrationsprozesse im Widerstreit* (Stuttgart, 1986), 397–414, table 1 (408).

Philip II, the situation underwent a change around 1550: Leyden took over the role of Louvain.[4]

How many Scotsmen went to Leyden? A few years ago R. Feenstra published some figures which are listed below with some additions.[5]

Scottish students at the University of Leyden, 1575–1800. (Figures in brackets refer to the number of Scottish law and medical students at Leyden)

		L	M			L	M
1575–1600	21	(9)	(–)	1701–1725	406	(187)	(167)
1601–1625	35	(10)	(6)	1726–1750	252	(115)	(98)
1626–1650	72	(24)	(20)	1751–1775	55	(26)	(21)
1651–1675	188	(89)	(49)	1776–1800	12	(1)	(9)
1676–1700	419	(235)	(122)				

4 Ibid., 397–98, and A. Murdoch, 'The Advocates, the Law and the Nation in Early Modern Scotland', *Lawyers in Early Modern Europe and America*, W. Prest, ed. (1981), 147–63, who writes at p.150: 'It seems that the landed classes did not just accept the law and the courts; they also began to send their sons to the bar, and to Holland to be educated in civil law. In the immediate past those who went abroad to study civil law had gone to French universities, but the advent of a firmly Catholic, absolutist regime in France caused a shift to Holland'. R. Feenstra, 'Scottish-Dutch Legal Relations in the Seventeenth and Eighteenth Centuries', *Scotland and Europe, 1200–1850*, T.C. Smout, ed. (Edinburgh, 1986), 128–42 draws attention to the fact that in the sixteenth century many Scottish law students continued to go to France. From the 1530s they seem to have preferred the university of Bourges, the centre of Humanist Jurisprudence. In 1572 the heyday of Bourges came to an abrupt end; during the Massacre of St. Bartholomew Hotman and Donellus fled from this town, op. cit., 129.

5 Feenstra, 130, table 1. For the total student numbers Feenstra took his figures from H.T. Colenbrander, 'De herkomst der Leidsche studenten', *Pallas Leidensis* MCMXXV (Leyden, 1925), 275–303, particularly from table II (294–95). Using the Leyden matriculation lists W.J. Liberton arrived at lower figures. According to him sixteen Scotsmen matriculated between 1582 and 1600; 1601–1625, twenty-four; 1626–1650, sixty; and between 1651 and 1662, sixty-one. See W.J. Liberton, 'Schotse studenten aan de Universiteit te Leiden (1582–1662)', *Mededelingenblad van de Caledonian Society* (1985–86). Liberton relied on the *Album studiosorum Academiae Lugduno-Batavae*, MDLXXV-MDCCCLXXV (The Hague, 1875). This album is also the basis of E. Peacock, *Index to English Speaking Students who have graduated [sic] at Leyden University*, Index Society Publications, xiii (1883). For every person Peacock indicates whether he is mentioned in the album as an *Anglus, Scotus, Americanus* etc.; unfortunately he did not extract the faculty classification from the album. A comparison of Liberton's chronological list with Peacock's alphabetical one shows that they contain roughly the same names. We also have at our disposal for the law students a typed list of 'Schotse Studenten in de Rechten te Leiden', made by Mrs. O.C.D. Idenburg-Siegenbeek van Heukelom in the early 1950s; a copy is available in the Academisch Historisch Museum, Leyden University. This list comprises about 690 names. So far as I know there are no comparable lists for other Leyden faculties. The figures which occur in Frijhoff's book always concern the 'Anglais et Ecossais' or the inhabitants of the 'Iles britanniques' taken together; therefore they have no bearing on our theme.

This gives a total number of 1460 Scottish students and of 696 law and 492 medical students, but the figures are very rough. The matriculation lists are far from complete, and not everybody studied for any length of time in Leyden.[6] Ten years after Leyden university the Frisian academy of Franeker was founded. It attracted relatively few Scots, around fifty during its whole existence, of whom about twenty also matriculated in Leyden.[7] Groningen (1614) was not much more popular than Franeker: sixty Scots between 1614 and 1800, of whom about ten were also enrolled at Leyden and only one or two at Franeker.[8] The only university that – at a respectful distance – competed to some extent with Leyden was Utrecht (1636). According to the (incomplete) matriculation lists up to 1800 at least 101 Scotsmen studied at Utrecht; of them about thirty matriculated simultaneously at Leyden. Although the faculty in which students matriculated is not mentioned in these lists, we can calculate by means of other sources that twenty students at least studied law and thirty-one at least medicine.[9] To all appearances Utrecht found favour with foreigners only towards the end of the seventeenth century; that favour was not always a steady one:

[6] In the appendix to his article: 'Lawyers, Landowners, and the Civic Leadership of Post-Union Scotland', *Jurid. Rev. N.S.*, xxi (1976), 97–120, N.T. Phillipson arrives at a total of 634 Scottish law students matriculating at the law school of Leyden, 1660–1790. As for Utrecht, for the same period he gives 104 law students and for Groningen (from the year 1691) sixty-one. As will be shown below the figures for Utrecht and Groningen are incorrect: Phillipson took his figures from lists which were prepared for him 'on the instructions of the Deans of the three Law Schools'. Unfortunately Utrecht and Groningen provided him with lists of Scottish students in all faculties (Feenstra, op. cit., 131).

[7] *Album studiosorum Academiae Franekerensis (1585–1811,1816–1844)*, I, *Naamlijst der studenten*, S.J. Fockema Andreae and Th.J. Meijer, ed. (Franeker, 1968). I counted twenty-seven law students and five medical students but point out that the matriculation lists are very deficient in the matter of faculty designation. They seem to be reliable for the total number of matriculated students; see J.A.H. Bots and W.Th.M. Frijhoff, 'De studentenpopulatie van de Franeker academie: een kwantitatief onderzoek (1585–1811)', *Universiteit te Franeker, 1585–1811: Bijdragen tot de geschiedenis van de Friese hogeschool*, G.T. Jensma et al., ed. (Leeuwarden, 1985), 56–72 at p.56. According to Feenstra (op. cit., 132) between 1661 and 1751 thirty-two Scottish law students matriculated at the University of Franeker; twenty of them were later admitted to the Faculty of Advocates in Edinburgh. H. de Ridder-Symoens, 'Buitenlandse studenten aan de Franeker universiteit, 1585–1811', *Universiteit te Franeker*, 73–89, counted twenty-four law and three medical students (75, continuation of table 1).

[8] *Album studiosorum Academiae Groninganae* (Groningen, 1915). I counted thirty-one law students and two medical students. According to Feenstra, op. cit., 132, between 1661 and 1751 thirty-two Scottish law students matriculated at the University of Groningen; eighteen of them were later admitted to the Faculty of Advocates in Edinburgh. Franeker and Groningen's lack of popularity is also demonstrated by the fact that more than half of their law students who were later admitted to the Faculty of Advocates also matriculated at Leyden, see Feenstra, op. cit., 132.

[9] *Album studiosorum Academiae Rheno-Traiectinae, 1636–1886* (Utrecht, 1886). I used the excerpt from this album and of the *Album promotorum* mentioned below, which was made up in 1985 by Mr. G.C. Kaim for the Caledonian Society. For the reconstruction of the division into faculties one can use *The Faculty of Advocates in Scotland, 1532–1943, with Genealogical Notes*, F.J. Grant, ed., Publications of the Scottish Record Society, part cxlv (Edinburgh, 1944) and *Album promotorum qui inde ab anno MDCXXXVIo usque ad annum MDCCCXVum in Academia Rheno-Traiectina gradum doctoratus adepti sunt*, F. Ketner, ed. (Utrecht, 1936). Feenstra, op. cit., 132, reaches a slightly higher figure for law students (twenty-seven). In general, however, the Utrecht *Album* is notoriously incomplete for the years after 1657; see Bots and Frijhoff, op. cit., 71, n.10.

Scottish Students at the University of Utrecht, 1636–1800. (figures in brackets refer to the number of Scottish law and medical students at Utrecht)

		L	M			L	M
1636–1650	3	(1)	(–)	1701–1725	38	(1)	(23)
1651–1675	6	(1)	(–)	1726–1750	2	(1)	(–)
1676–1700	50	(16)	(9)	1751–1775	1	(–)	(–)
				1776–1800	1	(–)	(–)

Details derived from diaries and letters illustrate the competition between Leyden and Utrecht. As an example from the seventeenth century Feenstra cites the letters of Colin Mackenzie of Coul to his uncle John Mackenzie, one of the Clerks of Session. Colin began to read law at Utrecht (1692), but he ended his studies at Leyden (1698).[10] Van den Bergh's book on Gerard Noodt provides us with another example. On 8 August 1712 the famous Romanist Noodt, who was several times secretary of the Leyden academic senate, in this capacity delivered to the city council of Leyden the complaints of senate and students regarding the academic printer (appointed after the death of Abraham Elzevier), 'concerning the bad paper and letters, as well as the increase in the price of printing theses, which caused many students to take their degree in Utrecht and other neighbouring Academies'.[11]

Later we shall see whether Scottish students also suffered from the high prices and the poor quality of the paper of the academic printer of their theses. Van den Bergh states that the complaint that masses of students were migrating to Utrecht was raised again by Noodt in the senate on 17 December 1716. The occasion was another quarrel with the burgomasters of Leyden, concerning the fact that the decisions of the academic court were much too mild towards students, much to the distress of Leyden shopkeepers. This time the bailiff had taken action against some students, in blatant violation of the *privilegium fori*. Noodt urged that the numerous and rich English (in fact mainly Scottish, says Van den Bergh) students in Leyden might very well take refuge in Utrecht, if the academic jurisdiction was impaired. This seems a good argument, but we happen to know that in this case Noodt's threat was just a trick. In Utrecht there was no *forum privilegiatum* for academics at all.[12] At a later period a further point of difference between Leyden and Utrecht may have been the middle-class mentality of the former town. On the advice of Sir David Dalrymple, James Boswell – who studied law in the Dutch Republic

[10] Feenstra, op. cit., 133. On 13 February 1701 Sir Colin Mackenzie of Coul, Bart., was admitted to the Faculty of Advocates in Edinburgh, see Grant, op. cit., 135.

[11] G.C.J.J. van den Bergh, *The Life and Work of Gerard Noodt (1647–1725): Dutch Legal Scholarship Between Humanism and Enlightenment* (Oxford, 1988), 81.

[12] See Van den Bergh, op. cit., 81–82.

in 1763–64 – chose Utrecht instead of Leyden: '. . . it was hoped that he might also improve himself generally in culture and in manners; and for this purpose Utrecht was thought to offer advantages over Leyden'.[13]

In its matriculation lists the Academy of Guelderland at Harderwijk shows the names of twenty-two Scotsmen, all provided with the epithet 'M. Cand.' that is, *Medicinis Candidatus*. All these people came to Harderwijk only to take their doctorates, as the *Album promotorum* shows us.[14] At least seventeen of them had enrolled at Leyden before and so we have reason enough to assume that in reality not one Scotsman studied at Harderwijk. When we add the figures of all the aforementioned universities, we reach a rough total of around 1600 Scots students at Dutch universities; as far as we can verify, about 750 of them studied law, about 500 medicine while the remaining Scots were students of divinity and in the faculties of Arts.[15] Because some matriculation lists contain no indication of the faculty at all (Utrecht) or very deficient ones, it is impossible to determine the field of studies of many students; in fact the figures for law and medical students may have been slightly higher.

Following this discussion of Scots in the Netherlands, the institution of the *disputatio* or *dissertatio* calls for our attention. Its oldest form, the *quaestio disputata*, had its origin, as far as we can determine, in the practical exercises in disputation in the classroom; perhaps it is as old as universities themselves. Within the scope of this essay I cannot go into the origin and the evolution of the disputation at length,[16] but have to confine myself to the fact that in seventeenth-

[13] See Feenstra, op. cit., 133, citing *Boswell in Holland, 1763–1764, Including his Correspondence with Belle de Zuylen (Zaalide)*, F.A. Pottle, ed. (Melbourne-London-Toronto, 1952), 3. Boswell's (unfavourable) opinions on Utrecht can be looked for under Utrecht in the index of the book. On 29 July 1766 James Boswell of Auchinleck was admitted to the Faculty of Advocates in Edinburgh, see Grant, op. cit., 18.

[14] *Album studiosorum Academiae Gelro-Zutphanicae,* MDCXLVIII–MDCCCXVIII: *Accedunt nomina curatorum et professorum per eadem secula*, D.G. van Epen, ed. (The Hague, 1904); *Het Album promotorum van de Academie te Harderwijk*, O. Schutte, ed., Werken uitgegeven door Gelre, Vereniging tot beoefening van Gelderse geschiedenis, oudheidkunde en recht, no.xxxvi (Arnhem, 1980). The *Album studiosorum* does not seem to contain any names of Scottish law students, Feenstra, op. cit., 138.

[15] In his article on Leyden Colenbrander notes that the number of Scottish students was still rising in the period 1651–75 which contrasts with many other groups of foreigners: 'Many Scotsmen, enemies of Cromwell, stayed then in our country'; the peak was reached in 1676–1700. For law students Colenbrander's figures correspond with a remark of Murdoch, op. cit., 150: 'It appears that the number of Scots students matriculating at Dutch law schools peaked in the years 1681–1700'. At Leyden and Utrecht universities the numbers of medical students rose to a peak in the first quarter of the eighteenth century. Cf. for the influence of Boerhaave, Frijhoff, op. cit., 103–7.

[16] H. Coing, 'Die Gelehrten Rechte und die Gesetzgebung', *Handbuch der Quellen und Literatur der neueren europäischen Privatrechtsgeschichte. Erster Band: Mittelalter (1100–1500)*, H. Coing, ed. (Munich, 1973), 75; S. Kuttner, 'The Revival of Jurisprudence', *Renaissance and Renewal in the Twelfth Century*, R.L. Benson and G. Constable, ed. (Oxford, 1982), 299–323; and B.C. Bazan et al., *Les questions disputées et les questions quodlibétiques dans les facultés de théologie, de droit et de médecine*, Typologie des sources du Moyen Age occidental, fasc. xliv–xlv (Turnhout, 1985).

and eighteenth-century education and teaching dissertations or disputations – defended in public or privately – occupied an important place. For prospective jurists in particular, disputing counted as an outstanding practical exercise: in the Faculty of Medicine in the long run it became obsolete as a teaching method.[17] On the occasion of an alteration he made in the faculty curriculum the famous Leyden professor of medicine Herman Boerhaave abolished the compulsory practice disputation in the early part of the eighteenth century.[18] In eighteenth-century Louvain medical students were obliged to participate in six practice disputations before taking the licentiate's examination but could evade that obligation by paying a sum of money.[19]

In the nature of things disputing was done orally although perhaps on the basis of written moot points or theses. After the disputation had taken place the proceedings might be put down on paper. After the middle ages we see a gradually increasing importance given to the written piece that lay at the root of the oral disputation or discussion; after the *theses* which the professor *praeses* propounded, the paper written by the student himself appeared and took over the name of *disputatio*.[20] Connected with this evolution is the emergence, particularly in the seventeenth century, of the practice of writing some textbooks in the form of a collection of *disputationes* or *exercitationes*.[21] In these exercise disputations the subject matter, for instance a title of the Digest, was treated

17 I have the impression that the literature on the history of faculties of medicine has paid little attention to the subject of 'practice disputations'; see e.g. R. French, 'Medical Teaching in Aberdeen: From the Foundation of the University to the Middle of the Seventeenth Century, *History of Universities*, iii (1983) 127–57. With regard to the German faculties of medicine one can refer to E. Horn, *Die Disputationen und Promotionen an den Deutschen Universitäten vornehmlich seit dem 16. Jahrhundert, mit einem Anhang enthaltend ein Verzeichnis aller ehemaligen und gegenwärtigen deutschen Universitäten*, Elftes Beiheft zum Centralblatt für Bibliothekswesen (Leipzig, 1893). In the seventeenth century the medical students of Professor J. van der Linden (1639–51) in Franeker University regularly disputed in public '*exercitii causa*'. A bound series of fifty-nine numbered *disputationes physiologicae* dating from the period 1648–50 is held in the British Museum; see G.A. Lindeboom, 'Johannes Antonides van der Linden (1609–64), medisch hoogleraar te Franeker en te Leiden: Zijn betekenis voor de Friese hogeschool', *Universiteit te Franeker*, 356–70 at p. 361.

18 Boerhaave was appointed lecturer in 1701 and professor in 1709; he held this position till his death in 1738.

19 See C. Bruneel, *Répertoire des thèses imprimées de l'Université Louvain (1425–1797). Première partie: Faculté de Médecine*, Université Catholique de Louvain, Catalogues, inventaires et répertoires de la Bibliotheque centrale, iii (Louvain, 1977), VIII, XXIII. Cf. for the early seventeenth century the text of the *Visitatio* of 1617, in J. Molanus, *Historiae Lovaniensium libri XIV*, P. de Ram, ed. 2 vols. (Brussels, 1861), ii, 971, para. CXX: 'in quibus disputationibus et repetitionibus [Facultatis Medicae], ne fraus committatur, observari volumus ea, quae superius in disputationibus et repetitionibus juris studiosorum stricte praecepimus'. I owe the references in this and the preceding note to my colleague Hilde de Ridder-Symoens, of the Free University, Amsterdam.

20 On the development of *theses nudae* through *theses vestitae* into treatises which are divided into chapters see K. Mommsen, *Katalog der Basler juristischen Disputationen, 1558–1918. Aus dem Nachlass herausgegeben von W. Kundert, Ius Commune*, Sonderhefte, ix (Frankfurt/Main, 1978), 42–57.

21 E.g. for the famous Frisian lawyer, Ulrik Huber, T.J. Veen, 'Disputationes Huberianae', *It Beaken*, xlvii (1985), 236–37, with supplementary material in *Tijdschrift voor Rechtsgeschiedenis*, lvii (1989), 206, n.18.

in the form of a number of theses or propositions.[22] Under the chairmanship of the author-professor the *theses* had to be defended against the opposition of other students by one or more student-respondents chosen for the task.[23] In this style of teaching publicly defended dissertations for the purpose of obtaining an academic degree (the degree of doctor) also formed a natural part of the examination requirements.[24] We then find at the Dutch universities two main types of this genre of literature, *disputationes pro gradu* and *disputationes exercitii gratia*. Most probably works of the former category were written by students themselves, in any case not by the professor *praeses*; in the second category one can distinguish the practice disputations which were published in volumes under the name of the professor and those which were printed and published separately.[25] In this last group we find disputations in which the student calls himself only *respondens* and others in which he is described as *auctor et respondens*. In this second case the student was probably the author, or at least the *praeses* did not write the text, whereas the designation of the student as a mere *respondens* points to the authorship of the professor-chairman.[26]

What *dissertationes* of Scots students in the Netherlands are to be found? Let us start with the *disputationes pro gradu*. The figures which Colenbrander collected for Leyden do not give a very promising picture of the frequency of doctoral degrees.[27] From 1575 to 1795 33,189 'Netherlandish' students matriculated at Leyden and 24,102 'foreigners'. Of the 'Netherlandish' group 7,615 students took an academic degree (23 per cent); of all 'foreigners' together 2,254 (9.3 per cent). Among the some 1,460 Scots students Colenbrander discovered seventy-five degrees: 5.3 per cent. In view of the fact that many Scots enrolled at two or more universities I have added the degrees taken at all Dutch universities:[28]

[22] For the structure and the system of these volumes of collected (legal) practice disputations, R. Feenstra, 'Jacobus Maestertius (1610–1658): Zijn juridisch onderwijs in Leiden en het Leuvense disputatiesysteem van Gerardus Corselius', *Tijdschrift voor Rechtsgeschiedenis*, l (1982), 297–335.

[23] A.M.M.Canoy-Olthoff, 'Een onderzoek naar de inhoud van een aantal zeventiende en achttiende eeuwse dissertaties over vruchtgebruik', *Acta Falconis*, lviii/3 (Antwerp, 1983), 15–33.

[24] W. Allweiss, 'Von der Disputation zur Dissertation', *Dissertationen in Wissenschaft und Bibliotheken*, R. Jung and P. Kaegbein, ed., Bibliothekspraxis, xxiii (Munich-New York-London, 1979), 13–28.

[25] On the 'loose' disputations as the counterparts of the collected ones, Feenstra, 'Maestertius', at p.311, particularly n.89.

[26] Canoy-Olthoff, op. cit., 26, and Feenstra, 'Maestertius', 90. For some practice disputations which were published at the Nijmegen Kwartierlijke Akademie in the course of the last quarter of the seventeenth century under the name of law students as *respondentes*, A.M. Ruuls came to the conclusion that the students 'dressed up' an outline the professor had given them and/or used a bibliography he provided; see A.N. [=M.] Ruuls, 'Vier vragen omtrent de disputaties, binnen het juridisch onderwijs aan de Nijmeegse kwartierlijke academie verdedigd onder Petrus de Greve (periode: 1663–1676), benevens een poging tot beantwoording', *Batavia Academica*, vi (1988), 31–51.

[27] Colenbrander, table IV.

[28] For Leyden university we do not have a complete *Album promotorum* at our disposal. *Bronnen tot de geschiedenis der Leidsche Universiteit*, P.C. Molhuysen, ed. 7 vols. Rijks Geschiedkundige Publicatien,

Continued

Scottish Graduates at Netherlands Universities, 1575–1800
(Figures in brackets refer to the number of Scottish law and medical doctorates)

		L	M			L	M
1575–1600	1	(1)	(–)	1701–1725	40	(1)	(39)
1601–1625	3	(2)	(1)	1726–1750	16	(–)	(14)*
1626–1650	3	(1)	(2)	1751–1775	13	(–)	(13)
1651–1675	14	(1)	(13)	1776–1800	13	(–)	(13)
1676–1700	42	(1)	(41)				

* In the period 1726–50 two degrees of Phil. Dr. et A.L.M.

The total comes out at 145 Scots taking academic degrees, seven of whom took a law doctorate and 136 a medical one. When we remember that around 750 Scotsmen studied law and about 500 medicine, the discrepancy between the faculties becomes very clear. Scottish divinity students (about 130 of them were enrolled at Leyden alone) did not take a degree at all;[29] of the jurists barely one per cent obtained a doctorate.[30]

In fact the situation of the jurists was even sadder. Let us examine the seven doctors of law more closely. The first was Iacobus Ramsaeus, *Scotus, Logices Professor extraordinarius*. On 20 March 1593 he received – at Leyden – the degree of *doctor iuris honoris causa*.[31] Joannes Mordisonius (John Murdison or Murdisson) was next to graduate, at the same university, which he did on 19 May 1604. He had matriculated as a law student at Leyden in 1599, became a lecturer in physics in the same year and a professor of logic in 1603.[32] In 1604 he took a law degree: as a *licentiatus iuris* 'creatus est D[octor] Iuris in

[28]*Continued*
Grote Reeks, xx, xxix, xxxviii, xlv, xlviii, liii and lvi (The Hague, 1913–24) contains a list of graduates for the period 1575–1610 (in the appendices of vol. 1) and a '*Catalogus promotorum*' from 19 September 1654 to 1811 in the appendices of vols. 3 ff. The list of doctoral degrees 1610–54 has to be reconstructed using other sources. For the Utrecht *Album promotorum*, see n.9; for Harderwijk, n.14. See for Franeker, *Album promotorum Academiae Franekerensis (1585–1811)*, Th.J. Meijer, ed. (Franeker, n.d.[1972]); for Groningen, 'Lijst van Promotien', *Album studiosorum*, cols. 445–622.

[29] Colenbrander, op. cit., 291.

[30] Feenstra, 'Legal relations', 131: '. . . many (law students) would not have troubled to take a degree of any kind'.

[31] See Molhuysen, *Bronnen*, i, 460*. James Ramsay matriculated at Leyden as a law student on 6 April 1588 (*Album studiosorum*, col. 23). In 1588 he also became an extraordinary professor of logic. He died in 1593. Cf. A.J. van der Aa, *Biographisch woordenboek der Nederlanden, bevattende levensbeschrijvingen van zoodanige personen, die zich op eenigerlei wijze in ons vaderland hebben vermaard gemaakt*, 21 vols. (Haarlem 1852–78), xvi, 66.

[32] See *Album studiosorum*, col. 270 (matriculation 24 November 1599 of 'Joannes Mordisonus, Scotus, [Aet.] 31, J[uris]'); Van der Aa, xii–II, 1167 and P.C. Molhuysen et al., *Nieuw Nederlandsch Biografisch Woordenboek* [N.N.B.W.], 10 vols. (Leyden, 1911–37), ii, cols. 967–68.

Senatu Academico per Magnificum D. Rectorem, D. Bronchorstium'.[33] Did this professor write a dissertation?[34] We may ask the same question about Guilelmus Mackdowall, that is William Macdowell, who took the degree of *doctor iuris* at Groningen on 20 May 1625. From 1614 until 1627 he was a *professor ordinarius* of logic (until 1620), physics, metaphysics and (from 1620 also) ethics.[35] Again at Leyden, the highest degree in law was conferred on Guilelmus Hagius or William Haig by Professor Maestertius, acting on behalf of his colleague Bernardus Schotanus (12 July 1645). This time we know with certainty that Haig disputed publicly.[36] Unfortunately for the time being at least I have been unable to trace either a copy of the disputation or its subject. On the other hand two libraries possess a copy of the *disputatio inauguralis* which Robertus Hamiltonus defended successfully at Leyden on 25 August 1671; it is entitled *Disputatio politico-juridica, inauguralis, de Aerarii publici necessitate, ac pleno principum vectigalia, etc. imponendi iure*.[37] The *auctor et defendens* Hamilton dedicated it to '*Carolus II, Magnae Britanniae, Franciae, ac Hiberniae Rex, Fideique Defensor, Pius, Felix, Inclytus*'. As appears from his text Hamilton was a pure royalist. Not only does he regard his birth in a monarchical kingdom as a privilege,[38] but he also denies to parliament all right of interference with the imposition of taxation.[39] Thus the young doctor

[33] 19 May 1604. See Molhuysen, *Bronnen*, i, 153. Cf. Feenstra, 'Legal relations', 137, n.21.

[34] Strangely enough Murdison's promotion is not mentioned at all in Bronchorst's diary; see *Diarium Everardi Bronchorstii sive Adversaria omnia quae gesta sunt in Academia Leydensi (1591–1627)*, J.C. van Slee, ed., Werken uitgegeven door het Historisch Genootschap, Derde serie, xii (The Hague, 1898), 112–15. The Advocates Library, Edinburgh, possesses a pamphlet containing the congratulations of Murdison's friends Baud, Daniel Heinsius and Petrus Scriverius on his doctorate of law, *Vota et gratulationes amicorum quum Nobilissimus Doctissimusque Vir Iohannes Murdisonius Scotus Naturalis Philosophiae in illustri Batauorum Academia Professor post licentiam in utroque jure summum in eadem facultate gradum assumeret (Lugduni Batavorum, Ex Officina Thomae Basson*, 1604).

[35] See 'Lijst van promotien', col. 448. Cf. *Dictionary of National Biography* [D.N.B.], L. Stephen and S. Lee, ed. 22 vols. (1908–9), xii, 511; and N.N.B.W., ii, col. 862.

[36] See Molhuysen, *Bronnen*, ii, 292. Jacobus Maestertius himself was the son of a father of Scottish origin, Adam Mesterton or Masterton, cf. Feenstra, 'Maestertius', 297–98. 'Guilelmus Haig, Scotus, [Aet.] 49, J[uris] Cand[idatus]' matriculated at Leyden on 1 May 1635 (*Album studiosorum*, col. 270). The interval between the matriculation and the promotion seems odd.

[37] See Molhuysen, *Bronnen*, iii, 315*. Copies of this disputation (printed *Apud Viduam & Haeredes Joannis Elsevirii*, Leyden) exist in Leyden University Library and the Advocates Library, Edinburgh. On 2 November 1668 'Robertus Hamilton, Scotus, [Aet.] 24' matriculated at Leyden as a law student (*Album studiosorum*, col. 551).

[38] *Disputatio*, fo.B verso: '. . . verum cum mihi, quae mea est felicitas, in aere Monarchico nasci contigerit, contra omnes & quosvis Monarchomachos evincere conabor, Monarchae cuivis vere sic dicto, qui unus & solus imperat, cuique caeteri parent, . . . competere potestatem'.

[39] See e.g. *Disputatio*, fo.B 3 verso: 'Concludimus . . . Vectigalium, Tributorum & Taxationum impositiones esse legitima illud (sc. Aeraria bene constituta) fovendi & augendi media, hasque imponendi potestatem plenam atque absolutam summae in Republica competere Majestati independenter ab omni inferioris alicujus Magistratus assensu, quidquid hi enim habent vel dignitatis vel potestatis a summa Majestati mutuantur . . .'

challenged the powers of the Cavalier Parliament.[40]

On 24 August 1680 Guilelmus Blakader, *Scotus*, was next, also at Leyden; he disputed about '*Lithiasis*'.[41] Because the Greek word *lithiasis* means 'stone' or 'gravel' we are very probably dealing with a medical dissertation and a mistake in the *Catalogus promotorum*. The last comer was Hugo Reid, a 'Scoto-Britannus'. He matriculated at Leyden in 1721 and took his degree in law on 13 August 1722 disputing *de Praeparatione bilis in hepate*.[42] The subject of the disputation, the preparation of the bile in the liver, indicates that this is again a doctorate of medicine and a mistake in the *Catalogus*: during two centuries not seven but only five Scotsmen took the highest law degree at a Dutch university. The number of medical doctorates amounted to 138 in all. In this figure is included the doctorate of Duncan Cuminius, conferred on him on 30 June 1684 after a public defence of his dissertation, *De Cerebro eiusque pathologia in genere*. The steps the English envoy took before Professor Drelincourt to prevent the promotion were frustrated by the Academic Senate:

> iudicavit Senatus ad se non pertinere iudicium de rebus politicis, sed de eruditione in qualibet facultate, idque liberum semper fuisse Academiae, neque illam libertatem aut posse aut velle abnegare.[43]

Our Scots law students were likely to be innocent of *disputationes inaugurales aut pro gradu*: they went abroad because it was considered more honourable to pass the Faculty of Advocates' examination in civil law, which included an examination on a title of the Digest by a committee of examiners appointed by the Faculty.[44] For admission to the Faculty of Advocates it was not necessary to take a law degree abroad but a Latin thesis had to be written which would be discussed at the examination. Did the Scots law students prepare themselves for these theses by active participation in so educative a practice as disputing *exercitii gratia*? Answering this question is not very easy because the disputations at issue have not been preserved systematically. In so far as they were written by the professors *praesides* and published in volumes under their names, library catalogues give some help; on the 'loose' disputations of which sometimes the student was *auctor et respondens* and which might inform us about his personal contribution, a researcher can very rarely set eyes. As yet in my investigation of Scottish students I have not produced

[40] G.M. Trevelyan, *A Shortened History of England* (Harmondsworth, 1959), 342–43. Hamilton praises the light burden of English taxation: 'In Anglia sunt levissimae (sc. taxationes), etiamsi tot quotidie de eorum oneribus audiantur querimoniae & murmura' (*Disputatio*, fo.B 3 verso).

[41] See Molhuysen, *Bronnen*, iii, 332*. I did not find William Blakader in the matriculation lists. Cf. D.N.B., ii, 578 (Blackadder).

[42] Molhuysen, *Bronnen*, iv, 284*. On 17 June 1721 'Hugo Reid, Scotus, [Aet.] 20' matriculated at Leyden as a medical student (*Album studiosorum*, col. 874).

[43] See Molhuysen, *Bronnen*, iv, 26 and 195*.

[44] Feenstra, 'Legal relations', 131 and n.22. Murdoch, at p.150, says that the Faculty of Advocates' examination included a lecture to the judges of the Court of Session on a title from the Digest assigned by the Dean of Faculty. It was not until 1750 that advocates were required to pass an examination in Scots law. Those who chose the examination in Scots law introduced in the previous century did not give a lecture before the judges.

particularly spectacular results. After consulting the card index of Dutch disputations, dissertations and academic orations set up by Professor S. van der Woude and placed in the university library in Amsterdam, and after going through many volumes of collected disputations,[45] and examining library and publishers' catalogues,[46] I have tracked down only five legal practice disputations:

Robertus Sinclair, Scoto-Britannus. *Respondens.*
[Disputatio] de dividuis et individuis.
Divided into thirteen theses. Added are 10 *parerga.*

[45] Besides the two undermentioned collections in the names of Maestertius and Pagenstecher I went through: E. Bronchorst, *Methodus feudorum quatuor publicis disputationibus in illustri academ. Ultraj. repetita notisque et moribus illustrata, autore et praeside Cypriano Regneri ab Oosterga* (Utrecht, 1652) listed in M. Ahsmann and R. Feenstra, *Bibliografie van hoogleraren in de rechten aan de Leidse Universiteit tot 1811*, Geschiedenis der Nederlandsche Rechtswetenschap, Deel vii, Afl. 1 (Amsterdam-Oxford-New York, 1984), no.103; J. Maestertius, *Analysis juris feudalis sex disputationibus comprehensa, quas in Batavorum Academia exercitii gratia sub praesidio Iacobi Maestertii publice disquirendas proposuerunt sex candidati, quorum nomina singulis disputationibus adscripta sunt* (Leyden, 1637) (Ahsmann and Feenstra, no.342); B. Schotanus, *Disputationes juridicae ad seriem materiae Pandectarum conscriptae a Bernardo Schotano, quibus fundamenta iuris per rationes decidendi ac dubitandi explicantur* (Amsterdam, 1653) (Ahsmann and Feenstra, no.591); C. van Eck, *De sectis et philosophia iurisconsultorum* (Jena, 1724) (not mentioned in R. Dekkers, *Bibliotheca Belgica Juridica, een bio-bibliographisch overzicht der rechtsgeleerdheid in de Nederlanden van de vroegste tijden af tot 1800*, Verhandelingen van de Koninklijke Vlaamse Academie voor Wetenschappen, Letteren en Schone Kunsten van Belgie, Klasse der Letteren, Jaargang xiii, no.14, (Brussels, 1951), 50; A. Matthaeus [II], *De judiciis disputationes quindecim* (Utrecht, 1639) (Dekkers, 111, no.3); idem, *De judiciis disputationes septendecim in illustri academia quae est Trajecti ad Rhenum publice propositae ab Anth. Matthaeo* (editio posthuma, Amsterdam, 1665) (Dekkers, 111, no.3); idem, *Disputationes de obligationibus XLII, de criminibus VII, de servitutibus VII etc.* (ed. posthuma, Utrecht, 1660) (Dekkers, 112, no.1, mentioning, however, A. Matthaeus III as the author); idem, *Disputationes de successionibus XX, de matrimoniis XIII, de tutelis V etc.* (Utrecht, 1652) (Dekkers, 111, no.5); C.R. ab Oosterga, *Censura Belgica seu novae notae et animadversiones quibus omnes et singulae leges, quae continentur in XII libris Codicis, moribus praecipue Belgii . . . confirmantur etc. Hisce ob connexionem causae accedunt ejusdem auctoris disputationes juridicae* (Utrecht, 1666) (Dekkers, 126, nos.17 and 18); P. Voet, *Disputationes IX de justitia et jure in Acad. Ultraj. publice ventilatae* (Utrecht, 1654–58) (not mentioned in Dekkers, 181–82); A. Matthaeus [I], *Collegia juris sex: unum fundamentorum juris, alterum Institutionum, tertium & quartum earundem, quintum Pandectarum, sextum Codicis; quibus adjectae sunt disputationes quaedam extraordinariae* (Groningen, 1637) (Dekkers, 111, no.15). Moreover I went through six boxes containing 'loose' disputations from several Leyden faculties which are held by Leyden University Library and bear the signatures 236 A 12; 236 B 3; 236 B 8; 236 C 12; 237 B 3; 238 A 5.

[46] I examined the catalogues of the Koninklijke Bibliotheek, The Hague, of the Leyden and Utrecht University Libraries and of the Advocates Library in Edinburgh (*Catalogue of the Printed Books in the Advocates Library [before 1871]*). Among the Elzevier catalogues I mention C.F. Walther, *Catalogue méthodique des dissertations ou thèses académiques imprimées par les Elzevir de 1616 a 1712, recueillies pour la première fois dans la Bibliothèque Impériale publique à Saint-Pétersbourg etc.* (Brussels, 1864); and H.B. Copinger, *The Elzevier Press: A Handlist of the Productions of the Elzevier Presses at Leyden, Amsterdam, The Hague and Utrecht, with References to Willems, Berghman, Rahir and other biographers* (1927). Walther mentions the disputations of Sinclair and Leirmonthius, Copinger the ones of R. Hamilton and G. Burnet, but not the disputation of R. Cook.

Publicly defended at Leyden on 24 February 1646.
Praeses: Professor Jacobus Maestertius.
Printed: *Ex Officina Bonaventurae & Abrahami Elsevir*, Leyden.[47]

Thomas Leirmonthius, Scoto-Britannus. *Respondens*.
[Disputatio] de qua fide et modo Justinianus, vel (cujus opera potissimum usus est) Tribonianus leges et constitutiones Romanas retractavit aut novas edidit.
Divided into twenty theses.
Publicly defended at Leyden on 28 February 1646.
Praeses: Professor Jacobus Maestertius.
Printed: *Ex Officina Bonaventurae & Abrahami Elsevir*, Leyden.[48]

Robertus Cook, Fiffano Scotus. *Auctor [et Respondens]*.
Disputatio juridica de inofficioso testamento.
Divided into twenty-eight theses. Added are four *corollaria*.
Publicly defended at Leyden on 14 March 1676.
Praeses: Professor Antonius Matthaeus [III].
Printed: *Apud Viduam & Haeredes Joannis Elsevirii*, Leyden.[49]

Gilbertus Burnet, Scotus. *Auctor et Respondens*.
Disputatio juridica de belli causis, secundum jus naturae et gentium, justis et injustis.
Divided into a *prooemium* and two *capita* (subdivided into twenty-five sections or 'paragraphs'). Added are ten *annexa*.
Publicly defended at Leyden on 9 July 1701.

47 Published as *Disputationum juridicarum Centesima-vigesima-secunda* in a volume under the name of J. Maestertius: *Illustrium materiarum prima rudimenta,* CXLV *disputationibus comprehensa publicoque examini in Alma Leydensi Academia subjecta respondentibus jurisprudentiae candidatis, quorum nomina una cum materia quam singuli defenderunt sequens pagina indicat* (Leyden, 1646). See Ahsmann and Feenstra, no.351. Cf. Feenstra, 'Maestertius', 333–34. 'Mr. Robertus Sintclarus, Scotus, [Aet.] 21' matriculated at Leyden as a law student on 6 September 1645 (*Album studiosorum*, col. 361). He dedicated his paper to Ioannes Sinclair, 'Eques Baronneta a Steinstoun, Patruus suus magnus'. On 9 July 1647 he (Sir Robert Sinclair, of Longformacus) was admitted, and on 7 January 1676 readmitted, to the Faculty of Advocates in Edinburgh, see Grant, op. cit., 192.

48 Published as *Disputationum juridicarum Centesima-trigesima-septima* in Maestertius, *Illustrium materiarum*. 'Mag. Thomas Leermontius, Scotus, [Aet.] 21' matriculated at Leyden as a law student on 6 September 1645 (*Album studiosorum*, col. 361). He dedicated his paper to Robert, 'Comes de Roxburgh, Dominus Ker, Cesfurd, Cavertoun, etc., A privatis Regii Consiliis ac Regni Scotiae Secreti Sigilli Custos'. On 14 January 1648 he (Thomas Learmonth) was admitted, and on 8 January 1676 readmitted, to the Faculty of Advocates in Edinburgh, see Grant, op. cit., 122.

49 Copy in Österreichische Nationalbibliothek, Vienna. Cook matriculated (as 'Robertus Kuck, *Scotus*, [Aet.] 23') at Leyden on 3 May 1675 as a philosophy student (*Album studiosorum*, col. 597), on 29 November 1675 at Franeker as a law student (*Album studiosorum*, 218). He dedicated his paper to Alexander, 'Comes de Kellai, Dominus de Pittinueem, et Serenissimi Magnae Brittanniae Regis apud Scotos ex Secretis Consiliarius meritissimus, Maecenas suus'. On 13 November 1677, Robert Cook was admitted to the Faculty of Advocates in Edinburgh, see Grant, op. cit., 40.

Praeses: Professor Philippus Reinhardus Vitriarius.
Printed: *Apud Abrahamum Elzevier*, Leyden.[50]

Georgius Sharp de Hoddon, Scoto-Britannus, and Christoph. Schiffart, Emdanus. [*Respondentes*].
Julius Paulus.
Publicly defended at Groningen between August 1708 and September 1712.
Praeses: Professor Alexander Arnoldus Pagenstecher.[51]

Three of these five disputations were written by the professors *praesides*, Maestertius or Pagenstecher respectively. Here the only personal contribution of the student *respondens* is to be found in the dedication. Probably Robert Cook and Gilbert Burnet wrote their own disputations. Do these papers evidence a 'Scottish' background or character? Cook's treatise, consisting mainly of a discussion of the ideas of Bachovius, contrasts in no way with the products of his continental colleagues.[52] Burnet on the other hand makes a personal contribution. Treating the preliminary question whether any war at all can be considered lawful or justified he quotes the Gospel (Matthew, v, 38, 39);[53] he then refers *inter alia* to a 'librum nuperrime editum, cui titulus, *An Exposition of the Articles of the Church of England, Expositio articulorum fidei Ecclesiae Anglicanae*, auctor est Burnetus Salisburiensis Episcopus *articulo 37, pag. 388 in fine & 389. in princ.* ubi accuratissime, ut solet, Salvatoris nostri verba exponit, & dissentientium argumenta inde desumpta refutat'.[54]

My tentative conclusion is that the Scots law students in the Netherlands did not suffer much from the high prices and the poor quality of the paper of

[50] Copy in Leyden University Library. Burnet matriculated (at the age of 20) at Leyden as a law student on 8 September 1699 (*Album studiosorum*, col. 755). He dedicated his paper ('Theses') to Thomas Burnet, 'Eques auratus, Serenissimi nostri Regis Medicus Primarius, Pater suus optimus' and to Gilbert [Burnet], bishop of Salisbury, 'Patruus suus'. On 1 July 1703 Burnet was admitted to the Faculty of Advocates in Edinburgh, see Grant, op. cit., 25.

[51] Published as number nine in a volume containing ten dissertations under the name of A.A. Pagenstecher, *Sylloge Dissertationum. 1. De Jure Naturae. 2. etc.* (Bremen, 1713). I owe this reference to my Leyden colleague, R. Feenstra. Copies in Ghent University Library, and Advocates Library, Edinburgh. This book of Pagenstecher is not mentioned in Dekkers, 128. On 2 December 1712 George Sharp, of Hoddam, was admitted to the Faculty of Advocates in Edinburgh, see Grant, op. cit., 190.

[52] See R. Bachovius ab Echt, *Notae et animadversiones ad disputationes Hieronymi Treutleri*, 3 vols. (Heidelberg, 1617–19).

[53] 'Audistis dictum fuisse, oculum pro oculo, et dentem pro dente. Ego vero dico vobis, ne resistite malo, sed caedenti te in dexteram maxillam alteram quoque obverte' (*Disputatio*, 12).

[54] *Disputatio*, 13. Another reference to the famous *Exposition of the Thirty-nine Articles* (1699) is found in section 24 (p.21); for the rest Burnet leans heavily on P.R. Vitriarius, *Institutiones juris naturae et gentium in usum Christiani Ludovici marchionis Brandenburgici ad methodum Hugonis Grotii conscriptae* (Leyden, 1692) (cf. Ahsmann and Feenstra, no. 1001) and H. Grotius, *De iure belli ac pacis libri tres, in quibus ius naturae et gentium, item iuris publici praecipua explicantur* (Paris, 1625). Cf. on Bishop Burnet, D.N.B., iii, 394–405 and R. Chambers, *A Biographical Dictionary of Eminent Scotsmen*, 3 vols. T. Thomson, ed. (rptd. Hildesheim-New York, 1971), i, 243–48.

the academic printers of their theses. If they participated in educational programmes it must have been been under private instruction.[55] The mere handful of graduating law students contrasts sharply with the diligence of their medical colleagues. Their participation in the practice of defending theses *exercitii gratia* seems meagre too. However, the rare disputations we possess enable us to catch a glimpse of some individual views and convictions.[56]

[55] Cf. Phillipson, at p.107: 'Instead of educating their sons in the rudiments of law at home, they [sc. the Scottish men of rank] sent them abroad in increasing numbers, notably to Holland, above all to Leiden, to academies in which men of rank could study politeness and good manners as well as the law'.

[56] For their help in the preparation of this paper I am indebted to Dr. Nicholas Phillipson, Department of History, University of Edinburgh, to Mr. William Kelly, National Library of Scotland, to Mr. W. Otterspeer, Academisch Historisch Museum, Leyden University and to Mr. G.C. Kaim, Hoevelaken, a member of the Dutch Caledonian Society. Misses Nicole Hagemans, M.A. and Carolien van Haren, LL.M., research assistants, gave me exceptional help in collecting biographical and bibliographical data.

I would also refer to the recently published Leyden thesis of M.J.A.M. Ahsmann, *Collegia en colleges: Juridisch onderwijs aan de Leidse Universiteit, 1575–1630 in het bijzonder het disputeren*, Rechtshistorische Studies, Nieuwe Reeks, no. 1 (Groningen, 1990), which is important for the general history of Dutch legal education and deals inter alia with Ramsay and Murdison (p. 102 above). It was not available to me at the time of writing.

Chapter 8

James Greenshields and the House of Lords: A Reappraisal

Richard S. Tompson

The Greenshields case is a paradox in Anglo-Scottish legal history. Most modern citations tell us that the case established Scottish appeals to the House of Lords. That can be disproven by a review of the chronology of appeals. Yet when we look closely at the case, its aftermath and its subsequent interpretation there is actually more to be learned about the connections between the English and Scottish legal systems than the older view appeared to tell us.

This essay has four parts: the first is a correction of the conventional view; the second is a description of the case (1709–11); the third is a study of the surprising aftermath (1711–14); and the fourth is a sketch of how *Greenshields* disappeared from legal memory in the eighteenth century, and how it reappeared and was reinterpreted in the nineteenth and twentieth centuries.

First, the modern citations. A number of authoritative works tell the same story. Maurice Bond, in introducing volume nine of *The Manuscripts of the House of Lords*, said the case 'set the precedent of appeals from Scotland to the House'. In *The Oxford Companion to Law*, Professor Walker said it 'established the right of the House of Lords to hear appeals from the Court of Session'. Similar assessments appear in the leading modern texts.[1]

The correction is not too difficult. Scottish appeals were attempted as early as 1707. The first one heard by the House of Lords was in February 1708, and the peers made their first order on Scottish appeal procedure in April 1709. In the case of *Brand* v. *Mackenzie* the House ordered that upon receipt of an appeal 'from any decree given or pronounced in any court in Scotland', after a respondent had been served notice 'the sentence or decree so appealed

[1] *The Oxford Companion to Law* (1980), 540; *The Manuscripts of the House of Lords*, N.S., ix (rptd. 1965), xxii; see also J.H. Baker, *An Introduction to English Legal History*, 2nd ed. (1979), 32; D.M. Walker, *The Scottish Legal System*, 5th ed. (Edinburgh, 1981), 127–28; Enid Marshall, *General Principles of Scots Law*, 4th ed. (Edinburgh, 1982), 32. For other recent references, see below, nn.50–54. Baker omits the reference in his third edition (1990).

against, from such time, [may] not be carried on into execution by any process whatsoever'.[2]

Just about the time of this ruling, James Greenshields was opening his first meeting house in Edinburgh. Whatever he may have done there, he certainly was too late to inaugurate Scottish appeals.[3]

Greenshields was imprisoned in September 1709 for conducting divine worship without the authority of the Presbytery of Edinburgh and in violation of an order from the Provost and Magistrates. He presented a bill of suspension to the Court of Session which was refused in November. Greenshields then presented a reclaiming petition which was also refused, and at the end of December he sent 'a protest for remeid of law' to the queen and the House of Lords.[4] His appeal reached the House in February 1710 and it was formally received on 25 March. The hearing however was not until 1 March 1711.

Greenshields' offence was only unique in his willingness, even eagerness, to be convicted. There was no law of uniformity in Scotland. A majority of Episcopalians in 1689 was probably reduced to a large minority by 1707. In that year Daniel Defoe published a list of 160 Episcopal ministers 'who have not complyed with the present church government of Scotland'. He also counted at least fifteen meeting-houses in Edinburgh alone.[5] In 1711 an anonymous observer listed 113 Episcopal ministers 'who enjoy churches or benefices in Scotland'.[6] According to contemporaries, the English liturgy was used in many of the churches and meeting houses.

The lack of legislated uniformity and the divisions in Scottish society in the early eighteenth century help to explain the nervousness of the officers of the established Presbyterian church and the civil magistrates. Any of their

[2] The early attempts are noted in Fountainhall, ii, 367–68; the first hearing (*Rosebery* v. *Inglis*) is printed in *The Manuscripts of the House of Lords*, N.S., vii (1921), 554 and the ruling in *Brand* v. *Mackenzie* is in *The Manuscripts of the House of Lords*, N.S., viii (rptd. 1966), 273.

[3] The most thorough recent study of the origin of Scottish appeals to the House of Lords does not even mention *Greenshields*, which omission is entirely correct, A.J. MacLean, 'The 1707 Union: Scots Law and the House of Lords', *Journal of Legal History*, iv, no.3 (1983), 50 reprinted in *New Perspectives in Scottish Legal History*, A.J. Kiralfy and H. MacQueen, ed. (1984), 50. The same author does deal summarily with *Greenshields,* and deny its priority, in 'The House of Lords and Appeals from the High Court of Justiciary, 1707–1887', *Jurid. Rev., N.S.*, xxx (1985), 195.

[4] Fountainhall, ii, 523. The records of the Court of Session are curiously silent on the case. The entry books have a gap from July 1708 to June 1710 (S[cottish] R[ecord] O[ffice], CS 16/1/46 and CS/1/47). The Clerks' Minute Books fail to supply the deficiency (CS 47, 50, 53, 59, 62, 71, 74, 77 and 80).

[5] *An Historical Account of the Bitter Sufferings and Melancholy Circumstances of the Episcopal Church in Scotland, under the Barbarous Usage and Bloody Persecution of the Presbyterian Church Government* . . . (1707), 26 ff.

[6] *The Case of Mr. Greenshields, as it was printed in London, with remarks upon the same; and copies of the original papers relating to that affair* . . . (1710), 59–60. An excellent portrait of Greenshields' colleagues is in Bruce Lenman, 'The Scottish Episcopal Clergy and the Ideology of Jacobitism', *Ideology and Conspiracy: Aspects of Jacobitism, 1689–1759*, Eveline Cruickshanks, ed. (1982), 36–48.

Episcopal neighbours might be Jacobites, though doubtless the majority were not. In 1708 a fleet of thirty French ships with about 5,000 men had entered the Firth of Forth, only to be chased away by a British fleet. This attempted Jacobite invasion was followed by arrests, acquittals in Edinburgh treason trials, the removal of high-ranking suspects to London, and their return without conviction. The major sequel was the import of the English law of treason in 1709, over the unanimous opposition of Scots in Parliament.[7]

Greenshields entered this tense arena in early 1709. He claimed to be a native of the city and he said he had studied at the University. He had been ordained by the deposed bishop of Ross in 1694. A few years later Greenshields went to Ireland where he held a cure in the diocese of Down and then one in Armagh. He remained in Ireland for twelve years and during that time he took oaths of allegiance to the English sovereign. There were conflicting explanations for his return to Scotland. Greenshields said that he was in Edinburgh on family business, and that while there his rector in Ireland died and his curacy was taken from him. On the other hand Daniel Defoe reported a rumour that Greenshields had been paid £80 to come and set up in the city.[8]

Greenshields admitted that he was encouraged by 'the desire of some English gentlemen, her Majesty's servants here, and some other well-affected persons'. The curate took a private chamber in the Canongate, where he held services. When his first landlord was threatened with higher taxes, Greenshields moved to another site. The second landlord sued Greenshields in the court of the Dean of Guild for unauthorized remodelling; the curate was once again forced to vacate. The Commission of the General Assembly met on 5 August and made a decree against 'innovations in religion' aimed at preventing the use of the English liturgy. This decree was read from all pulpits on 21 August, and several meeting houses were ordered closed.[9] Nevertheless, at the end of August Greenshields was preaching in a new meeting-house – only this time it was 'just opposite to the great church of Edinburgh'.[10]

At this affront the Presbytery summoned Greenshields, who appeared on 7 September. He declined their jurisdiction and was found in contempt and ordered not 'to exercise any part of the office of holy ministry'.[11] This ruling was passed to the magistrates who summoned Greenshields on 10 September

[7] 7 Anne c. 21 was formally titled 'An Act for Improving the Union of the Two Kingdoms'. See P.W.J. Riley, *The English Ministers and Scotland, 1707–1727* (1964), 104–19; and Bruce Lenman, *The Jacobite Risings in Britain, 1689–1746* (1980), 108.

[8] *A Review of the State of the British Nation* (no.80), 8 October 1709.

[9] Bishop Nicolson to Archbishop Tenison, 29 August 1709. British Library, Add. MS 6116, fo.15.

[10] The details of Greenshields' experience are given in a number of contemporary pamphlets, the most useful being *The Case of Mr. Greenshields* (n.6 above). The last quotation comes from the respondents' case in the House of Lords, cited by Richard Colles, *Cases in Parliament*, 429 and reprinted in *E[nglish] R[eports]*, i, 357.

[11] S.R.O., Presbytery Minutes CH 2/121/7, 195.

and ordered him not to conduct services. When he defied this order on the following Sunday, he was recalled, admitted his guilt and committed to the Tolbooth on the 15th. Two days later a printed pamphlet appeared called 'A True Copy of a Letter from the Reverend Mr Greenshields from the Gaol of Edinburgh where he now lies, only for reading the English Liturgy'. The essay was addressed to 'a clergyman in the City of London', but in fact the 'letter' was promptly distributed to all the bishops of the Church of England. Nicolson of Carlisle received the pamphlet and 'a long history of [Greenshields] under his own hand'. He wrote to Archbishop Tenison that:[12]

> [Greenshields] tells me that the chief strength of the inhabitants of Edinburgh (in quantity and quality) are on his side, and are now framing a petition to her Majesty, setting forth the state of religion in those parts, and praying the allotment of salaries to a sufficient number of well qualify'd episcopal divines, to carry on the good work, which he has successfully begun; not doubting but they shall likewise be able to procure for them an Act of Toleration in the very next sessions of parliament.

On the last point, Nicolson was less than sanguine. He told the archbishop:

> May your head never ach (nor mine be broken) til this man's prophesies are accomplish'd! I am afraid this project will hardly be carry'd on without Blows.

Even as he was writing, the situation in Edinburgh was more complex than Nicolson realized. We see it in the behaviour of the Edinburgh Presbytery itself. In the same month that Greenshields was incarcerated another Episcopalian, James Walker, was cited before them. Walker did not appear. In October the attorney who had represented Greenshields appeared for Walker, but was not allowed to speak. In November Walker failed to appear again and a committee was sent to the magistrates. Finally, on 7 December, another committee visited the Lord Advocate regarding Walker, and 'his Lordship said there would be no difficultie as to him, he not being qualified according to Law' [i.e. not having taken oaths]. But there was further trouble. On 21 December the Presbytery learned that Walker had been cited earlier and was on probation. No further record of his case appears in the minutes.[13] In short, not all ministers accepted their punishment as readily as Greenshields.

During the last months of 1709 Greenshields continued his legal action. He presented a bill of suspension to the Lords of Council and Session in October. In it Greenshields claimed the protection of the law as an ordained minister; he argued the incapacity of the Presbytery to convict him, or of the magistrates to punish, or of the General Assembly to make rules for those not Presbyterians; and finally he asked to be freed under the terms of the 1701 Act against

12 Bishop Nicolson to Archbishop Tenison, 13 October 1709, British Library, Add. MS 6116 fo.17.

13 S.R.O., Presbytery Minutes, CH 2/121/7, 197–258.

Wrongous Imprisonment.[14] The magistrates answered that his orders were invalid and called him a'lay-man' and 'a Landloper from Ireland, pretending to be a lawful minister'.[15] The full bench of the Court of Session ruled against him on 8 November. Then Greenshields put in a reclaiming petition arguing that his ordination was a new issue, not raised initially by the Presbytery. This was also rejected and Greenshields presented his 'protest for remeid of law' on 30 December. The 'protest' had a superficial resemblance to the old form of appeal to the Scottish Parliament before 1707, although by 1709 the newer Scottish appeals were beginning to adopt English features.[16] This was the seventh case to go up since the Union; only nine months earlier, the first instance of a reversal of the Court of Session had occurred.[17]

The Greenshields petition came up in the House of Lords in February 1710. There was a considerable amount of interest for such an early stage of an appeal. The motion to send for the proceedings prompted an amendment to call for transcripts of all orders and for the personal attendance of Greenshields and some of the magistrates. This in turn produced a division, in which those seeking the added testimony lost and then lodged a formal protest.[18] A second motion was then debated, and the House voted to hear the case upon receipt of the documents. On 17 March the House decided that the case would be taken up 'as soon as the proceedings on the impeachment of Dr. Sacheverell now depending are finished'. The formal receipt of the Greenshields petition was recorded on 25 March, and the respondents were ordered to answer by the opening of the next session. In addition, the order of the House said that counsel for the respondents 'shall be at liberty, upon the hearing of this cause, to argue, in the first place, whether the said appeal be regularly and properly before this house, or not'.[19]

The hearing was delayed for nearly a year, first for the conclusion of

[14] The text of the Bill was printed in *The Case of Mr. Greenshields,* 9–12. In an earlier case, one Adam Peacock was arrested in Stirling in 1704 for intruding into the parish church, being under a sentence of deprivation by the General Assembly. Peacock raised a process under the Act of 1701 which failed in part because of the exception in the Act allowing magistrates 'to imprisone parties disobedient and contumacious to church censures' so long as they had the chance to make bail or demand a speedy trial. According to Fountainhall, Peacock's was 'the first [case] raised upon that new act of parliament', Fountainhall, ii, 209; Mor. 17065.

[15] Ibid., 52.

[16] As David Robertson pointed out a century later: 'They were still in Scotland stiled Protestations for remeid of Law. In Appeals brought after the Union, the form previously used in Appeals from Courts of Equity in England had apparently been adopted: But the old form of taking a Protest against the decision of the court, and declaring the grounds of Appeal by an instrument under the hand of a Notary Publick was continued for a considerable period after the Union. When the effect of an order of the House of Lords upon a Petition of Appeal came to be generally understood, the Protestations for remeid of Law were gradually discontinued, and for many years have been wholly left off', *Reports of Cases on Appeal from Scotland* (1807), xiv–xv.

[17] The reversal was in *Gray* v. *Hamilton,* in *The Manuscripts of the House of Lords*, vii, cit. sup. n.2, 12; and Robertson, *Reports of Cases on Appeal*, 1.

[18] H[ouse of] L[ords] J[ournals], xix, 68.

[19] H.L.J., xix, 127.

the Sacheverell case, then for the dissolution and new election, after which parliament reconvened in November 1710. The Edinburgh magistrates procrastinated and did not answer the Greenshields petition for about ten months.[20] Greenshields used the interval more productively and cultivated his contact with Bishop Nicolson of Carlisle. During a September visit, Nicolson wrote a testimonial for the curate to take to the archbishop of Canterbury:[21]

> The bearer is Mr. James Greenshields of whose late sufferings at Edinburgh yr Lordship has already heard a great deal, and will shortly hear much more. His case is widely different from that of a daring and seditious incendiary, as it has been industriously represented by some of his countrymen . . .
>
> I have convers'd with the gentleman for almost a week together, and I cannot find but that he's a person of great modesty & humility notwithstanding the temptation he is under of boasting: and that both the man himself and his cause have a just title to our compassion. I doubt not but that you will be of the same sentiments.

Greenshields delivered this letter to Archbishop Tenison, and when Nicolson came to London to attend the House of Lords in December, the Scot was there to meet him. Nicolson's London diaries show that the two worked closely on the case, meeting at least twenty-two times in the three months before the hearing. Nicolson wrote in his diary on 27 February:[22]

> . . . there being then with me Lord Summers, Lord Cowper and the Bishops of Bangor, Lincoln and Norwich, consulting on the case of Greenshields; which is to be restrained to the civil part, without touching on the Authority of the Kirk.

This was a vital tactical decision. It probably secured the reversal by diminishing the threat to the kirk. Ironically, the decision did not produce meaningful discussion of the role of the Lords in reviewing judgements of the Court of Session.

The first aspect became clear when the magistrates' counsel Peter King tried to raise the issue of church court jurisdiction in the first stage of the hearing. King said:[23]

> The Presbytery was only a subordinate ecclesiastic judicatory, from which appeals in course lie to the superior judicatories of the provincial synod and general assembly; and if the appellant thought himself grieved by the sentence of the Presbytery, and omitted this known and proper remedy, he could not in law, or good order, appeal from the Presbytery to the Lords.

Moreover, King pointed out that:

> No proper defenders or contradictors were summoned or called, and the Presbytery's sentence could not be reviewed, unless they themselves were called to

[20] *The Manuscripts of the House of Lords*, viii, cit. sup. n.2, 358, under 10 Jan. 1711.

[21] British Library, Add. MS 6116, fo.26.

[22] *The London Diaries of William Nicolson, Bishop of Carlisle, 1702–1718*, Clyve Jones and Geoffrey Holmes, ed. (1985), 551.

[23] Colles, 430; E.R., i, 357.

answer for it, and that the respondents [the magistrates] were not the persons to make answer in the case: and that although appellant pretended only to appeal from the decree of the Lords of Session, and the sentence of the magistrates, he directly libelled the sentence of the Presbytery, as groundless and illegal, and therefore to be reviewed, which upon the matter, was an appeal from the Presbytery against it.

The Lords ignored this argument. Indeed, according to Robertson's report, 'the appellant's argument on this preliminary point does not appear'.[24] This seems to have been part of the strategy, and Bishop Nicolson evidently felt they had some success, as his diary entry of 1 March reported:[25]

In the House, Mr. G.'s case heard; and the sentence of the Magistrates and Decree of Lords of Session, unanimously Reversed. There was little or no Debate on the main Subject ['Authority of the Kirk'?]. But a Division happened on a Question for Adjournment, after half the Counsel were heard; which was carryed (for sitting on) by 68 against 32. Some weak efforts were, after the Lawyers had done, made for adjournment of the Sentence till tomorrow; but the Cry was so loud for Reversing (20 Bishops present and concurring) that the Curate prevailed against the Lord Provost and Magistrates of the good Town of Edinburgh, who were undeniably in the wrong. N.B. The first point (i.e. Whether the Appeal lay Regularly before the Lords?) was quickly agreed, almost Nemine Contradicente; and then the Great Lords divided (as above) for goeing to Dinner. The Second part, being the Merits, held till near 7 at night; when my Land Lord and I dined together at home.

By this account it appears that the issue of the right of appeal attracted very little of the peers' attention. The only traces of the arguments used survive in the manuscript minutes of the Lords, a sketch of which appears in the published manuscript volume. Greenshields' counsel argued that 'the right of appealing was settled at the time of the Union'. The respondents' counsel claimed that 'there never was any appeal to the House of Lords in Scotland, and your Lordships have no more power than they'.[26] After these illuminating points, the house emphatically voted for its own jurisdiction. There was hardly any discussion of the alleged assumption of authority over the College of Justice.

Several possible explanations may be offered for the silence. In the first place, it is consistent with our finding that the case was not breaking new ground. Also, if the managers deliberately avoided a confrontation on the question of church judicatories, this might be a similar deliberate avoidance. This can be connected to two further points. The action of the magistrates was the main target, but it received no more discussion than the role of the peers in relation to the Court of Session. Finally, the two orders of the Court of Session may have caused some confusion in the House. The ruling of the full court in November and the order on Greenshields' reclaiming petition appeared to have unequal authority. Eventually the House would hear appeals from

[24] Robertson, 14.

[25] Jones and Holmes, *The London Diaries*, 553.

[26] *The Manuscripts of the House of Lords*, viii, cit. sup. n.2, 357.

all orders, but at this point the distinction may have prompted caution or confusion.[27] There may be no way to rank these explanations, but it should be noted that even the title of the case obscures the role of the Court of Session: *Greenshields* v. *Provost and Magistrates of Edinburgh*.

The main point in our context is that the issue seen by modern citators is very hard to locate in the sources and may be non-existent. Yet the case had great significance for Anglo-Scottish legal relations, if not in the way we have been told. We can better appreciate that significance when we look at the aftermath of the case, when some surprising things happened.

There was a uniformly negative reaction to the judgement in Scotland. The Presbytery of Edinburgh appointed a committee to respond. It drafted a letter to the Secretary of State to protest at what were called 'judicatories cloathed with any supream power' and it voiced the fear of 'a design to restore patronages which would be attended with the greatest disorders in this church'.[28] On the civil magistrates' side, there were continued arrests of Episcopal clergy. One pamphlet of 1711 reported at least half a dozen cases, in Aberdeen, Perth, Crail, St. Andrews and Orkney.[29] The author accused the Lord Advocate (James Stewart) of persecuting them 'with all the violence in his power' in spite of the Lords' verdict. He further charged that in November the Lord Advocate ordered the Provost to close all meeting-houses, which the latter refused to do without a royal command.

The reaction of the Court of Session was much less obvious. There is no record or report or other acknowledgement of the case after the two entries in Fountainhall under 1709. The other contemporary reporters, Forbes and Dalrymple, make no mention of Greenshields. Indeed, appeals to the House of Lords were not well reported at this stage. David Robertson, the leading student of this early period, wrote that:[30]

> Questions decided on appeal, after the time of the Union, though they excited attention, do not seem at first to have been more regarded as precedents, than the Questions appealed in the Parliament of Scotland had before been.

However important those older appeals had been, under the new regime a new range of problems appeared. Robertson described the records of early appeals in the following terms:[31]

[27] See Maurice Bond, *Guide to the Records of Parliament*, 114: 'At first Scottish appeals were received from final decrees only, and it was not until 1726 that H.L. began to hear also appeals against interlocutory orders'.

[28] Minutes of 25 March 1711 (S.R.O., CH 2/121/8, 32).

[29] *A Letter from a Gentleman in Edinburgh to his Friend in London, giving an Account of the Present Proceedings against the Episcopal Clergy in Scotland for using the English Lyturgy There* (1711).

[30] *Reports of Cases on Appeal from Scotland*, xv.

[31] Ibid., xvi–xvii.

> Many cases have been appealed which are not to be found among the decisions of the Court of Session hitherto published. In sundry instances, also, where Judgments of the Court of Session have been reversed in parliament, the original decisions still remain as precedents (and these in some questions of much moment) in the Collections of Decided Cases, in the Dictionary of Decisions, and in the works of Law Writers of authority. The instances where such reversals are properly stated in this period [1707–27] are so few as only to form exceptions to the general practice.

The same strictures were repeated and broadened by William Tait in the notes to his index of the cases collected by Morison:[32]

> The protestations of the Scottish parliament for remeid of law, often mentioned in Fountainhall's journal, are not referred to in the index, no procedure upon these protestations having been preserved.

Tait added that when the Faculty Collection commenced in 1752 the almost total neglect which the proceedings in appeals experienced from the reporters of decisions has been succeeded by a regular, although inadequate, degree of attention to the issue of the appeals of such cases as had been reported in the collection.

Not only was there a blank in reporting and/or publishing. In the view of at least one contemporary observer, Greenshields might be ignored by practitioners. The anonymous author of *A Seasonable Caution to the General Assembly* in 1711 pointed out the 'sovereign judicature' of the General Assembly 'in which the queen being always present by her commissioner, matters are determined without any appeal, except to the Bar of Heaven'. It was therefore safe for Scottish advocates and magistrates to believe that:[33]

> The peers of Great Britain having considered the commitment of Greenshields and reverst it does not at all disable and consequently ought not to discourage any magistrate from acting in their station according to law; it only extends to this particular case in which, whether some omission, some slip or some illegal step has been made is not for me to examine here, their lordships not suffering their proceedings to be printed or examined in print by anybody: but if in another case which may come before them, such slip or omission or illegal step cannot be found, such other case will receive no prejudice from this.

In short, this author was sure that Greenshields was no precedent. Those who disagreed would find their job more difficult without printed reports of the peers' proceedings. Such publication was discouraged by a Standing Order of 1698:[34]

> That it is a breach of the priviledge of this House for any person whatsoever to print or publish in print any thing relating to the proceedings of this House without the leave of this House.

32 *Index to the Decisions of the Court of Session* (Edinburgh, 1823), 528.

33 *A Seasonable Caution*, 5–6, 8.

34 *The Manuscripts of the House of Lords*, N.S., x (1953), 21.

The Scottish printer (the Heirs and Successors of Andrew Anderson) had no difficulty producing the documents sent to London in 1710.[35] The printed cases were required for appeals to the House of Lords. But there is no evidence of an attempt to print the proceedings in 1711. Presumably leave could have been obtained, yet the Scottish authorities may have had little desire to take the initiative. In summary, the effect of the case in Scotland was anything but decisive. The same was not true in London.

James Greenshields followed his legal victory in a way that few appellants have a chance to do. He became a successful lobbyist at the House of Lords, promoting both the Toleration Act and the Patronage Act of 1712. Bishop Nicolson's diary records at least fifteen meetings with Greenshields during the time the Acts were being debated. We also have the curate's own comments in a small collection of letters to his patron, Dr. John Colbatch, professor of Moral Theology at Cambridge. In December 1711 Greenshields reported taking up residence in Westminster 'to be near Parliament'. On 1 March 1712, the anniversary of his victory, he told Colbatch:

> I was 5 times with my Ld Treasurer about this [toleration] bill . . . I gave his Lo[rdshi]P w[ha]t information I could as to the expediency and necessity of it and all the court lords were very cordial in it.

At one point an amendment was proposed:

> . . . that no magistrate should putt in execution any ecclesiastical censure of the kirk agt any person either of the Episcopal or Presbyterian communion

but Greenshields reported that:

> Two thirds of the bishops [were] against it, because they feared it might be an ill precedent to deprive them sometime or other of the magistrates assisting in executing their censures.

When the Commons proposed an amendment to require oaths on all sides, Greenshields approved:

> It will do considerable service to the [Episcopal] church there, and . . . more of the Episcopal ministers will comply with taking the oaths then of the Presbyterians, in proportion to their numbers.

Greenshields neglected to comment on another feature of the Toleration Act which would be very important in the future. If a minister did not pray for the queen and Princess Sophia, he was liable to a £20 fine for the first offence:[37]

> . . . and for the second offence every minister of the established church in that

[35] *The Case of Mr. Greenshields, as it was printed in London* (op. cit. n. 6 above). These papers match the originals in the House of Lords Record Office, (see Appeals and Writs of Error, i, 88; Main Papers, 2651). They were printed sometime after January 1710, as the preface mentions Greenshields having spent 'four months' in prison.

[37] 10 Anne c. 2, s. 11; emphasis added.

> part of Great Britain called Scotland, being thereof convicted by the oaths of two sufficient witnesses *before the lords of justiciary*, shall be ipso facto deprived and declared incapable of any church or ecclesiastical living, during the space of three years, and every episcopal minister allowed and protected by this act, being thereof in like manner convicted, shall from thenceforth forfeit and lose the benefit of this act and be declared incapable of officiating as pastor of any episcopal congregation during the space of three years.

Thus the Toleration Act made penalties milder and more predictable, and it insured that any future Greenshields would find it much harder to appeal, as the case would be heard in the High Court of Justiciary, where appellate jurisdiction was going to be harder to establish.[38]

In 1712 Greenshields was also active in working for the passsage of the Patronage Act. In 1690 lay patronage had been replaced by a system of nomination by heritors and election by Presbyteries. When reform was proposed, it was to return to the old system of lay patrons, and since the General Assembly was not consulted, this Act, even more than its companion, violated the Act of Security and the terms of the Union. Presbyteries still approved nominees, but a serious element of friction was introduced which would disturb the kirk for several generations. One very important case in 1713 seemed to draw together most of the elements of animosity we have been studying and may serve as a conclusion to our sketch of the aftermath of Greenshields.

In Elgin the old cathedral church was used by the parish, and an adjoining chapel, called 'the Little Kirk', was also furnished for divine service. The chapel was used prior to 1704 by an Episcopal minister, with the approval of the magistrates. Later the Presbyterian ministers of the burgh obtained an order from the Privy Council and took over the chapel. The magistrates resumed possession in 1712 and asked another Episcopal clergyman, a Mr. Blair, to perform divine service in the Little Kirk. At this point, John Dundas, the Procurator for the Church of Scotland, with the concurrence of the Lord Advocate, brought a criminal action against the provost, the baillies, the sexton and Mr. Blair, on the ground that this was an intrusion contrary to the Acts of 1695 (c. 22) and 1712 (c. 7) and demanded restitution and damages.[39]

During the proceedings the Lords of Justiciary decided to remit one question to the Court of Session, namely to determine whether the Little

[38] There was of course no way to foretell this difference in 1712. The best discussion of this side of the appellate issue is in A.J. MacLean, 'The House of Lords and Appeals from the High Court of Justiciary, 1707–1887', *Jurid. Rev., N.S.*, xxx (1985), 192–226. Some early unsuccessful appeals in cases like Greenshields are noted at pp.193–94: William Duguid, 1713; William Black, 1714; Alexander Robertson, 1718. At this time, parliament had already meddled with several aspects of justiciary business; this was invited by art. XIX of the Treaty of Union and the qualifications it imposed; then 8 Anne c. 16 discharged the required attendance of several categories of people at the circuit sessions; 10 Anne c. 2 required practisers of law in North Britain to take oaths of allegiance and abjuration; 10 Anne c. 33 reduced circuits to once a year.

[39] *Provost and Baillies of Elgin* v. *Ministers of Elgin* (1713) Rob. 69.

Kirk was 'a parish church or part of the parish church of Elgin'. The arguments on this point dealt with both the physical position of the chapel and with its past usage. The Court of Session held that the Little Kirk was a part of the parish church, and the Lords of Justiciary held for the Presbyterian ministers that this was an intrusion and subject to an award of damages.

The magistrates appealed both the orders of Session and Justiciary to the House of Lords. The appellants argued that the Session decree was incorrect, namely that the chapel had been separate for thirty years and that the Lords of Justiciary had given them no chance to answer the decree. The respondent ministers relied on the original construction plan for the cathedral and on the evidence of the use of the space as an annex to the parish church. The peers:[40]

> . . . ordered and adudged that the said appellants be quieted in the possession of the Little Church in Elgin it being no part of the Parish Church; and that the said respondents do repay to the said appellants the costs and fine adjudged by the said Lords of Justiciary to the said respondents.

The Elgin decision turned out to be a unique example of a successful appeal of a justiciary ruling. What it shows in our context is the continuing power of the elements present in the Greenshields case. Given time, those elements might have produced an appellate power over the High Court of Justiciary, for it is likely that such appeals were considered 'legal' in the early eighteenth century. But the circumstances changed dramatically in 1715. Criminal appeal did not thrive thereafter, but civil appeals continued to grow.

The number of Scottish appeals, especially from the Court of Session, grew steadily in the eighteenth century. Even so, the Greenshields case slipped into obscurity during the same period of time. The loss and recovery of the case offer an instructive conclusion to our study.

Judging from the manuscripts of the House of Lords, appeals increased at a modest rate at first. Between 1708 and 1714 there were 144 appeals in all:[41]

	1708–1710	1710–1712	1712–1714
English	22	31	30
Scottish	6	14	18
Irish	7	6	10

The Scottish appeals clearly showed the most rapid growth, and Fountainhall's explanation has been followed by most writers. In February 1711, on the eve of the Greenshields decision, he wrote:[42]

> Towards the end of this session there were sundry more appeals given in to the

[40] Rob. 74–75.

[41] *The Manuscripts of the House of Lords*, N.S., viii–x. The English figures do not include writs of error.

[42] Fountainhall, ii, 643.

> Lords for remead of law to the British Parliament . . . I have marked no less than ten protests this winter session; they are turned more frequent and numerous since the Union then [sic] they were before, though access now is both more difficult and expensive than the discussing them before our own parliaments were. The reason may be, 1st to concuss the victor to a composition rather than undertake a tedious uncertain journey to London; 2do they have this advantage now, that how soon it is tabled in the House of Peers, all execution is stopt, whereas with us they were not suspensive of the sentence, but only devolutive.

By the following year, Fountainhall was even more concerned. He noted thirteen cases in his entry for 29 February 1712 and said 'by this number of appeals, we see they increase every year to the great impoverishing and detriment of this nation'.[43]

Yet if Scottish appeals were becoming more popular and widely-used, why would the record of an important one such as *Greenshields* seem to be lost? In the first place, the decision was reduced in value after 1715 and more so in the decline of the Jacobite cause after 1746. The result of the rebellions was a sharp reduction in the number of Episcopal ministers and a dramatic increase in the level of their political reliability. In the second place, disputes within the kirk assumed a far greater importance than fears of prelacy and prayer books. Where Greenshields was remembered, it was as a decision relating to church censure.[44]

However, *Greenshields* was not included in Lord Kames' *Dictionary of Decisions* in 1741. When Lord Swinton made a collection of appeal cases based on the House of Lords Journals (1708–73), he too omitted Greenshields. Finally in the works of solicitors or writers such as George Urquhart and Thomas Smith there was no mention of *Greenshields*, although both authors presented elaborate discussions and ample citations on appellate procedure.[45]

The recovery of the Greenshields case coincided with yet another link between the English and Scottish systems. By the end of the eighteenth century, the number of Scottish appeals had grown dramatically. Moreover, the Union of 1801 brought Irish appeals back to the House of Lords. Over the next few years growing numbers, and a lop-sided Scottish majority, caused attention to be turned to reform of the process. The House had already added many days of hearings, so the next logical site for reform was the Court of Session. These efforts culminated in an Act in 1808.

One of the products of this renewed interest was the collection of appeal cases by David Robertson, a barrister of the Middle Temple. Robertson's work covered only 1707–27. *Greenshields* appeared in the collection as

[43] Fountainhall, ii, 734.

[44] See an incomplete 'Table to the Most Remarkable Points in printed cases upon appeals to the House of Lords since 1701 [sic]' composed in the 1730s, under 'appeals', National Library of Scotland, Adv. MS 28.3.3.

[45] Kames, *Dictionary of Decisions* (1741); Swinton, *Collection* (printed in Morison, *Dictionary of Decisions: Supplemental Volume* (Edinburgh, 1815), separately paginated); G. Urquhart, *The Experienced Solicitor* (Edinburgh, 1773); T. Smith, *Forms of Procedure* (Edinburgh, 1821).

case number six. This was the first published version of the case since 1711, but it was not followed by rapid entry of the case into wider legal reference. When the case appeared in Kinnear's *Digest of House of Lords Cases* in 1865 it was under 'appeal (jurisdiction)' where it said that:[46]

> . . . appeal lay from an order of Court of Session refusing a suspension of a judgment of the magistrates, and also from such judgment . . .

The next direct reference in a formal legal work was the entry in the *Scots Digest of Appeals in the House of Lords from 1707 and of Cases in the Supreme Courts of Scotland* which began appearing in four volumes from 1908. One of the entries under 'Process – appeal' cited *Greenshields* this way:

> In an appeal to the House of Lords from a sentence of imprisonment for breach of an order of a presbytery, pronounced by the Magistrates of Edinburgh, and an interlocutor of the Court of Session refusing a suspension of the same, an objection to the competency of the appeal, in respect that it was in reality a direct appeal from the presbytery's order, *repelled*.

In other words, the digest noted the argument of the respondents which was set aside by the peers, but made no comment as to the impact on civil appeals.

As for the official record of the case, the documentary work of the Historical Manuscripts Commission was launched in the last quarter of the nineteenth century. Soon calendars of manuscripts such as those of the House of Lords were being produced, but the volume with the *Greenshields* documents only appeared in 1923.[47]

Turning to the work of historians at the beginning of this century, William Law Mathieson described the *Greenshields* case entirely as a part of the prayer book controversy. Greenshields had 'set up a meeting house, in order, as he himself explained, to see whether his political qualifications would protect him in using the Book of Common Prayer'.[48] It is not clear where Greenshields gave this explanation, but he probably knew that the protection would not work, and that he could provoke a test case. Mathieson made no suggestion that the case involved significant civil and constitutional questions. Peter Hume Brown wrote soon afterward:[49]

> Here then was the jurisdiction of the church, supposed to be for ever safeguarded by the union, set at naught in its prime concern. Henceforth the limits of that jurisdiction would be determined not by the constitution of the National Church, but by a House of Lords, of which Anglican bishops formed a component part.

46 J.B. Kinnear, *Digest of House of Lords Cases on Appeal from Scotland, 1709–1864*, (Edinburgh, 1865), 26; Shaw's *Digest* did not include the case because its coverage only began in 1726; the first instalment of the *Faculty Digest* began with cases from 1868. The case was also passed over by Charles Denison and Charles Scott in *Procedures and Practice Relative to English, Scottish and Irish Appeals* (1879).

47 *The Manuscripts of the House of Lords*, N.S., viii.

48 *Scotland and the Union* (Glasgow, 1905), 195–99.

49 *History of Scotland*, 3 vols. (Cambridge, 1909), iii, 146; (Cambridge, 1911), iii, 116.

G.M. Trevelyan confused the decisions in the Lords, and wrote that the question of competency was voted on 68–32, which 'ruling has ever since been accepted in Great Britain'. He added that henceforth 'the House of Lords was the judge of the limits of ecclesiastical jurisdiction in Scotland'.[50]

Arthur S. Turberville studied the House of Lords in the eighteenth century and in that institutional framework a similar conclusion emerged:[51]

> [the case] meant that in future the extent of the jurisdiction of the church of Scotland would be determined by the House of Lords.

Therefore it was:

> . . . easy to understand . . . Scots who . . . resented the determination of a case concerning the Presbyterian church by an assembly which contained an episcopal bench.

Turberville overlooked the juridical significance of the case and paid very little attention to the whole matter of Scots appeals.

Only after 1950 did the legal dimension begin to receive greater attention. The first full-length twentieth-century analysis of appellate jurisdiction was Andrew Dewar Gibb's *Law from over the Border* in 1950. While Gibb gave some contradictory views on the role of the bishops in the House of Lords, he was sure they were up to no good. He recognized that *Greenshields* was not the first case but called it 'one of the earliest and best-known [sic] of all Scots appeals'. He found the peers' judgement in error, because the appellant's case was 'loose and unconvincing' while the statutes cited by the magistrates 'exactly met the case'. In Gibb's view, *Greenshields* was a good early example of overbearing intervention in Scots law.[52]

Within a few years Professor T.B. Smith produced another analysis of *Greenshields*. He too saw the case as evidence of parliament's cavalier treatment of the constitutional guarantees of the Treaty of Union:[53]

> . . . Parliament from shortly after the Union till the present day has undertaken – without serious scrutiny of its powers – the purported variation by ordinary Act of Parliament of many of the conditions of Union . . .
> . . . Thus, for example, soon after the Union, the Toleration Act and the Patronage Act struck at Scottish religious feelings in a most vindictive way – as did the House of Lords in its judicial capacity when it assumed appellate jurisdiction in the *Greenshield's* [sic] case and supported the somewhat provocative actings of the appellant, an episcopal clergyman in Scotland.

[50] *England under Queen Anne,* 3 vols. (1930–34), iii, 238.

[51] *The House of Lords in the XVIIIth Century* (Oxford, 1927), 95, 147.

[52] *Law from over the Border* (Edinburgh, 1950), 8–12.

[53] *The British Commonwealth: The Development of its Laws and Constitutions*, G.W. Keeton, ed., 1, pt. 2, T.B. Smith, *Scotland* (1955), 646 and 11 (1962), 55; T.B. Smith, *A Short Commentary on the Law of Scotland* (Edinburgh, 1962), 55 (emphasis added).

There is some ambiguity here. Had the Lords assumed jurisdiction generally, or only in this case?

There is another kind of uncertainty in the Stair Society's *Introduction to Scottish Legal History*:[54]

> The right and power of taking such appeals was soon settled by a decision of the House of Lords in the case of *The Earl of Rosebery* v. *Pirrie* in 1708, followed by the case of Greenshields in 1710.

After this awkward re-entry in the 1950s, the case began to gain stature in the hands of text writers, a gain which may have been influenced by the growing attention to nationalist opinion. Whatever weight that had, there was no legal ground for the revival. In his latest incarnation Greenshields is still a provocative and elusive figure.

The *Greenshields* case is a curious example of the interaction of the English and Scottish legal systems. The following are among the significant features of that relationship:

1. An appellate connection existed before *Greenshields*, but the evidence around the case suggests that the connection was ill-formed and incompletely recorded.
2. The memory of *Greenshields* receded in the eighteenth century, despite the growing number of Scottish civil appeals reaching the House of Lords.
3. In the years around 1800 the number of Scottish appeals reached critical proportions and helped to force a closer look at the process; this meant recovery of past records and reform of future procedure.
4. With recovery of the story of the case, it was later employed to illustrate (a) persecution of the kirk and (b) invasion of Scots legal autonomy – both being English violations of the Treaty of Union.

These elements suggest that *Greenshields* has been a creature of the relationship between the two nations and their legal systems. As such, *Greenshields* was not a case which led in any area or on any principle. It did not 'establish' Scottish appeals, but it did reflect their role in the evolving relationship between the English and Scottish legal systems.

[54] G.C.H. Paton, 'The Eighteenth Century and Later', Stair Society, xx (Edinburgh, 1958), 55. The correct citation is '*Rosebery* v. *Inglis*'; see Fountainhall, ii, 438, which entry notes the resistance of the Scottish clerks to production of depositions, which resistance was the subject of Lord Rosebery's petition to the House of Lords on 6 March 1708, *The Manuscripts of the House of Lords*, vii, cit. n.2, 554.

Chapter 9

Default and Modern Process

Stephen C. Yeazell

Medieval and early modern English law lacked a procedural mechanism that modern legal process takes for granted: the default judgement.[1] Until 1725 a plaintiff could not secure a judgement in a personal action unless the defendant chose to appear in court and answer the charges. Only by the enactment of 12 George I c. 29 did it become possible to secure the entry of such a judgement in a personal action against a defendant who, properly summoned, nevertheless failed to appear. To untutored modern eyes the absence until modern times of a default mechanism seems puzzling. In modern English and American procedure the threat of a default judgement is the quiet hinge on which much adversarial process turns. Default compels the defendant to answer and keeps him in the game after it has started. Default enables modern process to place enormous burdens on adversarial shoulders in the confidence that they will not simply shrug them off. We think of medieval and early modern process as adversarial to a fault, yet it lacked this mechanism we regard as basic. The emergence of a default mechanism in eighteenth century England raises a question that can take two forms. One can ask why default emerged so late: how could medieval process function without a mechanism that seems to moderns so central? Alternatively, one can ask why default emerged at all: if English law functioned adequately without default for five hundred years, what changed? Both forms of the question yield insights into the development of a modern conception of legal process in early modern times.

Medieval law could function without default in personal actions because it did have default in real actions and because it had a variety of devices that compelled defendants to appear and answer in personal actions. Each of these devices yielded fees to the officials who administered them. One can understand the late adoption of default in personal actions as a tribute to the success of these compensating mechanisms, to the late development of a sharp distinction between civil and criminal processes, and to the hardiness of belief that office-holders held property in their fees. As wealth began to move from land to intangibles, personal actions (which dealt with such intangibles)

[1] I am grateful for the thoughtful comments of Paul Brand, Kenneth Graham, William McGovern, Mark Ramseyer, David Seipp and John S. Wiley.

came to dominate dockets in the seventeenth century. This shift in wealth and litigation patterns placed the compensating mechanisms under great strain. Simultaneously, the conceptions of office holding that protected them against change suffered erosion from the political changes that swept seventeenth-century England; a scandal in high places accelerated the erosion. Finally, as tort and crime became distinct categories, it was easier to contemplate the divergence of process in these newly separate spheres of law.

Parliament's adoption of default in 1725 did not mark a monumental change in process. It did, however, begin a transformation of the adversarial process, changing the state's role in litigation and moving the focus of litigation from the pleading stage to proof.

I. Medieval and Restoration Process

Default was both a very early and a late development in English law. On one hand common law placed almost transcendent importance on the appearance of the defendant. The plaintiff could get no relief unless the defendant appeared to answer the plaintiff's allegations. If the defendant did not appear, medieval process waited patiently while trying to make him do so. To force appearance it seized his property if it was available, and was prepared to seize his person as well. Here an ambivalence appears. If land was the object of the suit, the land was seized, 'and if the defendant . . . remain[ed] contumacious [in his refusal to answer], it [was] adjudged to the demandant'.[2] But if land itself was not the object of the suit, the defendant had to appear and respond to the plea if the plaintiff was to obtain any relief. If the defendant did not respond to seizure of his goods, or if the sheriff failed to locate either these goods or the defendant's person, medieval law declared him an outlaw, beyond the protection of society and liable to lose all his lands and goods. Yet in personal actions even this drastic step gave the plaintiff no relief: the recalcitrant defendant forfeited goods not to the plaintiff but to the crown. By failing to plead the defendant had offended the order of the realm but unless he did appear, the plaintiff got no remedy.

The writ of right, one of the most ancient forms of action, contained a default mechanism. Developed to try the ultimate title to land, the writ as understood by Bracton in the thirteenth century proceeded against the land itself. If the defendant failed to answer, the land, taken into the king's hands at the commencement of the action, was delivered to the demandant.[3] The writ of novel disseisin, which eventually supplanted the writ of right, employed the same mechanism. Both employed default in a way that seems limited to modern laywers. The defendant got the choice of appearing and contesting the action or defaulting and suffering the loss of the land. This

[2] F.W. Maitland, *The Forms of Action at Common Law* (Cambridge, 1936; rptd. 1976), 62.

[3] Ibid.

loss was not, however, irrevocable. A defendant who had thus lost his land could bring a writ of right against the former plaintiff, and in this action try the same question of title that would have been at issue had he appeared in the original lawsuit. The early writ of right thus gave plaintiff a remedy, but not the protection of *res judicata*.[4] Moreover, this remedy did not extend to the panoply of writs: it was limited to what have rather unsatisfactorily been called real actions.[5]

An elephantine process accompanied the writ of right. Even in the twelfth century litigants avoided it if they could. Each conceivable excuse for failure to appear constituted an essoin, which postponed the suit.[6] Novel disseisin was faster than the writ of right. Defendants could not avail themselves of essoins,[7] and the writ had a strong flavour of executive action. Combined with the availability of default, these characteristics made the new writ a powerful one. In consequence novel disseisin quickly supplanted the cumbersome writ of right and enjoyed great popularity for several centuries.[8] One of the advantages that prolonged its life into early modern times was precisely the availability of default judgements, a feature not at first attached to trespass, which might otherwise have been used as an alternative to the writ of right and novel disseisin.[9]

Medieval process thus knew the default judgement, but knew it best in processes available only to recover title to or seisin of land. For other actions only the defendant's appearance could produce a judgement. The law required submission – however unwilling – to its jurisdiction. Fortunately the medieval plaintiff did not have to rely on the defendant's good will. A series of devices aimed at producing the defendant's appearance: distress, attachment and arrest provided the most common means of compelling submission to the court. Distress, a self-help remedy available only to a landlord seeking rent, permitted the seizure of chattels, forcing a defendant desiring their return to sue in replevin. Attachment (available through the writ of *distringas*) extended the seizure of goods to claims other than rent actions. Armed with the writ, a plaintiff could ask the sheriff to seize the defendant's

[4] By contrast, modern default combines with broader notions of *res judicata* to protect against a second suit challenging the correctness of the first judgement. The defendant is limited to seeking to reopen the judgement, typically on the ground that he did not receive notice of the first action or was for some reason unable to respond to it. See, e.g., *Peralta* v. *Heights Medical Center, Inc.*, 108 S.Ct. 896 (1989).

[5] Borrowing terminology from Roman law, Bracton in the thirteenth century distinguished between actions that proceeded against a 'thing' (the real actions) and those that were against the person (personal actions). As many commentators have noted, the division never suited English writ-based law very well, and in consequence the boundaries between the real and the personal actions shifted over time. Fortunately we need not resolve the difficulties created by this borrowed terminology.

[6] F.W. Maitland, *Forms of Action*, 19–20.

[7] R.C. van Caenegem, *Royal Writs in England from the Conquest to Glanvill*, Selden Society, lxxvii (1959), 262.

[8] D.W. Sutherland, *The Assize of Novel Disseisin* (Oxford, 1973), 169.

[9] Ibid., 189.

goods, hoping that in order to regain his property the defendant would give pledges for an appearance in the action. Arrest (available with a writ of *capias ad respondendum*) operated straightforwardly: the sheriff would seize the defendant and hold him until the date for his appearance or until he bailed himself as security for that appearance. The final club held over the head of the recalcitrant defendant was outlawry. Originally 'the last resort of criminal law',[10] outlawry threatened the defendant with escheat of lands, corruption of blood, and legalized murder at the hands of any subject. Outlawry had its logic: the party who, having been thrice summoned, attached and sought for arrest to answer a claim, still refused to appear, was declaring himself beyond the dictates of even the most primitive system of peaceful adjudication. For society to wash its hands of him (and in the process to withdraw the protection of life and property) made sense. The law was punishing the outlaw for his failure to submit to royal jurisdiction.

None of these scarifying threats worked effectively. Distress was available only in an action seeking rent, and subjected the distraining landlord to liability for failure to care for the seized goods. Attachment and arrest required the cooperation of an often unwilling sheriff,[11] who, when faced with a difficult-to-execute writ, could report his inability to find either the goods or the person of the defendant – a return the plaintiff was unable to challenge. Moreover, even when successful, attachment and arrest required writs, and each writ involved fees to the officers who issued them. In the case of writs of *capias* (arrest) and *distringas* (attachment), the official was the filazer (or rather the filazer for the particular county in question). To this official a fee was due for each writ issued. Thus an action that proceeded through several attachments to an arrest would require multiple writs and multiple fees. Filazers, who by the seventeenth century at least had purchased their offices, jealously guarded the fees they produced.[12]

Outlawry worked no better. Its failure emphasizes the inadequacy of ordinary medieval process. Because distress and arrest often failed to secure the defendant's appearance, parliament between 1285 and 1504 extended outlawry to claims in account, debt, detinue, replevin and case.[13] These extensions testified to the weakness of other means of compulsion, but they also almost guaranteed that outlawry would fail as well. Precisely because the process was so drastic, judges were reluctant to apply it to what amounted to everyday disputes. Accordingly the law of outlawry became technical: a small slip in the steps leading to a judgement of outlawry sufficed to have it set

[10] T. Plucknett, *A Concise History of the Common Law* (1956), 385.

[11] One can sympathize with medieval sheriffs. Liable civilly for loss of seized goods and for escape of arrested prisoners, they can be forgiven a legendary lack of enthusiasm for performing either duty.

[12] C.W. Brooks reports that by the middle of the seventeenth century, 'there was a flourishing market in reversions for places as filazers . . .', *Pettyfoggers and Vipers of the Commonwealth: The 'Lower Branch' of the Legal Profession in Early Modern England* (1986), 230.

[13] Westminster II c. 11 (1285); 25 Edw. III, stat. 5, c. 17 (1352); 19 Hen. VII c. 9 (1504).

aside.[14] Worse, from the plaintiff's standpoint, by the sixteenth century the outlawed defendant could purchase a pardon for a few pounds – leaving him in possession of his lands and goods and the plaintiff still unsatisfied. And, like attachment and arrest, outlawry involved another set of officials and of fees; the clerk of the outlawries was an appointive office for which incumbents paid in the expectation of recouping their expenses in fees.

Understanding this array of drastic yet often futile efforts to compel defendant's answer requires us to understand why appearance was so important. In part the desire for appearance responded to practicalities: uncertainty of life and dreadful transportation remained constant facts of medieval English life. People did get sick, roads were often impassable. Any legal system that ignored these circumstances made unnecessary trouble for itself and compromised its fairness into the bargain.

Yet one can also perhaps see a theory lurking behind these practicalities.[15] A society that employed default judgements in its most solemn and final process had some use for the idea. One must account both for its presence in the real actions and for its absence in the personal actions. The key to both lies in understanding the position of the medieval English state. Though powerful by contemporary standards, English goverment was weak by modern standards. Its resources were spread thin and expending them required a strong justification. Controlling the primary form of wealth – land – supplied one such justification. To resort to default in real actions was no more than to accept necessity. On land rested not only the king's finances but also his sovereignty: 'All land whatsoever [was] held, mediately or immediately, of the Crown'.[16] Not just what we might now call dispute settlement but government itself would cease if a recalcitrant litigant were able to block adjudication of claims to the most significant form of wealth.[17]

Although necessity and political theory combined to make default acceptable in actions to recover title or seisin, extending default to other areas was another matter. It is a cliche to point out that modern English

14 As one seventeenth-century manual put it, 'Outlawries are but meer scare crowes, to disable both the Plaintiff and Defendant, in putting them to unnecessary Charge . . .', *The Practick Part of Law: Shewing the Office of a Compleat Attorney* (1653), 288.

15 The insistence on appearance tempts one to describe medieval justice as voluntary, a weak state offering justice as a service rather than as a command. Yet this explanation seems inadequate on a pair of grounds. First, the writs themselves take the form of commands, either to the sheriff or to the defendant; it is hard to fit a voluntarist notion of justice with the language of the writs. Moreover, attachment, distress, arrest and outlawry are not the stuff of gentle persuasion: they aimed at forcing the defendant to appear. That they often failed to accomplish their goal does not mean that they aimed at less than compulsion. Second, default did exist for those most solemn medieval proceedings – the real actions.

16 A.W.B. Simpson, *An Introduction to the History of Land Law* (Oxford, 1961; rptd. 1979), 1.

17 'Seisin was the cardinal point of land law. It was the basis of economic life. Land was everything to everybody. To lose one's land, or in other words, to be disseised of one's tenement, was as fatal a blow as losing one's job in a society which knows no unemployment insurance. It was, economically speaking, the worst thing that could happen to anybody', R.C. van Caenegem, op. cit. n.7 above, 262.

law grows out of a series of efforts to create truncated, simpler and therefore quicker forms of action. But speed in law is as dangerous as it is desirable: it enables error to infect the judgement, for wrong to triumph over right. In an adversarial system the chance for error will always be greatest when one side does not even appear to state its case. Moreover, the failure to appear makes more likely an error of special concern to a court – the possibility that it lacks power to hear and decide this case. Requiring such an appearance in the personal actions, though not in the real actions, reflects political theory. None seriously challenged the king's power to hear suits involving freehold: a series of solemn charters not only recognized but insisted on this jurisdiction. Beyond freehold, however, the royal power was less clear because less pressing. Was there another court that should hear the case? Was the controversy properly a matter for royal concern? Requirements that minimum amounts be at stake to invoke royal jurisdiction and the requirement that plaintiffs allege some royal concern (captured in *vi et armis* allegations that invoked the king's peacekeeping functions) attest to the proposition that all recognized royal jurisdiction was limited. To insist on appearance is to require submission to – or challenge of – the court's jurisdiction. A party who has argued his cause to the court has been forced either to consent to its power to judge the controversy or to challenge that power. A process that prevented the state from wasting efforts in producing a decree which would only prove the starting point for litigation challenging its efficacy may have seemed both a sensible way of allocating scarce bureaucratic resources and a politically wise precaution.

The character of the writs in personal actions offered another reason for caution. Medieval law, in some respects far more flexible than ours, drew no sharp distinctions between what we would now call civil and criminal matters. Not only dramatic examples like 'private' criminal prosecutions, but also the common 'civil' writs testify to the interpenetration of what have become separate legal and intellectual spheres. Many of the writs in personal actions grew from trespass, and their allegations spoke of a wrong to the king's peace. Even after no one took literally the allegations that bordered on felony, an air of seriousness clung to these writs. Indeed it was just this air of seriousness that made *capias* and *distringas* available as mesne process: the sheriff, a royal officer, ought to bestir himself to force these malefactors to answer. Yet this stance had an inherent limiting principle. If shrieval vigour in pursuing these complaints rested on their similarity to crimes, the same restraints limiting criminal process ought to apply to analogous civil actions, to use a pair of anachronistic categories. One such constraint involved the necessity of a defendant's appearing to answer charges. A criminal defendant could not be tried *in absentia*; indeed, even if present, he could not be convicted if he refused to plead. If a trespass was a serious wrong, though not so serious as a felony, could it be appropriate to come to judgement without so much as a response to the complaint by the defendant?[18]

Even when medieval English law took a step toward default in personal actions, it preserved this emphasis on the defendant's appearing to answer the plea. The Statute of Marlborough provided that in personal actions once issue was joined (that is, once the parties' exchange of pleading had formulated an issue for a jury) a defendant could have only one essoin.[19] Having taken that essoin, the defendant could have judgement entered against him if he failed to appear 'at the day given to him by the essoin'. This provision takes a half step toward modern default, according to which judgement can be entered after any failure by the defendant to respond in accord with procedural requirements. Marlborough's solution is more cautious, permitting default only after 'anyone hath put himself on the inquest'.[20] Both the words and the deed speak of a submission to royal jurisdiction generally and to a particular form of process. Once the stage at which the defendant would enter a responsive pleading had passed, medieval lawyers felt much more confidence in acting as if they had power to dispose of the case without the defendant. Until then, the defendant could be harassed, but judgement itself lay beyond the court's power.

II. Why Default?

This regime of appearance as a precondition of judgement changed in 1725. By 12 George I c. 29 Parliament made it possible to enter judgement against a defendant who failed to appear.[21] In place of arrest the Act provided

[18] I am indebted to David Seipp for suggesting this analogy.

[19] 52 Hen. III c. 13 (1267).

[20] The Latin of the statute's phrase is, 'postquam aliquis posuerit se in inquisicionem aliquam'.

[21] The Act provided that:

> . . . [F]rom and after the twenty fourth day of June one thousand seven hundred and twenty six, no person shall be held to special bail upon any process issuing out of any superior court, where the cause of action shall not amount to the sum of ten pounds or upwards . . . and that in all [such] cases . . . the plaintiff . . . shall not arrest or cause to be arrested, the body of the defendant . . . but shall serve him, her or them personally, within the jurisdiction of the court, with a copy of the process; and if such defendant . . . shall not appear at the return of the process or within four days after such return, in such case it shall and may be lawful to and for the plaintiff . . . upon affidavit being made, and filed in the proper court, of the personal service of such process as aforesaid (which said affidavit shall be filed gratis) to enter a common appearance or file common bail for the defendant or defendants, and to proceed thereon, as if such defendant . . . had entred [sic] his, her or their appearance, or filed common bail; any law or usage to the contrary notwithstanding.

For actions seeking more than ten pounds the Act permitted the institution of civil arrest to continue, but only if the plaintiff made a special affidavit of the amount in controversy, the sheriff being directed to take bail only for the amounts specified in the affidavit. In cases in which the plaintiff had made no such affidavit, no arrest was to take place, but the plaintiff could use the same combination of service of process and default if the defendant failed to appear.

that the plaintiff was required to serve the defendant with process. If he failed to appear on the date specified by that process, the plaintiff, having sworn that the defendant was properly served, could then make a common appearance for defendant – that is, the plaintiff could have his attorney appear instead of the defendant's and proceed to take judgement against the absent defendant. To be sure, the Act permitted civil arrest to continue to exist in larger cases if the plaintiff made a special affidavit of the amount owed. Nevertheless the adoption of this legislation marks a small turning in the procedural road; no longer did English courts have to have the defendant before them to enter judgement:[22] an opportunity to appear substituted for an actual appearance.[23]

If one accepts the argument so far, this development poses a problem the obverse of the one with which we started. Default's absence seems explicable, but its advent remains unaccounted for. In a system that attached so much importance to the defendant's appearance, why did Parliament in 1725 abandon the requirement of appearance in personal actions? I believe the answer has several parts, some broadly social and economic, others narrowly doctrinal and circumstantial.

To examine broader aspects, one has to go no further than the pair of seventeenth-century revolutions, which overthrew two kings, executing one in the process. These events made a difference in the fabric of political life and in political assumptions. The execution of Charles I and the expulsion of James II bespoke rejection of important aspects of royal policy. William and Mary, Anne and the Hanoverians accepted their subjects' conviction that there were unacceptable paths, particularly those of religion, into which a monarch could stray. The Act of Settlement testified to a general will to which even monarchs had to pay heed. The existence of that will had led to the rejection of a king and the resettlement of the crown on Protestant heads. Although it was not yet established that parliament was that sovereign (Blackstone assiduously denied it in 1775),[24] it could escape no one that the king was not all-powerful. The political revolution that followed the Glorious Revolution was carefully ambiguous about the exact location of sovereignty but the Commons were now among the king's rivals for power.

Drawing a direct line between these grand political themes and the development of a default remedy approaches the absurd. Nevertheless relationships can be suggested. For much of the seventeenth century the political classes of England had continually appealed to the common law as a bulwark against feared royal despotism. The common law usually failed them in the event, but it was a powerful rhetorical source. This rhetoric had procedural implications. If liberty lay in the scrupulous adherence to every

22 The Act did not apply to Scotland.

23 The 1725 legislation was renewed and amended in 1732. The amendments extended the time for defendant's answer to eight days and required the summons to be in English – it having been discovered that many small debtors could not understand the Latin summons, 5 Geo. II c. 27 (1732).

24 W. Blackstone, *Commentaries on the Laws of England*, 7th ed. (1775), i, 154–55.

turning of the writs, then almost any change in law was a threat to liberty. The settlement of 1688 changed the nature of the discourse. The nation had shown that it was able to guarantee in fact, not just in word and theory, what passed for liberty in seventeenth-century discourse. Under those conditions the rights of the English seemed to depend less on punctilious adherence to common law writs than on an active political vigilance.

One must not overstate this case. Sovereignty had been wrested from the crown, but the terms of the struggle showed how deeply ingrained was the course of common law in the political discourse of the nation. The Act of Settlement reads like the work of a family solicitor concerned to keep the property of a county dynasty in safe hands, and half a dozen of the abuses laid at the feet of James II in the Bill of Rights of 1689 were perversions of the procedures of common law.[25] Yet with the monarchy apparently tamed, it became thinkable to alter the course of the common law in minor ways.

The two seventeenth-century revolutions had other effects as well. Although the Commonwealth never achieved significant legal reform, repeated parliaments and commissions spoke of the pressing need for such reform. The best known of these, a commission appointed by the Rump Parliament in 1649 and chaired by Sir Matthew Hale, heard proposals that bear on our topic. One such pamphlet, *Proposals of Diverse Attorneys of the Court of Common Pleas*, attacked distress as a means of forcing defendants to appear in court as a 'costly', 'prolix', and 'neglected' process which should be discontinued.[26] The Restoration brought back the king but could not entirely turn back the clock on such thoughts. The proposal became the stuff of law reform in the seventy-five years following the Restoration.

Grand political themes affect people's thought about the design of petty details, but more immediate, often fortuitous events are also necessary. For default, one has to look no further than a statute enacted in the second year of the reign of William and Mary.[27] Coming in the midst of legislation dealing with high matters of state (statutes confirming the actions of the previous parliament, settling the income of various duties on William and Mary, reversing the unpopular judgement of *quo warranto* against London), the statute enlarged the power of distress by permitting the distrainer to sell the distrained chattels. The revision shifted the balance of power between distrainer and distrained, between plaintiff and defendant. No longer thrown back on successive coercive steps, the plaintiff who could distrain now had a mesne process that offered a remedy if the defendant did not answer: the plaintiff could simply realize the assets of the sold distrained chattels. The defendant was now faced with a choice: either appear and defend, or lose your chattels. For those actions in which distress was possible, this statute

[25] Seating unqualified jurors, requiring excessive bail, imposing excessive fines, inflicting unusual punishments and threatening fines and forfeitures before conviction.

[26] C.W. Brooks, op. cit. n.12, 129–30.

[27] 2 Wm. & Mary, c. 5 (1690).

virtually amounted to a default provision. It took the giant conceptual step of using compulsion, not just to force the defendant's appearance, but to give the plaintiff a remedy. To do so in all cases – as where, for instance, the defendant had lands but not chattels that could be distrained, or where the plaintiff sued on a writ on which distress was not available – might not seem a giant step. From this perspective, parliament in 1725 did no more than extend to all plaintiffs the remedy already available to landlords claiming rent.

Economic change belongs alongside grand political themes and shifts in the conceptions of office holding as a concomitant of legal change. In the century following the Restoration Britain underwent what P.G.M. Dickson has called a financial revolution, reorganizing its institutions of public credit.[28] The Bank of England was founded in 1694, and public speculation in the nascent stock market was enough to trigger the South Sea Bubble. It is tempting to write an account of default in which it marks a small step in the modernization of the legal system. The links in such an argument are not difficult to construct. The modern world runs on credit arrangements and creditors need a means of collecting the inevitable bad debts. Because time is credit's base, a speedy and inexpensive debt collection system will reduce the price and increase the availability of credit. The common law at the Restoration gave creditors a fierce remedy – civil arrest was an unpleasant prospect – but also a slow one. Arrest cost money and took time, all just to get the defendant to trial. After that, a plaintiff prevailing at trial still had to persuade the sheriff to execute on any available assets. Default judgement speeded the execution of judgements by eliminating steps in the process. Default judgements might thus mark a small movement toward a modern credit system. One can add to this skeletal argument the proposition that seventeenth-century wealth seems, slowly, to have commenced the move from land to intangible assets – various credit instruments and early forms of equity ownership.[29] In the nineteenth century the proliferation of such instruments accompanied the unleashing of industrial capitalism. Any move toward intangible obligations as an important form of wealth increased the importance of a reliable enforcement system; the holders of such instruments needed to be able to enforce the rights represented by these pieces of parchment and paper. In these terms the argument resembles that sketched by Douglas North and Robert Thomas in their *The Rise of the Western World*: readily transferable and enforceable rights in property unleashed initiative and created wealth.[30] The lesson for any legal system

[28] P.G.M. Dickson, *The Financial Revolution in England: A Study in the Development of Public Credit, 1688–1756* (1967).

[29] Shares were not an important form of this shift. Investors were more likely to hold either government obligations (once the national debt was reorganized) or to be participants in small partnerships, G.C.A. Clay, *Economic Expansion and Social Change, England 1500–1700* (1984), ii, 67–70, 79–80; L.A. Clarkson, *The Pre-Industrial Economy in England, 1500–1750* (New York, 1972), 189–90.

[30] Douglas C. North and Robert Paul Thomas, *The Rise of the Western World: A New Economic History* (Cambridge, 1973; rptd. 1985).

seems to be the importance of having a system of easily transferable ownership and of efficient enforcement. Default judgements contribute to the latter goal.

Straightforward though the argument is, the economic evidence will support it only in a limited form. In spite of the notorious South Sea Bubble, ownership of private shares was not a widespread form of seventeenth- or eighteenth-century wealth holding. The financial revolution of the eighteenth century came in public, not in private finance.[31] True, the Bank of England regularized national credit and enabled Britain to conduct several expensive wars without jeopardizing internal security. Its shares became a standard form of investment among the small class fortunate enough to have money to invest. But the important thing about the Bank was that it did pay its debts; it never tested the efficacy of legal enforcement mechanisms. Even if it had, one can scarcely imagine that the availability of default judgements would have swayed a prospective creditor of the Bank. If the Bank had failed, high politics, not creditors' remedies, would have determined the outcome.

Private credit was another matter, one more amenable to explanation in terms of the North-Thomas thesis. A wide network of small credit covered seventeenth-century Britain, made essential in part by the chronic shortage of currency:[32]

> Although the demand for credit was great, the market for credit was disorganized, particularly for long-term loans. Lenders were a motley collection, frequently indistinguishable as a group, for money-lending was a spare-time occupation for most people . . . farmers, shopkeepers, petty traders . . . merchants . . . widows.

Such a situation sounds like the stuff to bolster the North-Thomas argument in a carefully limited form. Petty credit in the aggregate can be important to a national economy, and default judgements would have significance in speeding the flow of petty debt collection: such debtors are the least likely to raise defences and such creditors are most likely to see a connection between legal remedies and debt collection. We have good evidence that such creditors made heavy use of the legal system. As C.W. Brooks' study of the lower branches of the bar argues, 'The single most important fact about the history of the profession (and the system within which it operated) during this period is that from the mid sixteenth century until the outbreak of the Civil War, litigation came flooding into Westminster Hall both suddenly and on an unprecedented scale'.[33] Actions of debt dominated this increase. In both King's Bench and Common Pleas, roughly 80 per cent of the seventeenth-century actions filed employed the writ of debt, a significant increase over the previous century.[34] Not all

[31] P.G.M. Dickson, op. cit. n.28, 489.

[32] L.A. Clarkson, op. cit. n.29, 48.

[33] C.W. Brooks, op. cit. n.12, 48.

[34] Ibid., 69. The proportion of debt actions in the total docket increased from 19 per cent (King's Bench) and 67 per cent (Common Pleas) in 1560 to 80 per cent (King's Bench) and 88 per cent (Common Pleas) in 1640. Ibid.

such claims represented simple debts.[35] Yet even if a third of these debt actions reflected transactions more complex than simple borrowing, the remainder still constitutes most common law actions for the period in question.

Brought for small amounts, such actions could be equally unsatisfactory both for the legal system and for the participants. Unless the creditor employed arrest, she (recall that many small creditors were widows) risked having the defendant ignore the action. But if the plaintiff did use arrest to secure a speedy judgement, the sheriff would be asked to seize the defendant for a debt that might be trivial. However much such an arrest inconvenienced the defendant, it assured the plaintiff only of the adversary's appearance, not of payment. The 1725 default legislation reflects frustration with such a simultaneously Draconian and futile procedure in its very title: 'An Act to prevent frivolous and vexatious arrests'. The wording suggests a picture of expanding credit pressing against the confines of a legal system not designed to handle such transactions. Arrest, after all, had been justified on the grounds that the defendant had committed a violent breach of the king's peace.[36] When such 'breaches' consisted of failing to repay twenty shillings, the system was no longer able to function. The coming of default judgements thus both reflected and eased the growth of credit. Expanding credit, particularly small, private credit, created the pressure; incorporating default judgements into the system made the collection of some debts slightly faster, even as they made it possible for the legal system to function without collapse.

The use of arrest to collect debts was coming to seem anomalous as well as vexatious. So long as felonies and trespasses were both prosecuted by private citizens seeking now revenge and now compensation the anomaly had not appeared. That world was slowly coming to an end in the seventeenth century.

[35] The conditioned bond was a very common contractual instrument through the end of the eighteenth century. Those binding themselves to contractual obligations did so by executing a bond calling for payment of an amount considerably larger than the value of the underlying contract. On the reverse of the bond was a condition, excusing its performance if before the date on which it fell due the obliger rendered some performance – the construction of a building or the repayment of a loan (the real obligation for which the bond was a security instrument).

[36] During the year preceding its enactment, the bill that became the default statute had been linked in parliamentary discussion with a companion bill for the relief of imprisoned debtors, *Journals of the House of Commons, October 9 1722 to May 15 1727* (rptd. 1803), xx, 311, 314, 603. This circumstance suggests another reason for avoiding arrest in personal actions, set forth in a petition of such prisoners:

> A petition of the poor and miserable Prisoners now lying in the Prison of White Chapel, in the County of Middlesex, on behalf of themselves and others, their Fellows, being about one hundred and twenty in number, was presented to the House and read; setting forth that the petitioners are imprisoned for very small debts; the charges of the Arrest, and fees of confinement amounting to more than the debt; which mostly have arisen from the Necessity of their Families to Tallymen, Pawnbrokers and others . . . Ordered, That the said Petition do lie upon the table until the bill to prevent frivolous and vexatious arrests shall be read a second time.

Ibid., 603. Tallymen advanced goods on credit, to be paid for in instalments.

One reason the seventeenth- and eighteenth-century English feared the crown was that it had become a more effective administrative force. Though a professional bureaucracy was centuries away, the Tudor and Stuart monarchs ruled the realm with a thoroughness that would have made their medieval colleagues envious. A sign of this thoroughness was the new apparatus that came into play for uncovering and prosecuting crime.[37] Although the instigation of private criminal prosecutions remained a staple,[38] the justices of the peace began to play a more active role in the interrogation of suspects and the investigation of crime.[39] High official bodies, the Privy Council and Star Chamber, began to take responsibility for investigating and prosecuting cases with political ramifications or those that threatened social order. With these developments, what we know as criminal law began to distinguish itself from complaints of subject against subject. As that distinction began to take hold, it became possible to design civil process with features that would have been unacceptable in a trial of criminal accusations. Default was one such change. Once trespass and its progeny were uncoupled from criminal process, one could consider innovations that would have been barred so long as they were linked. Such an uncoupling was natural in a world in which officials were beginning to take major responsibility for investigating and prosecuting crimes, which thus became distinguished from the causes prosecuted entirely by private parties.

To claim that change was constitutionally possible and perhaps economically useful in a small way does not, however, establish that it occurred. For centuries people had inveighed against the delay and expense of common law. Today the bar produces most of those costs and most of the impediments to change. In the seventeenth and eighteenth centuries, court costs were a larger element. One of the major impediments to any change in the procedures of common law and chancery were the men who held the offices associated with the courts: cursitors, filazers, the Six Clerks, the underclerks, clerks of warrants, clerks of fines, exigenters, prothonotaries and the like. These men were office holders, not modern bureaucrats. Their pay came, that is, not from a salary granted by the government, but from fees paid by litigants for processing routine transactions – so many shillings for an original writ, so many shillings for a *capias* and so on. The offices were valuable assets and their holders had generally purchased them from the patron – often a judge or similar high official – in whose grant they lay.[40] For example, at the end of the sixteenth century John Lennard purchased the office of *custos*

[37] J. Langbein, *Prosecuting Crime in the Renaissance: England, Germany, and France* (Cambridge, Mass., 1974) elaborates the argument.

[38] J. Langbein, *Torture and the Law of Proof* (Chicago, 1977), 79.

[39] '. . . [T]he Marian statutes both expanded and contracted the magistrates' office. The prosecutorial role occasioned the decline of the adjudicative', John Langbein, *Prosecuting Crime in the Renaissance*, 111.

[40] W.S. Holdsworth, *The History of English Law*, i, 7th rev. ed. (1956), 248–55.

brevium from William Cecil for an annual payment of £240; in spite of this tax on his income, Lennard died a wealthy man.[41] Because their income rose and fell with the number of litigants requiring the step in the legal process that lay in their control, these officials viewed with great distaste any proposal that eliminated 'their' step in the process. To put the matter specifically, the institution of a default judgement would put out of business those who issued *capias* and *distringas* writs and those who controlled the steps leading to outlawry. Moreover, because these petty officials had purchased their offices from the high judicial officers who controlled them, these great men also had much to lose if the steps of mesne process were accelerated. All through the seventeenth century, therefore, one finds sober warnings against any alteration in the course of common law. The loudest proponents of this argument were of course those who held positions in the judicial bureaucracy and who stood to lose from any change that made their offices inessential to litigants.

The argument also found sympathetic ears far from Westminster. Not just judicial officials, but powerful aristocrats, courtiers and petty office holders throughout the land held on such terms. One must recall that the modern English 'fee' derives from the word used to designate the grant of a fief. Medieval and early modern governments were perennially short of cash, a difficulty exacerbated by the long struggles between crown and parliament in the seventeenth century. Under such conditions, it was much easier to pay official salaries through the indirect taxation of the office-and-fee system than through direct taxation, the approval of which would require resolving the differences between king and Commons. Late medieval and early modern England was therefore shot through with sinecures and posts.[42] With so many people, so much of government dependent on the rights to payments that derived from the holding of offices, even those far removed from law would hesitate to support a principle that, if extended to them, would eliminate their livelihoods and might even threaten the political order.

There were countercurrents. G.E. Aylmer's elaborate studies of seventeenth-century office holders identified three sources: patronage, patrimony and purchase.[43] In the first two influence in high places secured a position for the holder. In the last the transaction involved simple sale of the office by the person holding the power of appointment. One must not draw too sharp a distinction between the three methods; patrons expected a show of gratitude

[41] C.W. Brooks, op. cit. n.12, 230–31.

[42] Consider, for example, the Fox family, whom J.A. Sharpe describes as 'mere gentry, who had progressed steadily since the restoration through office holding [until] Henry Fox, the first Lord Holland, secured the Paymastership in 1757', *Early Modern England: A Social History, 1550–1670* (1987), 157–58.

[43] G.E. Aylmer, 'Office Holding as a Factor in English History, 1625–1642', *History*, xliv (1959), 228; G.E. Aylmer, *The King's Servants: The Civil Service of Charles I, 1625–1642* (1961, rev. ed., 1974); G.E. Aylmer, *The State's Servants: The Civil Service of the English Republic, 1649–1660* (1973).

for their help and elaborate gifts or payments were a good way of showing a properly thankful stance. No matter how they had gained their offices, holders thought they had property in them. No thoroughgoing challenge to this conception appeared until the wars at the end of the eighteenth century forced on Britain some of the characteristics of modern bureaucracy. But from the sixteenth century forwards purchase of office was repeatedly, if unsuccessfully, condemned. A 1552 statute forbade the sale of offices connected with royal property, defence and justice,[44] but it safeguarded then-existing rights and was in any case widely ignored. Still, outright purchase and sale of offices was to many offensive, particularly when practised on a grand scale, as Thomas Parker, Lord Macclesfield, discovered in 1725.

Parker, who by 1714 had become the Chief Justice of the King's Bench, 'found favour with George I, receiving a peerage in 1716 and in 1718 the Lord Chancellorship'.[45] Well understanding the value of such a position, Macclesfield proceeded to dispense his powers of patronage over various offices with vigour and resolution, exacting the highest price available for any position. By the standards of the time he was doing nothing wrong in expecting payment from the grateful recipients of a post within his patronage, but Macclesfield erred in offering them for sale. He also had bad luck. The South Sea Bubble burst in 1718. In the wake of that financial collapse, it became apparent that the Masters in Chancery, appointed by the Lord Chancellor and charged with stewardship of various monies, had been speculating with them with disastrous results. These losses exposed the dangers of the office holding system in an especially salient way, for the masters had gone beyond the ordinary petty harassment represented by the fee system: whole estates had vanished. A parliamentary investigation which began with irregularities into care of funds went on to suggest that such speculation was likely when the Lord Chancellor had sold the offices to people who would feel the need to wring every opportunity for profit out of them. Macclesfield, who to the end had vigorous defenders (including George I), was impeached by Parliament and imprisoned until he had paid a fine of £30,000.

Scandal is an historical wild card. One cannot prove that without Macclesfield's disgrace there would have been no default legislation.[46] I want to make a more cautious statement: scandals like the Macclesfield affair are the sort of thing that can momentarily jar legislatures, causing them to do things to interests that would ordinarily be sacrosanct. Macclesfield's fall did not destroy office holding, which flourished for another century, but perhaps it enabled Parliament to engage in one of those tiny spasms that passed for procedural reform until the great tremors of the mid nineteenth century. Even

44 Stat. Realm, IV, i, 151–52.

45 *Biographical Dictionary of the Common Law*, A.W.B. Simpson, ed. (1984), 404.

46 In particular, I am not arguing that the 1725 legislation was aimed at the Chancery officers who had purchased their places from Macclesfield. Entirely separate officers issued the common law writs of *distringas* and *capias*. The link is rather with the general institution of office holding.

a society steeped in patronage can become outraged at the simple purchase of offices, the more so when its consequences seem to threaten the stability of family wealth, as the South Sea Chancery losses did.[47] The point stands out sharply because no charges of personal corruption blurred the issue in the impeachment trial. No one suggested that the Lord Chancellor had taken bribes in individual cases; indeed his probity and learning were admired. Parliament was still prepared to discharge him, testifying to its belief that offices should not be sold.

If Lord Macclesfield had not been impeached, would default judgements have entered common law in 1725? If Parliament had not expelled James II, would it have been prepared to alter the hallowed course of common law? If fewer people had brought actions of debt for small amounts, would the need for default in personal actions have seemed less pressing? If Marian bail reforms had not, almost accidentally, created an official mechanism for the prosecution of crimes, would civil and criminal process have remained linked and immutable? The argument so far has suggested negative answers to each of these questions. Putting the questions in stark form makes clear the fatuity of placing great confidence in any one of these asserted relationships. Taken together, however, they suggest a change in context that made default appear thinkable, a trivial but unthreatening reform. Default made available to all plaintiffs the remedy which for the previous thirty years had been available to plaintiffs who could distrain. Default posed no royal threat to liberty or property because the nation had in the previous century twice made it clear that it knew how to deal with royal threats to liberty and property. Default deprived no official of property in fees because it had become less clear that officials held property in their offices or their fees. Instituting default judgements in personal actions did not threaten the liberty of the subject, because criminal prosecutions now seemed a quite different matter from property and contract.

Removing objections to changes does not ensure that those changes will occur, but for changes in common law procedure removing obstacles does a great deal. Because there was no general theory justifying common law procedure, many of the objections to change at any point took one of two forms. Sometimes the claim was that the whole structure of the law constituted a marvellous, if unintended, bastion of liberty. Coke made this claim most strongly in the sixteenth century; Blackstone and Burke argued versions of this thesis in the eighteenth. If accepted, this argument struck a powerful blow against change – any change – because the system was greater than human understanding. One might tinker with an apparently innocuous aspect of process and unwittingly remove a keystone of the edifice. This argument was strongest at times of constitutional instability. The seventeenth century

47 In 1732, when parliament renewed the 1725 default legislation, it was still engaged in an investigation of the fees of court officers, with a special emphasis on Chancery, *Journals of the House of Commons*, op. cit. n. 36, xxi, 892.

was such a time; so was the later eighteenth, as various interests began to ask for parliamentary reform and revolution abroad challenged the nearest monarchy. The crisis of the Hanoverian settlement past, the early eighteenth century was, in contrast, a period of relative constitutional calm. Threats might come from plots, the Pretender was a fine bogeyman, but the Glorious Revolution had laid bounds to royal power and the Hanoverians did not seem disposed to challenge those bounds. The other argument against change in common law process is proprietary. Offices were wealth as well as power. To change the perquisites of office looked dangerously like depriving a man of his property. These arguments had lost some force by the eighteenth century. The eighteenth-century constitution linked patronage, office, and wealth, but the political classes were beginning to look with scepticism on the toll taken by claims of office holders. Three days before passing the 1732 renewal of the first default statute, the House of Commons received an elaborate report from a committee on fees received by officers in chancery.[48] The parliamentary committee recommended a resolution, that passed unanimously:[49]

> That the House doth agree with the Committee . . . That the Interest, which a great number of Officers and Clerks have in the Proceedings . . . has been a principal Cause of extending Bills, Answers, Pleadings . . . to the great Delay of Justice and the Oppression of the Subject.

Lord Macclesfield's error lay in failing to understand that what was tolerated in 1625 had a century later become impermissible at least when practised on a large scale. The growth of a credit economy, even one as anarchic as that which produced the South Sea Bubble, ate deeply into the undergirding of the fee system. Government itself was creeping toward a system of salaried officials rather than office holders paid by haphazardly accumulated fees. Regularly held parliaments (one of the new political understandings) meant that the legislature was available to levy taxes for those officials of whose duties they approved and to stop entirely the activities of others. The revenue system had been put on a sounder basis; a tax on land, still the preponderant form of wealth, made annual revenues predictable and made it possible to think in terms of a budget. Even the royal household, long unable to support government out of its wealth, had to depend on the Civil List for operating expenses.

In an atmosphere in which its adoption seemed to threaten neither individual liberties nor the constitution itself, default could exhibit its own modest virtues. The most considerable one was as a creditor's remedy. A standing complaint against common law process was that it gave the recalcitrant defendant a long list of ways to evade the plaintiff, even when the defendant had not a shred of merit in his defence. Especially as wealth came to depend as much on commerce as on land, as credit markets made the expense of delayed payment palpable and as many of the petty bourgeoisie

[48] Ibid., 892–95.

[49] Ibid., 895.

joined the creditor class, there was much to be said for a process that did not permit the defendant to ignore the plaintiff's complaint. Parliament in 1725 heeded these virtues, and common law has relied on default for the succeeding three and a half centuries.

III. Light on Modern Process

If default judgements are a small sign of shifts in greater social and economic spheres, they also mark a step toward a modern conception of process. Just as it is important not to exaggerate the directness of the link between grand socio-political movements and default, so one must avoid the temptation to portray the 1725 statute as a grand turning point. It was not. Common law process sailed on its leisurely course for another century and a half before thorough change overtook it. But one can responsibly argue that default judgements in personal actions were a small tremor that formed part of a larger shift in the design of process. Moreover, though historians have demonstrated that nothing ever marks the end of the medieval aspects of anything, default judgements did refocus litigation in a way familiar to modern lawyers.

Default is not an inevitable idea. Five centuries of common law process witness that it is possible to operate a judicial system – even a very durable one – without universally available default to drive the adversaries. It is therefore worth thinking about what the coming of default meant to common law process. Default drives modern civil procedure. Once the plaintiff has filed a complaint, default commands the steps of the minuet. A defendant who fails to answer will find a default judgement entered in plaintiff's favour. The force of default extends beyond compelling an answer: the defendant's failure to comply with any order of the court is one of the grounds for entering a default judgement. Together with the dismissal of the complaint – the plaintiff's analogue to default – it locks the antagonists together. The parties can break off the battle, but default assures that the decision not to continue the fight will be mutual. It enables the plaintiff to insist on its continuation even when the defendant is unwilling. Default also subtly alters the adversarial process. Until default, the focus of the state's efforts lay in compelling the defendant to submit to its jurisdiction. Medieval process involved two struggles: one between the state and the defendant; the second between plaintiff and defendant. Only when the state had won the first could the second occur. Medieval process aimed at compelling the defendant's submission, and adopted a civil version of *peine forte et dure* to achieve it, piling the rocks of attachment and arrest on the defendant until he submitted himself to the court's power. Only then could and did the focus shift to the plaintiff's claim. This stance suggests a doubt about the court's powers: the state expended its (and the plaintiff's) energies in compelling the defendant to submit. If the defendant resisted, the state punished him, but until it had won that contest would not move on to the plaintiff's claim. Modern process, by contrast, shows no doubts about its own right to exist. The court's power is assumed. Armed with this self-confidence, modern process declares victory without firing a shot in the battle for its own jurisdiction, moving directly to the second confrontation, that between plaintiff and defendant. Default also shifts the focus both of litigants' strategy and of the lawsuit. Before default, the defendant's best delaying strategy was typically a prolonged effort to avoid appearance and the necessity to answer. It may not be too strong to say that the major suspense in a medieval lawsuit was whether the defendant could be made to appear and answer: the merits became anticlimactic. By contrast, default causes defendants to conceive of delaying tactics more closely approaching the merits. Modern process is not less prone to delay than medieval: prolonged discovery (in the United States), flurries of procedural arguments, motions for summary judgement are all used by defendants fighting off the inevitable day of judgement. But these delaying tactics have a different focus: even procedural motions often have some reference to the merits of the claim (*forum non conveniens* arguments are a good example), and discovery and summary judgement approach the merits much more directly. In consequence even the defendant acting in bad faith must do so by immersing himself in the merits of the plaintiff's claim.

It is commonplace to mark the beginning of modern substantive law as coming in the early seventeenth century, as two of the three great medieval contractual writs collapsed into one another. Procedural change opened the way for the creation of a coherent idea of informal contract. If one turns to procedure, the historiographical tradition is different. The standard accounts suggest that process dwelt in a lingering medieval haze for another hundred and fifty years until the combined effects of Bentham, a reformed parliament, the transatlantic efforts of David Dudley Field and, perhaps, the muckraking of Charles Dickens wrenched it into modernity. Whatever the causes of change, however, the movement toward a recognizably modern procedure is generally thought to have come only in the mid nineteenth century, with the merger of law and equity and the abolition of the forms of action. I have offered a mild revision of this understanding. It is possible to see a glimmer of a modern idea of process emerging in 1725, the date of the enactment of the first default judgement statute. After that date, defendants in personal actions did not have to appear to have enforceable judgements entered against them. No longer did the plaintiff have to seek distress, *capias* or outlawry in order to compel the defendant to answer him in court. Delay was, as always in law, still possible, but the primary tactic of delay was no longer an effort to avoid or evade a defence on the merits. Instead a defence on the merits became the chief method of delaying what would otherwise be an immediately entered adverse judgement. The burden of litigation had shifted from the plaintiff to the defendant. The plaintiff still had to prove his case, but now the chief difficulties became those of proving the merits, not those of compelling the defendant to answer. The focus of attention comes closer to the merits of the claim. The movement to default suggests another change in the medieval idea of process, though now one must speak of effects rather than of causes. Default becomes an acceptable universal response to non-appearance only when people no longer believe that the forms of action matter. Until that time, different responses – now the seizure of land, now distress, now *capias* – seem to be called for. Only when people believe that the writs are much the same does it seem right to use a single response to the defendant's failure to appear. Here, however, we encounter a reversal of the usual process of evolution of English law, for substance has prepared the way for procedural change rather than the other way around. A sense that substantive law is, if not a unified field, then at least capable of being organized and comprehended, must precede the conclusion that there are universally applicable procedural devices. Writing in the latter part of the century, Blackstone took such a view; so did Bentham, who otherwise found little in common with Blackstone. The adoption of default in 1725 shares with these two great antagonists the view that English law could be comprehended whole.

Chapter 10

Macaulay's 'Utilitarian' Indian Penal Code: An Illustration of the Accidental Function of Time, Place and Personalities in Law Making[1]

K.J.M. Smith

This essay attempts to examine both the historical and intellectual forces responsible for producing Thomas Macaulay's 1837 Indian Penal Code, finally enacted in 1860. Macaulay's Code and its creative antecedents are worthy of our interest because together they constitute a curious and important episode in the development or evolution of criminal jurisprudence and, more generally, in nineteenth century intellectual history.

The shaping forces behind the Code included, most particularly, a dynamic mixture of time, place, and personalities: 'Time' in the sense of the 1830s being a period when a broad reforming spirit had infected at least some in positions of power and influence, and when commissions of enquiry, of one form or another, were much in vogue as the standard technique for ascertaining the nature, if not always the solution, of specific social problems; 'Place' in the sense that legislating for India obviously raised issues and necessitated meeting difficulties peculiar to that part of what later became the 'Empire'. The third, and perhaps most potent of these formative influences, were the personalities and individual philosophies of the leading participants: Macaulay, James Mill, then occupying a pivotal position in the East India Company, and the strong posthumous presence of Bentham, who died in 1832, two years before Macaulay's Indian interlude began.

I. The Circumstances of Macaulay's Appointment

Appreciation of the cardinal features of the political and philosophical climate in which the Code was produced is aided by a glance back at the immediate history of the 1833 Charter Act which created the post of legal member of the Governor-General's Legislative and Executive Council of India, first occupied by Macaulay.

Prior to the 1833 Act India enjoyed, or suffered, diversified government with no centralized Indian-based authority; the various provinces were ruled

[1] With acknowledgements to Bentham's 'On the Influence of Time and Place in Matters of Legislation', *Works of Jeremy Bentham*, J. Bowring, ed. (Edinburgh and London, 1843), (hereafter *Works*), i, 169.

and run independently of each other. This local autonomy of government was complemented (or aggravated) by separate systems of law, each made up of a mind-numbing jumble of Hindu or Muslim law generously overlaid with a mixture of English law and East India Company administrative 'regulations'. Since the late eighteenth century a London-based system of supervisory government existed entailing 'dual control' shared between the British government appointed Board of Control (to which Macaulay was briefly Secretary) and the Court of Directors of the East India Company. The Board of Control was responsible for the general supervision (with the power of veto) of the political and administrative activities of the East India Company; a peculiar set up persisting until the momentous political jolt delivered by the 1857 Indian Mutiny, which finally terminated residual attempts at a working compromise between Indian and European notions in matters of law and government.

The 1833 Charter Act functioned as the legislative foundation for the British government's policy of transforming the subcontinent from being a source of land rent revenues and some trade into a huge market of traders and consumers, capable of absorbing much of the vast manufacturing capacity generated by Britain's accelerating Industrial Revolution. Such a transformation was seen as contingent upon the government of the whole of India being placed on a centralized and unified basis. The natural, if not inevitable, corollary of this objective was a uniform structure of administrative institutions and laws.[2] However, considerable uncertainty persisted as to the proper pace or extent of this process of the Anglicizing or Europeanization of India. Right through to the Indian Mutiny nothing resembling a consensus view emerged on the degree to which Indian culture and institutions could and should be retained and accommodated within a modernized India. Opposite poles of opinion were represented by what might be termed the 'Burkean' or 'Romantic' concept of trusteeship and preservation of Indian institutions on the one side, and on the other, the out and out Anglicists, often fuelled by a heady blend of Evangelicalism and Utilitarianism;[3] probably the best known of nineteenth-century propellants

[2] For the system of 'dual control' of Indian government, see J. Fitzjames Stephen, *History of the Criminal Law* (1883) (hereafter 'H.C.L.'), iii, ch.xxxiii and E. Stokes, *The English Utilitarians and India* (1959), ch.1.

James Mill's extensive (115 full paragraphs) administrative 'Despatch' (10 December 1834) to the Governor-General's Council on the implementation of the Charter Act cites the problem of protecting the native population as being an important factor in introducing a uniform system of sound law to which all were subject. This became a pressing need with the 1833 Act allowing the 'free ingress of Europeans' into the country's 'interior' to hold land. Protection for natives was needed 'from insult and outrage in their persons, properties, religions and opinions' (para. 40); 'Eagerness of some temporary advantage, the consequences of power, pride of a fanciful superiority of race, the absence of any adequate check from public opinion' might lead to 'misbehaviour' (para. 41). Despatch reprinted in C.P. Ilbert's *The Government of India* (Oxford, London and New York, 1898), 492–532.

[3] See J.L. Clive, *Macaulay: The Shaping of the Historian* (1973), ch.xi–xiii; and R.D. Altick, *Victorian People and Ideas* (New York, 1973), ch.iv.

for accomplishing epic works of social and political reconstruction, whether at home or abroad. Evangelicals looked to flush out and revitalize native souls with Christian morality and English education; Utilitarians sought to satisfy their temporal needs by the provision of efficient government and sound laws.

It was into this situation, heavy with the expectation of social, economic and political developments in India, facilitated by the 1833 Act, that Macaulay was recruited to the central post of legal member of the Governor-General's Council.[4] Yet he was not an overwhelmingly obvious choice. Why Macaulay was chosen and why he accepted the appointment is far from self-evident. One can approach such questions by asking what qualities might be included in any specification for the post of legal member: most naturally, perhaps, a lawyer with substantial expertise in framing legislation; someone with experience and the demonstrated capacity for the routine grind and graft, so much a part of lawmaking; someone not unlike Sir James Stephen, then a highly influential and moderately reformist force in the Colonial Office.[5] Indeed, both his famous sons, Leslie and Fitzjames, testify that not only was he offered the post but that Macaulay 'strongly advised' him to take it.[6] Although Macaulay makes no recorded reference to this it seems highly unlikely that it is without some substance, and that Sir James was not at least sounded out on the possibility, if not actually made a firm offer. However, whether first or second choice, after initial resistance from a minority of directors of the East India Company Macaulay was appointed.[7]

Most clearly in his favour was a familiarity with Indian affairs, gained as Secretary to the Board of Control. He also brought to the position an unpromising intellectual flashiness, not obviously suited to years of solid legislative labour in service of the Company under an Indian sun. Macaulay's unusual intellectual capacities revealed themselves early in life. One famous

[4] The Council comprised the Governor-General and three member employees of the East India Company. The Council performed a dual function as both the legislative forum and the supreme executive body of India. The law member's function was intended to be exclusively legislative, and therefore did not entitle him to attend or vote at the Council meetings devoted to executive business. Macaulay, however, was allowed to take a full role at executive as well as legislative meetings of the Council.

[5] For example, P. Knaplund, *James Stephen and the British Colonial System, 1813–47* (1953); D.J. Murray, *The West Indies and the Development of Colonial Government, 1801–1834* (Oxford, 1965). By a combination of ability, appetite for work and unwillingness to delegate, Stephen 'virtually ruled the Colonial Empire'; Sir Henry Taylor, a friend and colleague at the Colonial Office, *Autobiography* (1885), i, 223. Stephen was known to some as 'Mr. Over-Secretary Stephen'.

[6] Leslie Stephen, *Life of James Fitzjames Stephen* (1895), 235, and Fitzjames Stephen, H.C.L., iii, 298, n.2.

[7] See, for example, Macaulay to his sister Hannah, 21 October 1833 in G.O. Trevelyan, *The Life and Letters of Lord Macaulay* (1876, New York, 1877), i, 296. James Mill, then Chief Examiner in the Company (and effectively the highest official below the two Chairmen of Directors) was 'consulted' and very 'handsomely' advised the Company to take Macaulay, Macaulay to Hannah Macaulay, ibid., 1 November 1833, 300.

occasion indicative of these powers was the four-year-old's response to a concerned enquiry after having hot coffee spilt over of his legs: 'Thank you, madam, the agony is abated'.[8] This infant phenonomen grew into an adult phenonomen possessed of considerable linguistic skills, an astonishing memory fed by a voracious eclecticism which produced great broad-fronted erudition. Equipped with such talents, the adult Macaulay quickly established himself as a spectacular conversationalist and, by his contributions to the *Edinburgh Review*, as a distinctly stylish and promising man of letters. By the age of thirty-three Macaulay had become a man of mark in society, literature and politics. His writing style, and what his friend Sydney Smith called great 'waterspouts of talk', both fascinated, intimidated and exhausted readers and listeners. Again, Smith tells us, Macaulay 'not only overflowed with learning but stood in the slops'.[9] According to another contemporary:[10]

> His voice is one of the most monotonous and least agreeable of those which usually belong to our countrymen north of the Tweed: pitched in alto and rather shrill, pouring forth words in inconceivable velocity: never stopping for words, never stopping for thoughts, never halting for an instant even to take breath, hauling the subject after him with the strength of a giant, till the hearer is left prostrate and powerless by the whirlwind of ideas and emotions that has swept over him.

Complementary to this high speed delivery was a deep reserve of literary and historical learning which Macaulay constantly and naturally drew on. The technique was eventually seen at work in House of Commons performances, something well described by G.M. Young:[11]

> Between the beginning and end of a very short speech [on the Anatomy Bill] Macaulay has touched on the habits of murderers, France, Germany, Italy, the peasants of Russia and their Tsar, . . . barbers, old women and charms, the squaring of the circle and the transit of Venus, Richard of England, Leopold of Austria, and the bricklayer who falls from a ladder. The listener has been borne at exhilarating speed, but in perfect security, through a variegated landscape and deposited at his destination before he has time to wonder where he is going.

As to political allegiance, he had entered Cambridge a Tory and left a Whig. Macaulay's political career began in 1830 as member of parliament for Calne, Wiltshire, a pocket borough within the gift of the Whig grandee Lord Lansdowne. His legendary reputation as a parliamentary debater got under way a year later with a speech supporting the second reading of the Reform Bill; a performance which, as well as opening the doors of Holland House, gained

8 Recently quoted by Owen Dudley Edwards, *Macaulay* (1988), 6.

9 Quoted by Hesketh Pearson, *The Smith of Smiths* (1984 ed.), 180. Smith also relates: Macaulay 'breakfasted both with me this morning in company with three other very clever men much disposed to talk, but it was not Macaulay's disposition that they should say a word, I might as well have had three Mutes from a funeral', *Selected Letters of Sydney Smith*, Nowell C. Smith, ed. (1956), 198.

10 G.F. Francis quoted by G.M. Young in 'Macaulay', *Daylight and Champaign* (1937), 12–13.

11 Ibid., 13, 'The speaker is thinking in images drawn from an inexhaustible store of historic reminiscence, and flashed on the mind of the listener with the force and dexterity of a born story-teller', 14.

Macaulay his first government post in June 1832 as Secretary of the Board of Control, supervisor of the East India Company's activities.[12] This, in turn, led to acquaintance with Indian affairs, with James Mill (Macaulay's sparring partner in political philosophy in the columns of the *Edinburgh Review*) and eventually to involvement in the drafting of the 1833 Charter Act.

Not only was the offer of the position of legal member to Macaulay surprising, his acceptance might appear similarly unexpected. Six years of legislative toil in a sometimes ruinous climate and exile from the literary and political society which had recently so firmly embraced him could hardly have been a compellingly attractive prospect. However, the Indian appointment had the irresistible attraction of a huge salary of £10,000 per year. Its irresistibility lay in Macaulay's own financial insecurity and his father's impecunious state, while shifting political forces made his parliamentary post and income by no means assured. With savings from £10,000 per annum, Macaulay expected to return to England at the age of thirty-nine with £30,000, 'a larger fortune I never desired'.[13]

After three months of travel, Macaulay reached Madras in June 1834, later moving on to Calcutta, the seat of the Governor-General and Indian government.

II. The Code's Production and Influences

The 1833 Charter Act made provision for the appointment of a Law Commission whose function was to advise on and propose schemes for an eventual comprehensive and homogeneous body of legal codes for the whole of India. Within a year of Macaulay's arrival a Commission was appointed with him as its head.[14] Choice of a penal code as the Commission's first task was in large measure Macaulay's and based on several considerations. Primarily, the influx of European settlers after the 1833 Act underscored the need for a uniform penal code with jurisdiction over both Europeans and Asians. Furthermore, practically speaking, criminal law reform was politically less contentious with few vested interests at stake and fewer toes to be trodden on. As Henry Maine (a later successor of Macaulay as legal member) observed 'nobody cares about criminal law except theorists and

[12] Clive, ibid., 220, notes that the position paid £1,500 a year and 'carried with it the privilege of unlimited franking – one greatly appreciated by this indefatigable letter-writer'.

[13] Macaulay to Hannah, 17 August 1833, Trevelyan, op. cit., 289.

[14] Besides Macaulay the Commission members were Charles Hay Cameron, John Macleod and G.W. Anderson. Cameron was an experienced colonial legislator of strong Benthamite leanings; Macleod's usefulness was in his powers as a 'hypercritic' of what others did; Anderson was a disaster, contributing not 'even a single hint of the smallest value'. Quoted by Clive, op.cit., 439. Furthermore, in Anderson's case, Macaulay later noted that the 'greatest service [Anderson] could render to the Commission' would be to 'keep to his bed all the week round', Macaulay to T.F. Ellis, 8 March 1837 in *The Letters of Thomas Babington Macaulay*, T. Pinney, ed. (hereafter *Letters*), iii (1976), 210.

habitual criminals'.[15] Finally, it was just this broad theoretical appeal found in the strong afterwash of the Enlightenment[16] which engaged Macaulay as criminal law:[17]

> . . . attracted the attention of philosophers [and] excites so general an interest among reflecting and reading men . . . a succession of men eminent as speculative and as practical statesmen has been engaged in earnest discussion on the principles of penal jurisprudence. There is perhaps no province of legislation which has been so thoroughly explored in all directions.

Composing a penal code was, then, appealing to Macaulay on intellectual grounds, with its universality and philosophical dimension greater than other areas of more earthbound and leaden law reform; and also attractive because of its higher profile in the world beyond lawyers and officialdom, with its promise of being most likely to keep him and his career not too far from the public eye during his exile.

Beyond the effects of his own political and wider philosophical attitudes, two main external channels of influence operated on Macaulay in the Code's production, both markedly utilitarian. First was the formal advice received from James Mill, both before and after leaving England; and second, the less tangible but seductive power of Benthamite thinking, then widely pervasive among sections of the East India Company.[18]

James Mill, as Chief Examiner of the East India Company, was responsible for communicating the will of the Company's Court of Directors in London to the Governor-General and Company officials in Calcutta. As author of the monumental *History of British India* (1817), Mill was an acknowledged authority on the subcontinent and, latterly, highly influential in modelling and interpreting the company's policies.[19] Mill, himself one of Bentham's

[15] Maine to Grant Duff, 22 December 1868 in Grant Duff Papers; private collection of S. Grant Duff, Skibereen, Eire.

[16] For a concise review of these European intellectual currents see O.F. Robinson, T.D. Fergus and W.M. Gordon, *An Introduction to European Legal History* (1985), ch.xv, particularly 408–13; and S. Collini, D. Winch and J. Burrow, *That Noble Science of Politics* (Cambridge, 1983), ch.1 for an exploration of the influential Scottish rationalist tradition, the 'Edinburgh Reviewers' and James Mill. On the particular climate of eighteenth century criminal jurisprudence and statutory reforms, see D. Lieberman, *The Province of Legislation Determined* (Cambridge, 1989), ch.10.

[17] Stokes, op. cit., 221–22. Bentham also favoured a penal code as a starting point to a general codification programme. See *Works*, iii and iv, 526–27. It appears that originally the first project of the Law Commission was going to be the far more mundane production of a code of civil procedure. But as a consequence of administrative delays in referring this topic to the Commission, the Penal Code was taken first, Stokes, op. cit., 220–21.

[18] For example, William Empsom was from 1824 Professor of 'general polity and laws' at the East India Company's administrative college at Haileybury. Empsom was a keen propagandist of Benthamite principles of law reform.

[19] On the eve of his departure to India in 1827 the reformist Lord Bentinck told Mill 'I am going to British India but I shall not be Governor-General . . . you . . . will be'. Quoted by Stokes, op. cit., 51.

most fervent propagandists, saw every aspect of Indian life as desperately needing vast changes. Its cultural institutions were deplorable:[20]

> . . . tainted with the vices of insincerity, dissembling, treacherous, mendacious, to an excess which surpasses even the usual measure of uncultivated society . . . disposed to excessive exaggeration with regard to everything relating to themselves . . . cowardly and unfeeling . . .

This perceived social and political degeneration was seen as reflected in Indian laws contemptuously dismissed by Mill as no more than a:

> . . . disorderly compilation of loose, vague, stupid or unintelligible quotations and maxims: selected arbitrarily from books of law, books of devotion, and books of poetry; attended with a commentary which only adds to the absurdity and darkness; a farrago by which nothing is defined, nothing established.

The utilitarian solution to this combination of chaos and impoverishment was decisive centralized government, a properly regulated system of land revenues and good, properly administered, laws.[21] However, whilst highly influential, Mill and kindred spirits were not in a position to set in train undiluted Benthamite reforms sweeping away all vestiges of Indian institutions; rather, the process could only be undertaken at a moderate pace. This is the kernel of Mill's 1834 'Despatch' setting out the implementation procedures and policies of the 1833 Charter Act, underlining that reforms should 'embody the abstract and essential principles of good government in regulations adapted to the peculiar habits, character, and institutions of the vast and infinitely diversified people under their sway'.[22] Macaulay translated this law making policy into a ringing epigram: 'Uniformity where you can have it; diversity where you must have it; but in all cases certainty'.[23]

As well as assisting in the preparation of the 1833 Charter Act, Macaulay also participated in parliamentary debates during its passage through the Commons. Here he offered a fair indication of his own as well as government thinking on India's destiny and the proper means of fulfilling it. Two strands of thought emerge: first, England's material return would be far greater if India were westernized:[24]

> . . . it is scarcely possible to calculate the benefits which we might derive from the diffusion of European civilisation amongst the vast population of the East. It would

20 *History of British India*, ii, 195. During his speech on the 1833 Charter Act Macaulay described Mill's *History* as 'not free from faults' but 'on the whole the greatest historical work which has appeared in our language since that of Gibbon'.

21 See also Mill's evidence before the parliamentary committee on the Charter Bill recommending centralized government and a uniform legal system, *Parl. Papers*, ix (1831–32), 44–45, 51.

22 Public Despatch, 10 December 1834, and generally paras. 15–28.

23 Commons debate on the Charter Bill, 10 July 1833; *The Complete Works of Lord Macaulay*, Albany ed. (1898) (hereafter *Works*), xi, 578.

24 Ibid., 583–86.

> be, on the most selfish view of the case, far better for us that the people of India were well governed and independent of us, than ill-governed and subject to us; that they were ruled by their own kings, but wearing our broadcloth, and working with our cutlery, than they were performing their salaams to English collectors and English magistrates. To trade with civilised men is infinitely more profitable than to govern savages.

Beyond frank materialistic calculation of this sort, there was the national moral achievement to be won by 'civilizing', by endowing India with European institutions and culture:[24]

> To have found a great people sunk in the lowest depths of slavery and superstition, to have so ruled them as to have made them desirous and capable of all the privileges of citizens, would indeed be a title to glory all our own . . . there are triumphs which are followed by no reverse. There is an empire exempt from all natural causes of decay. Those triumphs are the specific triumphs of reason over barbarism; that empire is the imperishable empire of our arts and our morals, our literature and our laws.

Though, presumably, Macaulay's reference to 'our laws' was not to be taken as meaning anything more than a system of laws devised and imposed by the British, for James Mill (and Bentham) transposing unreformed precedent-encrusted English law to India would be to invite chaos of a new variety; a move from the frying pan to the fire.[25]

In general political outlook Macaulay subscribed to Whig notions of steady and cautious social progress; accepting a gradualist or evolutionary view of social and political movement, whereby legislative intervention was a necessary catching up or adjustment process by government carefully 'watching the historical clock'.[26] Macaulay looked to a judicious compromise between innovatory speculation and well-grounded practicality. Thus for him 'the perfect law giver is a just temper between the mere man of theory, who can see nothing but general principles, and the mere man of business, who can see nothing but particular circumstances'.[27] But Macaulay's hostility towards radical Utilitarian political philosophy was never carried through to Benthamite jurisprudence. Indeed in the process of his noted dismembering of James Mill's Utilitarian a priori science of government,[28] (where Macaulay 'came forth like a Whig David to slay the Utilitarian Goliath') he had incidentally expressed admiration for Bentham's contribution to legal

[24] Ibid., 583–86.

[25] Mill, *History*, v, 425; Bentham, *Works*, i, 187–88.

[26] Collini, et al., *That Noble Science of Politics*, 192.

[27] *History*, *Works*, ii, 463 -64.

[28] A science of government deducible from the immutable features of human nature; attacked in Mill's 'Essay on Government' (1829), *Works*, vii, 365. Macaulay himself was later accused of the same sin of 'a priori reasoning' by T.C. Robertson, a member of the Governor-General's Council, Stokes, op. cit., 212.

science.[29] Furthermore, when in India Macaulay was happy to speak of Bentham as 'that eminent writer . . . from whose opinions on a question of jurisprudence it is rarely safe to dissent'.[30] And soon after being informed of his position as head of the Law Commission Macaulay breezily confided to a friend the 'immense reforms in hand . . . such as would make old Bentham jump [for joy] in his grave'.[31] Essentially, Macaulay brought to law-making an attitude which could be aptly described as a 'fusion of utilitarian clarity and rigour with Burkean pragmatism'.[32]

III. The Code's Nature, Style and Structure

Although nominally the product of the Law Commission, both Macaulay's personality and the Indian climate combined to ensure that the Code was predominantly Macaulay's creation. Work on the Code began in summer 1835, with the Draft Code and Report being presented to the Governor-General in October 1837. Macaulay and his team had embarked on their task with high enthusiasm and hopes of completion within a year.[33] However, of the original Commission only Macaulay's constitution proved sufficiently robust[34] to stay the course by resisting capitulation to the severe climate and high sickness rate;[35] thus making him almost solely responsible for the Code's drafting.[36]

The Code was remarkable stylistically, structurally and substantively, marking a radical and express departure from the approach of any English

[29] Leslie Stephen, *The English Utilitarians* (1900), ii, 85. And see 'Westminster Reviewer's Defence of Mill', *Edinburgh Review* (1829). For the collection of *Westminster Review* and *Edinburgh Review* articles centring around Mill's essay, see *Utilitarian Logic and Politics*, J. Lively and J. Rees, ed. (Oxford, 1978). As Leslie Stephen notes, 'Macaulay showed his gratitude for Mill's generosity in regard to the Indian appointment by declining to republish the [offending] articles' – although they were republished after Macaulay's death.

[30] Governor-General's Council's Legislative Minutes, 11 May 1835; Clive, op. cit., 323.

[31] Macaulay to T.F. Ellis, 3 June 1835, *Letters*, iii, 146.

[32] Collini et al., op. cit., 198.

[33] Macaulay to T.F. Ellis, 'I begin to take a very warm interest in this work. It is indeed one of the finest employments of the intellect that it is easy to conceive. I ought however to tell you that the more progress I make as a legislator the more intense my contempt for the mere technical study of law becomes', 25 August 1835, *Letters*, iii, 152.

[34] Macaulay to T.F. Ellis: 'I shall have been two years on Indian ground in less than a fortnight, and I have not taken ten grains of solid or a pint of liquid medicine during the whole of that time', 30 May 1836, *Letters*, iii, 174–75.

[35] Of the climate Macaulay wrote: 'We are annually baked for four months, boiled for four more, and allowed the remaining four to become cool if we can. At the moment the sun is blazing like a furness: the earth, soaked with oceans of rain, is steaming like a wet blanket . . . insects and undertakers are the only living creatures which seem to enjoy the climate', Macaulay to Mrs. T. Drummond, 20 September 1837, *Letters*, iii, 225. But the climate was 'beyond all comparison better than that of the House of Commons', Macaulay to T.F. Ellis, 8 February 1835, *Letters*, iii, 132.

[36] For example, letters of 30 November 1836; 8 March 1837; 18 December 1837; *Letters*, iii, 202, 210, and 237–38. See also *Council Minutes*, C.D. Dharker, ed. (1946), 253 and *Parl. Papers*, xxx (1852–53), 300.

statutory provision before or since. Its style was strenuously and self-consciously clear and as free from complexity as language and conceptual constraints would permit. Technical terms, some with pedigrees stretching back hundreds of years, were taboo.[37] Use of ordinarily comprehensible language with words and expressions maintaining a uniformity of meaning throughout the Code also facilitated codification programmes in other areas of law.[38] However, although as Bentham preached,[39] simplicity might be the 'handmaiden of beauty, wisdom, virtue – of everything that is excellent', simplicity sometimes had to surrender to precision: 'in our definitions we have repeatedly found ourselves under the necessity of sacrificing neatness and perspicuity to precision' and sometimes in pursuing the cause of precision resort had to be made to 'rugged or intricate phraseology'.[40]

This keenly sought-after simplicity was intended to serve two functions: first to make the law widely accessible and comprehensible to, at least, the literate population; and, secondly, to restrict narrowly the role of judicial discretion and creativity. The former goal also carried a broad educative function of moral reorientation, as Bentham,[41] and others,[42] believed law could and should have. Keeping 'Judge and Co.' out of law making was Bentham's great bete noire.[43] Judicial 'legislation' not only brought great uncertainty and complexity to the law, it was also an outrageous 'usurpation' of legislative power, permitting judges to insinuate their own ideas into the law; complexity also served to line the pockets and inflate the standing of judges and lawyers.[44] Though hardly rivalling Bentham's splenetic distaste for the common law,[45] Macaulay also hoped

[37] Similarly, Bentham, *Works*, i, 96 n.

[38] *Report*, 426. And see Bentham, *Works*, iii, 209: 'The same ideas, the same words. Never employ other than a single and the same word, for expressing a single and the same idea'.

[39] *Works*, x, 531; and iii, 464. Also law 'as a rule of conduct . . . cannot be too simple, too clear, too free from dispute', *Works*, ii, 356.

[40] Introductory report upon the *Indian Penal Code*, 14 October 1837 (hereafter *Report*), *The Works of Lord Macaulay*, G.O. Trevelyan, ed. (1866), vii, 422–23. In Council, Macaulay had observed: 'I am firmly convinced that the style of laws is of scarcely less importance than their substance . . . [I]t has been so much the fashion . . . to darken by gibberish, by tautology, by circumlocution, that meaning which ought to be as transparent as words can make it', Minute, 11 May 1835, Dharker, 148. Similarly, Fitzjames Stephen, (legal member 1869–72): in Macaulay's time, 'statutes were lengthier, more drawling and tedious, more crammed with surplusage [than] either before or since', H.C.L., iii, 302.

[41] For example, *Works*, v, 235–36; iii, 270–71.

[42] Particularly Fitzjames Stephen. See 'Codification in India and England', *Fortnightly Review*, xviii (1872), 644 at 659: 'the influence, as a mere instrument of education, of the codifying acts, can hardly be exaggerated'; also H.C.L., iii, 322.

[43] *Works*, v, 369. For the view that Bentham approached judicial 'adjudication' in a more constructive fashion than generally understood, see G.J. Postema, *Bentham and the Common Law Tradition* (Oxford, 1986), ch. 12. See also Austin's more measured utilitarian critique of common law, *Lectures on Jurisprudence*, R. Campbell, ed., 4th ed. (1879), ii, Lecture xxxix, 'Disadvantages of Judicial Legislation: The Question of Codification Discussed'.

[44] *Works*, ii, 2.

[45] See, for example, A.W.B. Simpson, 'The Common Law and Legal Theory', *Legal Theory and Common Law*, W.L. Twining, ed. (1986), 8, 16. See Postema, *Bentham and the Common Law Tradition*, generally for a reinterpretation of Bentham's attitude towards the common law.

to 'greatly limit the power which the courts of justice possess of putting their own sense on the laws', rendering them 'not only bulky, but uncertain and contradictory'.[46]

Reinforcing these twin aims and benefits of clarity was the Code's innovatory incorporation of illustrative examples.[47] Macaulay claimed:[48]

> . . . the illustrations will lead the mind of the student through the same steps by which the minds of those who framed the law proceeded . . . they also exhibit law in full action, and show what its effects will be on the events of common life.

He was the first British legislator to employ this technique,[49] a practice maintained in subsequent Indian codes.[50] Beyond illustrations, Macaulay assisted the Code's readers with a series of extensively argued explanatory 'Notes' on each provision. Contrary to Benthamite legislative notions, these 'Notes' were not part of the Code and were jettisoned after the Code's eventual

[46] *Report*, 424.

[47] Little, if any, credit for this technique can be attributed to Bentham. See consideration of the point by Stokes, op. cit., 330, n.Y.

[48] *Report*, 423. Anxious to underline the issue, Macaulay continues: the illustrations 'are not cases decided by judges, but by the legislature, by those who make the law, and who must know more certainly than any judge can know what the law is which they mean to make'. See the *First Report* on the Code, 23 July 1846, by C.H. Cameron and D. Elliott, 190–203 for judicial criticism of the restrictive effect on discretion of illustrations. As to the educative potential of the illustrations see J.S. Mill: 'bèsides great certainty and distinctness given to the legislators meaning [use of illustrations] solves the difficult problem of making the body of the laws a popular book, at once intelligible and interesting to the general reader. Simple as this contrivance is, it escaped the sagacity of Bentham, so fertile in ingenious combinations of detail', *Westminster Review* (1838), 393, 402. The article is signed 'S'; attribution to J.S. Mill by the *Wellesley Index to Victorian Periodicals, 1824–1900*, W.E. Houghton, ed. (Toronto and London, 1966–79), 591.

[49] As Professor S.H. Kadish rightly points out, ('Codification of the Criminal Law: Wechsler's Predecessors', *Columbia Law Rev.*, lxxviii (1978), 1,098 at 1,113) the American codifier Edward Livingston in his draft Louisiana Penal Code (1826) was the first to employ illustrations. Contra, W. Stokes, *Anglo-Indian Codes* (1881), 1, xxiv; E. Stokes, op. cit., 231; and Clive, op. cit., 444. Livingston's integrated and comprehensive system of penal law consisted of a 'Code of Crimes and Punishments; a Code of Procedure; a Code of Evidence; a Code of Reform and Prison Discipline; and a Book of Definitions', 'Introduction', vi, *Complete Works of Edward Livingston on Criminal Jurisprudence* (New York, 1873) (hereafter *Works*). This, he hoped, would eliminate the arbitrariness and complexity of existing penal legislation which was a 'piece of fretwork exhibiting the passions of its several authors, their fears, their caprices, or . . . carelessness and inattention', all of which was further aggravated by the 'crude and varying opinions of judges . . . usurp[ing] the authority of law', 'Report on the Plan of a Penal Code', *Works*, 11–12. The English Criminal Law Commissioners in their First Report, 1834, (focused on the law of theft) acknowledged Livingston's 'very able Digest' of theft.

[50] But rejected by the English Criminal Law Commissioners in their Fourth Report, 1839. Erudite and wide ranging, the Fourth Report considered the principles of penal legislation from Beccaria to Feuerbach, Bacon to the French *Code Pénal*. The use of illustrations was thought by the Commissioners to be redundant if the legal statement was sufficiently clear; if it were not, then the remedy lay in clarificatory redrafting. Moreover, 'none but plain and obvious examples are conducive even to the purposes of instruction; for predicaments to which the application of the proposed rule was doubtful, would serve to perplex rather than enlighten the mind', (Report, 16). R.S. Wright's relatively radical draft Jamaican Criminal Code, as originally drawn, made no use of illustrations. However, the final version did after a strong disagreement of principle between Wright and Fitzjames Stephen, employed as an advisor by the Colonial Office. See M.L. Friedland, 'R.S. Wright's Model Criminal Code', *Oxford Jour. Legal Studies*, i (1981), 307, 317.

enactment in 1860.[51] But Bentham's legislative philosophy does manifest itself in the order and layout of the Code's introductory chapters, where first come terminological definitions and explanations, after which are definitions of punishments, then general exceptions followed by complicity provisions.[52]

The Code's novel style should also be seen as the product of several other factors, particularly that rather than a revamping of any existing coherent body of criminal law it was a *de novo* creation, unhampered by any former structural constraints or expectations.[53] One obvious alternative solution to this would have been the wholesale and (where necessary) modified importation of English law. However, most importantly, English criminal law was then officially in very poor odour, with the English Criminal Law Commissioners having in 1837 pronounced it to be 'so defective that it can be reformed only by being entirely taken to pieces and reconstructed'.[54] Therefore, subject to broad political sensitivities, Macaulay was at liberty to enjoy the role of a first principles legislator. This he did by starting with an express acceptance of the twin Utilitarian axioms of suppressing crime with the smallest possible infliction of suffering and ascertaining truth at the smallest possible cost of time and money.[55] Beyond this, Macaulay openly acknowledged his intellectual indebtedness to the 'most celebrated systems of Western jurisprudence', and particularly to Livingston's draft Louisiana Code of which, in turn Livingston had credited Bentham with having provided

[51] Bentham advocated interweaving the rationale of a particular provision with the text, *Works*, iv, 543–45 and ii, 356–57. The technique was, however, employed in Livingston's Louisiana Code. Macaulay saw no practical way of following this practice because of the possible diversity of reasons held by a legislative body for enacting particular provisions. See E. Stokes, op. cit., 200–1. But the notes as used were, at least, an aid to enactment in that they revealed the policies behind the provisions.

[52] *Works*, iii, 174. See also the comments of Fitzjames Stephen, H.C.L., iii, 302–3 and W. Stokes, op. cit., 1, xxii–xxiii.

[53] The Report suggests that had there been an existing system, 'which the people regarded with particularity, we should have been inclined to rather ascertain it, to digest it, and moderately to correct it, than to propose a system fundamentally different', *Report*, 416. Bearing in mind the reforming ambitions of James Mill, Macaulay and others, and their views on English law, this comment has all the appearance of political window dressing.

[54] Letter from the Commissioners to Lord John Russell, cited by Macaulay, *Report*, 421. The Criminal Law Commission was set up by Brougham as Lord Chancellor in 1833 with the initial remit of examining the criminal law with a view to 'digesting' it. By 1837 it had produced three reports (First 1834, Second 1836) on various features of the law, each report lamenting the unprincipled, contradictory and chaotic state of English criminal law. In the First Report the Commissioners spoke with open contempt of, 'The want of general principles and rules defining and limiting the nature of offences; . . . considerable discrepancies . . . met with in books of authority in adoption of . . . subtle, refined and useless distinctions' (*Report*, 3–4). Their early, pre-Macaulay Code, Reports did not attempt to produce full scale comprehensive codification programmes. For an outline of the Reports see A.R.N. Cross, 'The Reports of the Criminal Law Commissioners (1833–1849)', *Reshaping the Criminal Law*, P.R. Glazebrook, ed. (1978), 5. For the abortive outcome of their labours see A.H. Manchester, 'Simplifying the Sources of the Law', *Anglo-American Law Rev.*, ii (1973), 395.

[55] Board's Collections, 1,555 (1835–37), No. 63,507, 7–9. India Office Library. Cf. Bentham's similar prescriptions, *Works*, ii, 355 and iv, 480.

the theoretical underpinnings.[56] Yet even without these formative influences, Macaulay's highly distinctive style of composition and dialectical devices, already well-entrenched before India, contributed enormously to the Code's shape and form. As many contemporaries testified, style was the man.

Leslie Stephen captured one feature of Macaulay's style perfectly when remarking that 'nobody can hit a haystack with more certainty' than Macaulay.[57] Pertinent to the use of illustrations is the comment by John Morley (J.S. Mill's great acolyte and Liberal statesman) on Macaulay's 'quality of taking his reader through an immense gallery of interesting characters and striking situations . . . the style of great literary knowledge [used in a] process of complete assimilation and spontaneous fusion'.[58] Furthermore, says Morley, 'He never wrote an obscure sentence in his life' partly because for Macaulay:[59]

> . . . the world was spread out clear before him, he read it as plainly and as certainly as he read his books; life was all an affair of direct categoricals. This was at least one secret of those hard modulations and shallow cadences.

These qualities, ill-favoured by critics of general literature, were clearly an indirect recommendation for a legislator; something which did not escape Fitzjames Stephen, who understood that the 'absence of shading, which is unnatural and unpleasing in a picture, is indispensable in a mathematical diagram, and the sharp contrasts which sometimes pall upon the reader of a history are just what are wanted in a penal code'.[60] Metaphorically uniting general literary style and the law, Leslie Stephen suggested:[61]

> Clearness is the first of the cardinal virtues of style; and nobody every wrote more clearly than Macaulay . . . he proves that two and two make four, with a pertinacity which would make him dull if it were not for his abundance of brilliant illustration. He always renders the principle which should guide a barrister addressing a jury. He has not merely to exhaust his proofs, but to hammer them into the heads of his audience by incessant repetition.

Indeed, there are occasions in the Code where Macaulay went too far in trying to 'anticipate captious objections' and over-defined elements of the Code; a failing characterized by Fitzjames Stephen as akin to attempting to 'rid a house of dust by mere sweeping. You make more dust than you

[56] *Report*, 421. See Kadish, loc. cit., 1,099–106, for an excellent account of Livingston's code and Bentham's influence on it. Also in 'The Model Penal Code's Historical Antecedents', *Rutgers Law Jour.*, xix (1988), 521, 523.

[57] *Hours in a Library* (1892 ed.), ii, 352.

[58] *Critical Miscellanies*, i (1913 ed., first published 1877), 253, 265–67.

[59] Ibid., 275 and 283. Similarly Walter Bagehot on Macaulay's literary style: 'It is too omniscient. Everything is too plain. All is clear; nothing is doubtful', *Literary Studies*, R.H. Hutton, ed., 4th ed. (1891), ii, 256. Matthew Arnold somewhat sniffily, attributed this to 'a dash of intellectual vulgarity'. Quoted by S. Collini, *Arnold* (Oxford, 1988), 66.

[60] H.C.L., iii, 302.

[61] *Hours in a Library*, ii, 364.

remove'.[62] Such blemishes fail to detract from the overall superb clarity which is the Code's hallmark; something encouraging belief in Macaulay's claim that in seeking the desired effect in several chapters he had 'changed the whole plan ten or twelve times, which contain not a single word as it originally stood'.[63]

IV. The Code's Substantive Nature

The Code's substantive provisions rival its style for innovation and progressiveness. A distinct rationalistic and subjectivistic approach is displayed in the culpability requirements and punishment provisions for offences. Throughout the Code a strong strain of legal modernism is recognizable, with some instances where the Code provisions are arguably more enlightened than equivalent areas of current Anglo-American law.

The key to subtle gradations and appropriate labelling of criminal culpability is clarity in the terminology of fault. These linguistic building blocks of liability received scrupulous and detailed attention: the meanings of 'intention', 'knowledge', 'negligence' are each methodically laid out.[64] Defined terms are then consistently employed throughout the Code. Much the same treatment is accorded to quasi-technical expressions such as 'fraudulent'.[65] This served Macaulay's objective of ensuring that fixed degrees of culpability could be accurately and reliably included in individual offence definitions and not subject to the infinite vagaries of applying indistinct common law notions. In turn this facilitated the Code's firm declared stance against the English

62 H.C.L., iii, 306. By far the most extravagant example of overdefinition in the Code is section 349 which defines force:

> A person is said to use force to another, if he causes motion, change of motion, or cessation of motion to that other; or if he causes to any substance such motion, or change of motion, or cessation of motion as brings that substance into contact with any part of that other's body, or with any thing which that other is wearing, or carrying, or with anything so situated that that contact affects that other's sense of feeling, provided that the person causing the motion, cessation of motion, or change of motion in one of the three ways hereinafter described: first, by his own bodily power; secondly, by disposing any substance in such a manner that the motion, or change or cessation of motion takes place without any further action on his part, or on the part of any other person; thirdly, by inducing any animal to move, to change its motion, or to cease to move.

63 Undated Council *Minute*, C.D. Dharker, ed., 253. Within a few weeks before completion Macaulay wrote to Ellis: 'Whether it is well or ill done heaven knows. I know only that it seems to me to be very ill done when I look at it by itself, and well done when I compare it with Livingston's Code, with the French Code or with the English [consolidating] statutes', 8 March 1837, *Letters*, iii, 210.

64 Austin was well aware of the necessity of carefully defining culpability terms and matters of *mens rea* generally. See 'Fragments of a Scheme of a Criminal Code', Lectures, op. cit., 1,086–100 and 'Tables 1 & 2', 1,103–4. Note also Bentham's discussion 'Of Intentionality', ch.viii, *Introduction to the Principles of Morals and Legislation*; *Works*, i. The English Criminal Law Commissioners in their Fourth Report (1839) were similarly concerned to achieve reasonable definitional precision although noting that 'metaphysical exactness is visionary and absurd' (xv).

65 One slip where the bad old (English) ways are resorted to is the use of 'malignantly and wantonly' in section 257. Noted by Kadish, loc. cit., 1,119 n.168.

law of constructive liability, most particularly the felony murder rule whose perverse operation Macaulay illustrated in characteristic fashion:[66]

> To punish as a murderer every man who, while committing a heinous offence, causes death by pure misadventure, is a course which eventually adds nothing to the security of human life . . . For example, hundreds of persons in some great cities are in the habit of picking pockets. They know that they are guilty of a great offence; but it has never occurred to one of them, nor would it occur to any rational man, that they are guilty of an offence which endangers life. Unhappily one of these hundreds attempts to take the purse of a gentleman who has a loaded pistol. The hand touches the trigger, the pistol goes off, the gentleman is shot dead . . . To send [this pickpocket] to the gallows as a murderer, appears to us an unreasonable course.

Constructive liability breached the adopted tenet that liability must reasonably relate to personal culpability. Accidental death where caused by negligence was to be punished, but only as 'involuntary culpable homicide'.[67] Overall, Macaulay's homicide provisions were an impressive model of progressive thinking and clear formulation quite outclassing the English Commissioners' contemporary efforts,[68] and capable, with very limited modification, of modern use.

The Code's punishment rationale was complementary to Macaulay's aim of grading offences predominantly on the basis of demonstrable culpability (whether subjective or objective) of actions rather than the chance occurrence of consequences where punishment would be 'superfluous' adding nothing to the 'security of human life'. Capital punishment is 'very sparingly inflicted', being restricted to murder and treason.[69] Macaulay's justifying discussion of death and the whole range of lesser penalties is recognizably infused with Benthamite precepts;[70] above all that punishment should be used economically and efficaciously. The original absence from the Code of a

[66] *Notes on the Indian Penal Code*, M, *Works*, vii, 508–9. Macaulay noted that 'Offences against the body' 'appears to us to require fuller explanation than almost any other' part of the code, ibid., 493. This example was used by the 1845 Criminal Law Commissioners, Second Report, (1846) when attacking the felony murder rule.

[67] Clause 305. Livingston also roundly condemned constructive liability as 'ex post facto law [and] an illegal assumption of legislative power', *Works*, 13. But vestiges of such liability are found in the draft Louisiana Code. Noted by Kadish, loc. cit., 1,019, n.167. A similarly disapproving attitude is displayed by the English Criminal Law Commissioners in their Fourth Report where constructive liability was characterized as 'forced constructions' and adaptations of definitions to meet judicially perceived needs as amounting to an 'exercise of legislative functions by judges' (xiv).

[68] See Fourth Report (1839), Homicide provisions (arts. 1–71). Even allowing for the fact that the provisions were a 'Digest' of the law, the Commissioners' remit permitted moderate innovation, as shown in some areas of digested law. Stephen's observation that obscurity in the Indian Code's definitions of culpable homicide and murder made them the 'weakest part of the Code' (H.C.L., iii, 313) is misleading. Stephen's comments relate to the Code as finally enacted which contained amended homicide provisions. Macaulay's version was undoubtedly clearer. To this effect, see A.R.N. Cross, 'The Making of English Criminal Law', [1978] *Crim. Law Rev.*, 519, 525–27. See also W. Stokes' critical remarks, op. cit., 40.

[69] *Report*, 429, note 'M'.

[70] Particularly as expounded in *Introduction to the Principles of Morals and Legislation*, ch.xiii-xv.

general crime of manslaughter based on negligence was a consequence of Macaulay's aversion to constructive liability which in turn entailed what he regarded as ineffectual punishment: it did not deter harmful action. As Whitley Stokes (legal member of the council from the late 1870s) critically noted in his commentary on the Code: 'The framers do not seem to have troubled themselves much about the rival theories of punishment respecting which German jurists and philosophers have written so copiously'.[71] This was a probable allusion to the various retributive schools of thought which rested punishment on notions of just deserts, whereby guilt was purged or annulled by proportionate punishment levels. Indeed Stephen's criticism of the omission of a general offence of negligence-based manslaughter was that the retributive aspect of punishment had been ignored. Therefore even though only 'bad luck' might distinguish one risk taker from another, punishment of the one accidently causing death 'gratifies a natural public feeling . . . for punishment of one who has actually caused great harm'.[72]

Two further instances may be briefly offered illustrating Macaulay's pursuit of a general rationale of founding liability and punishment largely on the culpability surrounding the defendant's act and paying less heed than English law to the chance occurrence of any harmful consequences. First, the Code introduced a series of offences where endangering actions without harm materializing was the basis of criminality.[73] A second example relates to criminal attempt where for some reason the full offence in the particular circumstances was impossible, such as in picking an empty pocket. The Code, at least in some cases, contrary to English law of the time, sought to remove impossibility as a bar to conviction; the implicit rationale being that the defendant's mental culpability remained unchanged whether the criminal objective was achievable or not.[74]

V. Delay in the Code's Enactment

Through a combination of external events (largely the politically highly contentious Afghan campaigns) and for reasons intrinsic to the Code, twenty-three years elapsed before it became law; by nineteenth- or even twentieth-century standards perhaps unremarkable. The history of the delay of an enterprise which began with such tremendous panache offers a classic illustration of the great dead weight power of governmental and administrative inertia, indolence and the desire for a professionally quiet

71 Op. cit., 26.

72 H.C.L., iii, 311. Arguably Stephen's own denunciatory theory of punishment was quasi-utilitarian in that it aimed at strengthening society's common condemnation of and aversion to harm causing behaviour, thus ultimately decreasing the incidence of such conduct.

73 Sections 279–89.

74 Section 511. But see W. Stokes, op. cit. n.49, 68–70 for the constructional difficulties of these provisions.

life, similarily responsible for a whole clutch of abortive domestic codifying efforts in the nineteenth century. Arguably, by such standards it might be seen as surprising that the Code was ever enacted.

Beyond the Code's revolutionary style and innovative substance, the first factor telling against its early enactment was a change of key personnel to individuals far less imbued with reforming zeal. This process began in 1835 with Lord Bentinck's replacement by the more cautious Auckland as Governor-General, and with James Mill's death in the following year. Macaulay left the subcontinent at the beginning of 1838, being succeeded by the solid Andrew Amos, first professor of law at University College, London and one of the English Criminal Law Commissioners appointed in 1833. Auckland had chosen Amos in preference to James Young whose credentials Auckland found uncomfortably progressive for his tastes, remarking that 'enough of pure Benthamism was already secured to our Code'.[75]

Reception of the Code was mixed, and on Amos's urgings Auckland gratefully referred the Code for comments to the Supreme Court judges of each of the Presidencies in Bombay, Madras and Calcutta. The consultative responses of the judiciary and other concerned officials,[76] were fed at an exceedingly leisurely pace to Cameron and Elliott, a pair of Indian Law Commissioners.[77] They eventually produced two huge and sympathetic reports,[78] which with considerable industry, patience and acumen refuted practically every objection as to the Code's nature and content. With only trivial amendments they declared the Code fit for enactment. Yet despite such searching and detailed scrutiny and final endorsement, the project stalled, partly in consequence of the Governor-General's (Dalhousie)

[75] Quoted by E. Stokes, op. cit. n.2, 240. Auckland's specification of the new law member included someone with 'good sense and temper, and address in conciliation in large proportions', Clive, op. cit., 466.

[76] Mill characterized much criticism as being made in the 'worst motives and spirit' and some of the Code's opposers as seeking to install themselves as a 'privileged oligarchy', *Westminster Review* (1838), 393, 404–5.

[77] Comments on inaction over the Code occasionally surfaced in the periodical press, such as the particularly sharp remarks in the *Edinburgh Review* (1841), 425, 457. The anonymous author was Ross Donnelly Mangles, a Chairman of the East India Company and, on Macaulay's recommendation, a member of the Indian Education Committee, *Letters*, iii, 125; attribution by *Wellesley Index*, 1,489. According to Frederick Millett (Secretary of Macaulay's Law Commission team) 'the voluminous comments . . . were allowed to go to sleep in the office of the Legislative Council for five years before they were referred to the Law Commissioners for examination and report'. Evidence to Select Committee of the House of Lords, *Parl. Papers*, xxx (1852–53), 124.

[78] Reports on the Indian Penal Code 1846 and 1847 by C.H. Cameron and D. Elliott. The thoroughness of the work can hardly fail to impress. The First Report extends to 697 full paragraphs; the Second to 544. Cameron and Elliott were required to take account of the English Criminal Law Commissioners' Seventh Report, which they did with advantage. Predictably much of the judicial criticism, in one way or another, related to the Code's lack of practicality and theoretical flavour, and restrictions of judicial discretion. Strong support for the Code, unsurprisingly, also came from J. Macleod, one of Macaulay's original Indian Law Commissioners in his *Notes on the Report of the Indian Law Commissioners on the Indian Penal Code* (1848).

preoccupation with annexation of the Punjab, and particularly because the implacable opposition of Drinkwater Bethune (Amos's replacement) to both the Code's substance and style.[79]

A build up of pressure to put British subjects under the criminal (as well as the civil) jurisdiction of the company's courts in the Indian interior eventually forced the Governor-General's hand, for the law applied in these courts was unappetizingly Muslim-based. The need to introduce a new criminal code was now awkwardly pressing. Rather than enact Macaulay's ready made Code, Bethune produced his own far more traditional model, eventually dispatched to London in 1851 along with Macaulay's for a final choice to be made. After more equivocation and rapid buck passing,[80] a special select committee of the Indian Legislative Council produced an interim report favouring Macaulay's work,[81] which, after limited revisions by Barnes Peacock, (Bethune's successor) was enacted in 1860 and operating from 1862;[82] apparently some Indian judges had jumped the gun and started using it in the early 1850s.[83]

VI. Evaluation of the Code

If longevity is a reliable indicator of high quality, then the standing of Macaulay's work is beyond dispute, with the current Indian Penal Code varying little from the 1860 version.[84] Less obvious is the Code's intellectual and theoretical pedigree. Over the years many have endorsed Stephen's well known claim that the Code was the:[85]

79 Drinkwater Bethune 'objected to the new language [and] opposed . . . illustrations, saw no use in setting aside the terms of English law . . . which had acquired a settled and definite meaning. He thought this was a mere whim, or love of singularity, which ought not to be indulged'. Evidence of David Hill (Madras administrator) to Select Committee of the House of Lords, *Parl. Papers*, xxx (1852–53), 335.

80 Stephen put this hesitancy down to 'the extensive aversion which for a long time before the the mutiny was felt by influential persons in India to any changes which boldly and definitely replaced native by European institutions. It appeared in every way the safer course to alter and interfere as little as possible . . .', H.C.L., iii, 299.

81 E. Stokes, op. cit. n.2, 262.

82 See 'Historical Introduction to the Indian Penal Code', *Indian Law Institute: Essays on the Indian Penal Code* (Delhi, 1961), 1, 33.

83 *Parl. Papers*, xxx (1852–53), 287, 296.

84 Stephen judged the Code as having 'triumphantly supported the test of experience', H.C.L., iii, 299; see also W. Stokes, op. cit. n.49, 71–72 and J. Bryce, *Studies in History and Jurisprudence* (1901), ii, 108.

85 H.C.L., iii, 300, also at 322; for him the theft provisions represented 'the law of England in its maturity, and freed from most of the intricacies which distorted it so strongly' (317); and in Trevelyan, op. cit., 303. Similarly, Pollock, 'The Indian Penal Code . . . is English Criminal Law simplified and set in order', *The Expansion of the Common Law* (1904), 16–17; G.C. Rankin, *Background to Indian Law* (Cambridge, 1946), 207; M.C. Setalvad, *The Role of English Law in India*, Lionel Cohen Lecture (Jerusalem, 1966), 14. But contra, S.G. Vesey-Fitzgerald, 'Bentham and the Indian Codes', *Jeremy Bentham and the Law*, G.W. Keeton and G. Schwarzenberger, ed. (1948), 222, at 226–28.

> . . . criminal law of England free from all technicalities and superfluities, systematically arranged and modified . . . to suit the circumstances of British India.

But a strong substantive resemblance to English law, though structurally and stylistically quite distinct, does not reveal or explain the process by which Macaulay reached his conclusions. He was, of course, the creature of his own political and philosophic outlook: India was to be endowed with the great prize of European culture, and inevitably for him this was to be of a predominantly English flavour. Yet although Macaulay could not escape from his own cultural dictates, crucially they did not run deeply in the case of law. Being merely a nominal lawyer (having eaten a few dinners at Lincoln's Inn), Macaulay had developed no reverence for the common law tradition; constructing a code from first principles carried no risk of emotional betrayal of a system of which he had been no more than an outside observer; he was free from those intellectual accretions often built up from membership of the legal fraternity and so frequently inclined to resist and write off even limited innovation. At least to this extent it is right to see him as an unhampered practitioner of a universal science of jurisprudence,[86] also believed by Macaulay to be of practical relevance for home consumption.[87]

Bentham is rightly credited with translating some of the broad notions of the European Enlightenment into concrete schemes for social and political engineering.[88] His great role in Macaulay's venture was imbuing in this relatively open-minded legislator a keen awareness of the link between law and social development, and the importance of a rigorous and systematized approach to law-making. Macaulay was hardly someone with a temperament constructed to serve as a mere conduit for the ideas of others. A common criticism was his forceful uncompromising faith in the infallibility of his own outlook. Morley accused him of a tendency to 'oracular arrogance . . . and declamation';[89] someone to be seen 'shouldering his way successfully through the troubles of the universe'.[90] As Macaulay on more than one occasion admitted, Bentham was the adopted inspirational force behind the Code, thus entitling him to share with Macaulay the considerable credit attaching to it.

By way of a concluding comment or postscript, in 1825, following Bentham's years of generally fruitless attempts at soliciting commissions for his schemes throughout the world, Hazlitt cruelly quipped that Bentham's name though little known in England was venerated in the 'plains of Chili and the mines of Mexico'.[91] Macaulay's efforts removed a good deal of the sting from Hazlitt's

86 Eric Stokes aptly describes 'this cast of mind that was of the eighteenth-century philosophe . . .', op. cit., 207.

87 Macaulay to James Mill, 24 August 1835, *Letters*, iii, 146–47. Though politically changes on the scale of Macaulay's Code were close to impossible, S. Amos, *An English Code* (1873), 384–85; Stephen, H.C.L., iii, 304.

88 See, for example, Robinson, Fergus and Gordon, op. cit., ch.xv.

89 Morley, op. cit., 257.

90 Leslie Stephen, op. cit., 374.

91 'Jeremy Bentham', *The Spirit of the Age* (1825), 3.

jibe. Without any direct effort on his part, Bentham achieved his most tangible codifying success in the form of the Indian Penal Code. Uncannily, Bentham forecast just this when claiming: 'I shall be the dead legislative of British India. Twenty years after I am dead, I will be a despot'.[92] Dying in 1832, Bentham was eight years out with his prediction.

[92] *Works*, x, 450. Quoted by E. Halevy, *The Growth of Philosophic Radicalism*, J. Plamenatz, ed. (1972), 510. Besides India, Macaulay's Code was indirectly employed in other British controlled territories including Israel (Penal Code 1938, adopted after independence in 1948). See N. Abrams, 'Interpreting the Criminal Code Ordinance 1936: The Untapped Well', *Israel Law Rev.*, vii (1972), 25. I am grateful to my colleague Mr. Alex Stein for this reference.

Chapter 11

The Development of Danish Joint Stock Company Rules during the Eighteenth and Nineteenth Centuries

Inger Dübeck

The kings of Denmark became absolute monarchs in 1660. This absolutism lasted until 1849, when a democratic constitution was adopted. Among the first legislative initiatives of the newly established absolute king, Frederick III, was the creation of a systematic corpus of Danish civil law, the so-called Danish Code which was not finished until 1683, by which time his son had succeeded him as Christian V. This code was the first real 'codification' in Europe written in a national language, and it was admired as such by Jeremy Bentham among others.[1] Many parts of the lawbook were simply taken from older and often more or less antiquated medieval sources; some rules were new. Very few were inspired by judge-made law or by legal practice. The influence of Roman law and other foreign legal systems was small. The lawbook was divided into six books: the first three dealt with procedural law, legal regulations for the Danish church, rules about persons and family relations and various secular problems. Book four dealt with maritime law and book five with the law of property and contract as well as the law of inheritance; book six was devoted to criminal law. The lawbook did not address many commercial and industrial problems, which then had to be regulated in other ways, for instance, by the grant of charters and privileges, or by specific statutes.[2]

The Danish Code was soon translated into Latin, German, English, Russian and other languages and thus became quite well known in Europe. In Denmark itself it was soon realized that many of the rules in the Code were out of date and would have to be supplemented with new legislation as developments in society called for changes. General rules on contracts, tort, associations, companies, patents and unfair competition were to be found neither in the lawbook nor in individual statutes until late in the nineteenth century. But the lawbook stressed the modern view of freedom of contract

[1] Jacques Vanderlinden, 'Code et codification dans la pensée de Jeremy Bentham', *Tijdschrift voor Rechtsgeschiedenis*, xxxii (1964), 45.

[2] Inger Dübeck, 'Alt hvis politien egentlig vedkommer . . .' (The Relation between the Danish Code and the So-called Police Order), *Danske og Norske Lov i 300 År*, Ditlev Tamm, ed. (Copenhagen, 1983), 145.

both in relation to form and content.

The seventeenth and eighteenth centuries had witnessed the appearance of many trading companies to handle the growing overseas trade with the Danish colonies in India, Africa and the West Indies (the Virgin Islands). The period also witnessed the appearance of iron foundries, textile factories and other industries, as well as a bank and some insurance companies, all of them normally organized as joint stock companies. But companies were not free to choose how they wished to organize production. In some matters the state (the king) had to guarantee special rights or privileges. Indeed one cannot really speak of industrialization in Denmark before the 1870s. The building of railways, steamships, canals, harbours and telegraphs and the founding of private banks were among the events of the 1840s and 1850s that created the conditions for Danish industrialization and the capitalism necessary for its success.

The joint stock company which has become such an important form of business organization in the modern western world is the result of a long development. Characteristic elements such as limited liability, free transferability of shares, a share capital or pool of stock were not features of eighteenth-century company law.[3] In some countries companies had to be incorporated by a grant, charter, privilege or concession, which secured special corporate rights. In others there were no such requirements for a company to be accepted as a collective entity. One of the early problems for legal theory was to define a joint stock company. Was it to be looked upon as a public agency or just as a private enterprise? This causes difficulties for the modern legal historian as well. In the legal doctrines of the nineteenth century the concept of corporation was reserved for those companies which fulfilled the conditions for being a moral or legal person (collective entity). In England, thanks to the Bubble Act, the modern business company seems to have evolved from joint stock associations organized under deeds of settlement rather than from the companies incorporated by royal charter or by act of parliament. Limited liability was not an essential component of the structure of English companies for a fairly long period. Charters of incorporation were difficult and expensive to obtain. This form of incorporation was mostly used by banks and by fire insurance, water and canal companies. After the American Revolution the thirteen states each received power to incorporate companies. Special acts of incorporation were granted more readily than in England, with the result that corporations became very common. The corporate form was used as a practical instrument not only for companies with public functions (banks,

[3] B.C. Hunt, *The Development of the Business Corporation in England* (Harvard, 1936); A.B. Du Bois, *The English Business Company after the Bubble Act, 1720–1800* (New York, 1971); K. Bösselmann, *Die Entwicklung des deutschen Aktienwesens im 19. Jahrhundert* (Berlin, 1939); K. Lehmann, *Das Recht der Aktiengesellschaft* (Berlin, 1898, 1904).

insurance companies and manufacturing enterprises) but also for private business associations.[4]

In Denmark the establishment of partnerships as well as of joint stock companies was looked upon as a form of contract or deed of settlement. The principle of freedom of contract was accepted early in these relations. Contracting was looked upon as a matter of private law while the grant of a charter was a matter of public law. Danish legal theorists distinguished between companies carrying out 'public' functions and operations and companies which were only 'private' societies. The first had to have charters which, among other things, gave them monopolies and other benefits such as freedom from taxes or from duties or customs. They acted in an official capacity and on behalf of the state. The grant of a charter might be regarded as providing a company with special public functions or a status as a public agency. In questions of property and contract the companies were regarded *inter partes* as subject to private law.

In Denmark as in England purely private companies, which did not attract much interest from the state, developed in parallel to the public ones. Their contracts or deeds of settlement were only of interest to public authorities if they needed some special rights or freedoms and therefore asked for a special privilege. In order to start a factory with monopoly or special patent rights something more than a contract or deed of settlement was needed. A charter was necessary in order to allow the factory to operate, but not in order to have the business recognized as a moral or legal person. The private deed of settlement in itself might, however, be given the king's confirmation in the form of a special grant, with the purpose and result that the contractual conditions were valid not only among the participants, but also in relation to third parties, the surrounding world of creditors and new contracting partners. Such confirmation gave a private deed of settlement the effect of legislation. Only those deeds of settlement (conventions, byelaws) which sought special privileges were given royal confirmation. Such privileges might be limitation of liability, free transferability of shares or protection against execution or pursuit by creditors. The practice of granting charters containing special privileges to all sorts of small or large enterprises became an administrative burden for the central civil service and the government in the course of the first half of the nineteenth century. Privileges became easy to obtain. A wish for legislation in the field of company law was put forward in public debate. The privilege system was originally a system of effective control and management of a kind in commercial and industrial matters for the government. The developing burden just mentioned made the control no longer effective. Everybody who asked for a grant was given it without further investigation, unless the enterprise had a special status or special functions, for instance, where it was a public utility. Railway companies

[4] Willard Hurst, *The Legitimacy of the Business Corporation in the Law of the United States, 1780–1970* (Charlottesville, 1970).

and other companies serving some public interest still underwent careful investigation and control.

In the eighteenth century some contracts of association had to be registered in local courts or by municipal authorities. Some of them even had to be published in newspapers as well. At present it is not clear under what specific conditions such registration or publication was necessary. Until 1862 there were a few unclear rules. The purpose of registration was to give publicity to the fact that such a contract had been made but it is doubtful whether it had the effect intended. The legal theorists of the early nineteenth century discussed whether publication in the traditional way by oral reading in the courts was of any legal effect whatever. It was also questioned whether the written registration in the records and files of the courts was of more or less legal effect than oral reading. A desire for a better system was growing in broad circles of commercial and political life in the middle of the nineteenth century.[5] The new democratic constitution of 1849 proclaimed many new liberties or civil rights. Freedom of association and freedom of business were specifically promised. To give effect to this promise new statutes were needed. One of the new acts concerned registration of firms (1862). It introduced a special register for 'anonymous' or joint stock companies and for trading companies which could be sued. The inspiration for this modern registration system was found in the English Company Acts of the same period. The Act of 1862 was, however, unclear as to which companies were to be registered as *sociétés anonymes* and which as ordinary companies with some limitation of their liability. During the discussions of the bill on registration of firms in the Danish parliament some members wanted it to be limited to questions about regulation of business, that is to matters of public law, while others wanted it to deal with problems of private law as well, for instance the question of liability. The latter group won the discussion and this led to an Act uncertain in content. The Act was replaced by a new Firms Act in 1889, which was not very clear either, but was a result of Nordic legislative cooperation and so set out some of the more generally accepted principles of regulation of firms.

These Acts were the only general legislation on joint stock companies until 1917. Danish industry and enterprises had a very high degree of freedom to develop rules and principles for their companies and manufacturing plants, acting almost as they themselves thought best. And some of them did so. A famous businessman, C.F. Tietgen, had a strong influence on the development of company law.[6] The only legal means of preventing fraud and the making of 'empty' companies were the rules on registration. But even if a company was

[5] A.S. Ørsted, *Haandbog over den danske og norske Lovkyndighed*, v (Copenhagen, 1832), 418; P.G. Bang, 'Udvikling af Læren om Interessentskab og de samme nærmest vedkommende Retsforhold', *Juridisk Tidsskrift*, xvi (1829), 15.

[6] R. Willerslev, *Studier i Dansk Industrihistorie, 1850–1880* (Copenhagen, 1952); Ole Lange, *Finansmænd, stråmænd og mandariner; C.F. Tietgen, Privatbanken og Store Nordiske, Etablering, 1868–76* (Copenhagen, 1978).

registered, one could never be sure that the contributions or the shares were paid up.

The problem of limited liability did not become fundamental for investors in England until the latter part of the nineteenth century. Rules on the liability of joint stock companies developed from the rules of partnerships. The deed of settlement became one of the instruments for promoting limited liability clauses. Another method of limitation was simply to put the word 'limited' after the joint stock company name. In this way the advantage of limitation was achieved without incorporation. In the U.S.A. limited liability was not at first very common outside financial enterprises and other firms performing public functions. However, at the beginning of the nineteenth century many general statutes had already provided manufacturing companies with limited liability (New York 1811; New Hampshire 1816; Connecticut 1818; Maine 1823).[7]

Among the theorists of the eighteenth century in Denmark mainstream opinion predominantly favoured the principle of joint and several liability, liability *in solidum*, for members of private societies. In judicial practice before 1827 one can find a quite clear distinction between liability of the participants in internal questions (among each other) and liability in external questions (in relation to creditors). The *inter partes* liability was looked upon as *in solidum*, and the external one was seen as a *pro rata* liability, though often in the form that the participants would not be forced to pay until the pool of assets, the funds of the society, was empty. A couple of the eighteenth-century judges in the Danish Supreme Court opposed this view, leading the opinion that joint and several liability was such an immense interference with a man's whole economic welfare, that it should only be accepted under special circumstances, for instance, on the basis of an expressly formulated promise. If this was not the case, a *pro rata* liability should be supposed to be agreed upon. But the majority of the judges followed the general principle of solidarity (1769). In 1827 the Supreme Court decided that the anonymous funds of a company were to be seen as an artificial person with the consequence that the participants should not be liable personally or *in solidum*, but only with the funds. Although the contract or deed of settlement of the company in question had not described the character of its organization in clear terms, the court did not consider this to be an essential problem. The court undoubtedly was influenced by the new French law (*Code de Commerce* 1806) on '*sociétés anonymes*' and German legal theory. The case and the decision itself did not cause much of a revolution in business life at the time. Nor did legal theorists, who discussed the decision and derived from it a clear principle of limited liability, attract much attention in practical commercial life. In the 1840s a small boom in the formation of companies took place largely inspired by some members of the newly established Danish Industrial Association and furthered

[7] Lawrence M. Friedman, *A History of American Law* (New York, 1973), 166 and 446.

by the favourable economic situation. But the really big boom in industrial settlements using limited liability companies did not occur until the 1870s. For a very long time the terminology and concept of liability was dominated by more or less indistinct definitions. Joint and several obligation was identified with personal obligation, and *pro rata* with limited obligation. The modern distinction between personal versus limited obligation in the sense of which part of one's property is affected (one's property as a whole or only one's shares) and the corresponding distinction between *in solidum* and *pro rata* in the sense of for which proportion of the debt of the association each member is bound, seems to have been unknown to both legal theorists and practical men in the mid nineteenth century. Also in the years to come during the second half of the nineteenth century there was still much uncertainty in practical business life as to the difference between a *pro rata* clause and a limited clause. The 1889 Firms Act for the first time seems to have clarified this problem in some measure.

The nineteenth century was dominated politically and economically by the liberal principle of 'laissez faire' and legally by the principles of freedom of contract and freedom of competition. The new demands for freedom which were included in the Constitution of 1849 in the chapter on civil rights also covered the right of creating companies and corporations. Denmark responded readily to this demand. No strict rules on joint stock companies were laid down until 1917. Business life was in practice left very free to make its own conditions. The same picture of legal development can be seen in relation to much of the new business legislation. Statute law on patents and trademarks appeared late in the nineteenth century together with the law on regulation of unfair competition, in a period when influence from foreign law was increasing together with growing international contact in the course of trade. A specific maritime and commercial court was instituted in 1861. It was to deal only with merchants, others engaged in commerce, enterprises and maritime matters. A modern Bankruptcy Act was passed in 1872, in the same period as the real industrial boom in Denmark began. The period between 1840 and 1870 had seen quite a number of companies which were unable to survive and had gone bankrupt.

With freedom of trade came freedom for craftsmen and industrial workers. The new class of free workers gained the freedom to sell their capacity to work in an open labour market. But the new conditions for workers relying on wages resulted in social weakness and vulnerability to sudden economic catastrophe. A short period of unemployment might lead to poverty and starvation. The new free labourers were forced to create their own associations, the trade unions. The development of trade unions started in the 1860s in Denmark and by around 1900 the whole labour market system was fully organized, with collective bargaining between employers' federations and the federations of the labour force.

The principle of freedom of association has thus led to two sorts of associations: modern corporations and trade unions. The legal regulation of modern commercial and business life did not come into existence until the negative aspects of unregulated freedom had convinced a majority of the Danish political parties that legislation was necessary to afford some protection against the abuses of the most unethical and uninhibited enterprises in the Danish financial and industrial world.[8]

[8] Inger Dübeck, 'Dänemark: Allgemeine Einleitung und Gesetzgebung', *Handbuch der Quellen und Literatur der neueren europäischen Privatrechtsgeschichte* III*: Das 19. Jahrhundert. 4ter Teilband. Die nordischen Länder*, Helmut Coing, ed. (Munich, 1987), 21 ff.; 37 ff.

Chapter 12

The Influence of Butch Cassidy on the Development of English Company Law

Roger Gregory and Frank Sharman

One of the most remarkable things about the legends of the Wild West is that many of them are true or based very closely on the truth. There really were bad men who went by names like Billy the Kid, Bloody Bill Anderson, Black Jack Ketchum and Three-Fingered Jack; they did rustle cattle and rob trains, and hide out in places with names like The Hole in the Wall; and they did retreat to Mexico when the U.S. Marshal came too close. Judge Parker did sentence 160 men to death, of whom seventy-nine actually made the drop. Naturally the stories have become embroidered and the characters in them romanticized. There was a gun fight at the O.K. Corral, but there was as little to be said for Wyatt and Virgil Earp and Doc Holliday as there was for the Clanton gang; the affair was short and messy and over in a few seconds.

With all legends it eventually becomes difficult to discern what truth, if any, lies behind them. The purpose of this essay is to try to discover what truth lies behind one of the stories which has become attached to the name of Butch Cassidy. This story is one which occurs not only in the Wild West and the fervid imagination of Hollywood but in east Kent and the court of Chancery.

The authors of this essay first heard the story from one of their law students, Reginald Scragg. He told it in a tutorial which was considering the case of *Hickman* v. *The Kent or Romney Marsh Sheep Breeders' Association*.[1] The story is curious and remarkable and suggests that had it not been for Butch Cassidy this case would never have been brought and that, therefore, the course of English company law might have been different. To assess what truth there is in this proposition we must start by assessing the place of the case in the development of English company law.

[1] [1915] 1 Ch. 881; The Public Record Office, Chancery Lane, Chancery Records, Classes J 4 and J 15.

I. The History of Hickman v. *The Kent or Romney Marsh Sheep Breeders' Association*

The Kent or Romney Marsh Sheep Breeders' Association was established in 1895.[2] At about that time very many pedigree societies for all sorts of farm animals were set up. Breed societies had been formed throughout the nineteenth century but there was a new spate of formations at the time of the great agricultural depression. These new societies not only gave a fillip to farming in their areas but were also useful in the development of export trade.[3] One of the main functions of the Association, as it is of any such pedigree society, was to certify animals as being genuine examples of their breed. In the case of Romney Marsh sheep, flocks were regularly inspected and all pure bred young animals were tattooed on the ear and their details recorded in the flock book. It was another important function of such an Association to issue pedigree export certificates; these were issued not for flocks but for individual sheep and they were, obviously, important to export sales.

Alfred John Hickman, the plaintiff in this case, was a flockmaster on Romney Marsh. (His nephews, Percy and Alfred Hickman, still are). The Kent or Romney Marsh Sheep Breeders' Association was registered as a company limited by guarantee on 23 April 1895. Hickman applied to join on 11 November 1905 and was elected on 12 December 1905. The first inspection of his flock took place in May 1906. There seems to have been no problem at first; indeed Hickman was elected to the Association's council in February 1912. But the fact that he resigned from the Council in December 1914 indicates that things had started to go wrong and that a dispute had arisen between Hickman and the Association. On 18 December 1914 Hickman issued his writ claiming a variety of declarations and injunctions. It appears from this writ that the dispute was a furious one. Hickman asks for the Association's secretary, Chapman, to be sacked; he wants the Association to stop trying to expel him. And there was another dispute, presumably related. Hickman claimed that the Association's minutes were not a true record; in particular it was he, Hickman, who proposed the appointment of a committee to inspect and tattoo his sheep, not Chapman. But the main point of the writ appears to be Hickman's asking for an injunction ordering the Association to register his sheep. (Why Hickman thought that a Chancery judge would be a good person to assess whether or not his sheep were pure bred Romneys does not appear in the court records).

When Hickman applied for his injunctions, declarations and orders, the Association immediately argued that he could not bring such a court action. The reason for this was said to stem from the fact that the Association was not

[2] The Association's name was changed, about twenty years ago, to the Romney Marsh Sheep Breeders' Society, to bring it more in line with the nomenclature of similar societies.

[3] Examples of such breed societies for sheep are Shropshires (1883), Oxfords (1889), Hampshires (1890), Lincolnshires (1892).

a mere unincorporated association but a registered company. It was therefore constituted by its Memorandum and Articles of Association and governed by the Companies Acts. The Articles of Association of the Kent or Romney Marsh Sheep Breeders' Association contained a provision, in Article 49, that all disputes between the Association and any member would be referred to arbitration. Now the Arbitration Act 1889 provided in effect that, if the parties to a dispute had entered into a 'written agreement' to submit such disputes to arbitration, then they could not bring an action in court about that dispute without going first to arbitration. The Association argued that Article 49 of their Articles of Association was such an agreement between them and Hickman and that therefore these Chancery proceedings must be stayed and Hickman must go to arbitration. Hickman argued that the Articles of Association were not an agreement between him and the Association and therefore he had not entered into an agreement to go to arbitration and the court could not stay these proceedings. The issue therefore became the apparently straightforward one: do the articles of association of a company constitute an agreement between the members and the company?

The problem that *Hickman* had to settle concerned the relationship between a company and its shareholders and, in particular, what is known as the statutory contract, which used to appear in s. 20 of the Companies Act 1948 and now appears in s. 14 of the Companies Act 1985. The wording of this section has not changed much since it first appeared in the Companies Act 1856. At the time of *Hickman* the relevant words were in the Companies (Consolidation) Act 1908, s. 14(1) and read as follows:

> The memorandum and articles shall, when registered, bind the company and the members thereof to the same extent and as if they had respectively been signed and sealed by each member, and contained covenants on the part of each member, his heirs, executors and administrators, to observe all the provisions of the memorandum and of the articles, subject to the provisions of this Act.

The problem which this provision creates is whether or not it has the effect of creating a contract between the members *inter se* and a contract between each member and the company. In 1937 Lord Greene admitted, in *Beattie* v. *E. and F. Beattie Ltd.*,[4] that this provision had proved controversial in the past and was likely to continue to be controversial in the future. The origins of the controversy are not difficult to trace. Because of the restrictions imposed by the Bubble Act, many business organizations were set up under deeds of settlement. Almost invariably an indenture, incorporating the association's constitution, was executed by every member and the trustees of the association. Therefore there was no problem in identifying the parties to the contract: the indentures established the contract between the members and the association. When incorporation by mere registration became possible under the Companies Act 1844, the problem still did not arise for that Act

[4] [1938] Ch. 708

required each shareholder actually to execute an indenture with a trustee of the company, and that indenture had to incorporate or refer to the company's constitution. A shareholder was defined as a person who was on the register of shareholders and who had executed such a deed.

That provision created a new problem. In the nineteenth century it was the common practice for shares not to be fully paid up. A company traded on its share capital and, where more was needed, further calls were made. When a company went into liquidation the liquidator was in the happy position of being able to call in all unpaid amounts on the shares. Shareholders receiving such calls soon discovered that, if they were on the register of shareholders but had not executed the requisite deed, they were not in fact shareholders and therefore not liable on the liquidator's calls. That, of course, was unsatisfactory and the Companies Act 1856 attempted to resolve the position by abandoning the need for an indenture actually to be signed and providing that such a deed should be implied to have been signed. That started the problem because the draftsman did not state in terms that the shareholder impliedly covenanted with the company. (He may have been justified in doing so, assuming that since the company had executed the registered deed and it was that registered deed that the shareholders were deemed to have executed, such a statement would have been otiose).

Since then all the successive Companies Acts have contained this sub-section. It is one of the most fundamental of all the provisions of company legislation because it binds the company to the members and the members to the company's constitution, ties that constitution to the Act and gives the whole thing life and force through the law as to deeds. It is odd that such a fundamentally important sub-section should be controversial. The problem for the judges stems from the fact that the sub-section says that the company and members are bound as though the shareholders had executed the deed but it does not expressly say that the company is deemed to have executed the deed. It was not too long before the significance of the apparent omission impressed itself upon the judges. One need look no further than the judgements of Kindersley, V.-C. in *Binney* v. *Ince Hall Coal and Canal Co.*[5] (under the 1844 Act) and in *Hutton* v. *Scarborough Cliff Hotel*[6] (under the 1856 Act) to see what happened. In the former case the whole judgement proceeds on the footing that the company and members are bound by the deed, whereas in the latter case no mention is made of this and the contract is described as being between the members *inter se*. Even the greatest of judges were perplexed. Lord Lindley confessed his uncertainty on more than one occasion. Farwell, J. decided in one case that the articles were 'a series of mutual covenants entered into by all the shareholders *inter se*' but, eight years later, when he was Farwell, L.J., he recanted. Stirling, J. expressly held in *Baring-Gould* v. *Sharpington Combined Pick and Shovel*

[5] 35 L.J. Ch. 363
[6] 34 L.J. Ch. 643

Syndicate[7] that section 20 did not create a contract between a company and its members, thus contradicting his widely quoted dictum in *Wood* v. *Odessa Waterworks*.[8]

Thus, up until 1909, it had been held that the company was not a party to the statutory deed at all and, as a result, it could not enforce its constitution against its shareholders, nor have the constitution enforced against itself;[9] but it had also been held that the company was a party and that the constitution was enforceable by and against the company.[10] At the same time other judges had held that the statutory deed operated both as between the company and its members and as between the members *inter se*.[11] Most of the cases were decisions of the Court of Appeal and could lead one to question the strength and effectiveness of the doctrine of precedent in those times.

In 1909 the House of Lords put an end to the dispute in the case of *Quinn and Axtens Ltd.* v. *Salmon*.[12] They held that the company was a party to the implied deed under s. 14(1) and that the company's constitution was enforceable both by and against it. That, of course, should have been the end of the matter; but *Hickman* started a whole new controversy. Mr. Hickman's case depended on the article requiring arbitration to be unenforceable against him. His counsel relied particularly on four cases where the courts had refused to enforce the articles. In his judgement Astbury, J. analyzed these cases with some care and claimed to find a distinction between them and another group of cases where the articles had been enforced. His lordship found that in the *Eley* line of cases the plaintiff had been seeking to enforce an article which did not give him rights qua shareholder. For example Eley wanted to enforce an article which appointed him solicitor to the company, Melhado sought payment of promotion fees and expenses as set out in the articles and Browne claimed that a provision in the articles gave him security of tenure of office as a director. But in the other line of cases, Astbury, J. concluded, the plaintiff had sought to enforce articles which gave them rights qua shareholders, for example the right to vote at shareholders' meetings or to receive share certificates or dividends. His lordship therefore concluded that the law was that:

> . . . first, no article can constitute a contract between the company and a third person; secondly, no right merely purporting to be given by an article to a person, whether a member or not, in a capacity other than that of a member, as solicitor, promoter, director, can be enforced against the company; and, thirdly, articles regulating the rights and obligations of the members generally as such do create

[7] [1899] 2 Ch. 80

[8] (1889) 2 Ch.D. 636

[9] See, for example, *Eley* v. *Positive Government Security Life Assurance Co.* (1876) 1 Ex.D. 88; *Melhado* v. *Porto Alegre Railway Co.* (1874) L.R. 9 C.P. 503; *Baring-Gould* v. *Sharpington Combined Pick and Shovel Syndicate*, supra.

[10] See, for example, *Pender* v. *Lushington* (1877) 6 Ch. Div. 70; *Moffat* v. *Farquhar* (1878) 7 Ch.D. 591; *Boschoek Proprietary Co.* v. *Fuke* [1906] 1 Ch.148.

[11] See, for example, *Wood* v. *Odessa Waterworks*, supra.

[12] [1909] A.C. 442.

> rights and obligations between them and the company respectively.

From this it followed, according to Astbury, J., that since, in the present case, the provision for referring disputes to arbitration regulated the rights and obligations of members generally, the Chancery proceedings would be stayed so that the matter could be referred to arbitration.

This interpretation of the sub-section, whilst settling Mr. Hickman's case, did little to settle the law, for it is loaded with more problems than confronted the judiciary before 1909. Firstly, it is impossible to reconcile it with the wording of the Act, since s. 14(1) says that the covenant extends to 'all' of the provisions of the constitution and the effect of *Hickman* is to limit it to some. Secondly, it cannot stand with the House of Lords' decision in *Quinn and Axtens Ltd.* v. *Salmon*, where the article in dispute related to Salmon's powers qua managing director. Thirdly, it puts all those provisions in a company's articles which deal with directors, secretaries or auditors outside the scope of s. 14(1). Fourthly, Astbury, J.'s distinction is only sound if there were no cases where 'outsider-right' articles were not enforced; but there is a number of such cases. Finally, it lacks common sense: for example, a shareholder is properly interested in seeing that the company's directors carry on its business in accordance with its articles and yet Astbury, J.'s reasoning puts those articles outside the scope of enforcement.

Despite all that, the case has been widely accepted ever since as a correct statement of the law. This case may not have absolutely settled English law on this point but even those who doubt its correctness treat it as the basic starting point for all discussion of the topic. So how did this important case come about and what did Butch Cassidy have to do with this valuable decision?

Clearly, whatever the legal niceties, there was a dispute about whether or not Hickman's sheep were pure bred Romneys and clearly that was very important to him. Had it not been for that, the case would never have been brought. Obviously the reason why he needed the sheep registered was in order to sell them – and to sell them as certified and tattooed Romneys.

II. Butch Cassidy's Contribution

The story of Butch Cassidy's involvement is that Hickman urgently wanted certified Romneys because he had the chance of landing a large contract for the sale of Romneys to some sheep farmers from Utah. The sheep farmers from Utah were in trouble. Their existing flocks could not withstand the poor, thin and salt-laden grasses of Utah. So why were they in Utah? They were in Utah because they had been driven out of their original grazing in Wyoming by the cattle ranchers. And the cattle ranchers had driven them out by the simple expedient of calling in Butch Cassidy, who had shot up the sheep farmers until they fled westward into Utah. Since then the sheep farmers had been all round Europe looking for salt resistant sheep. They had been sold many animals, of many breeds and none, all of which turned out to be as intolerant of salt as their original flocks. The only sheep of which they could be certain were the Romney Marsh sheep which, because of their origins on the Marshes, were salt resistant. The sheep farmers were now hardened by their previous experiences, and would only buy properly certified Romney Marsh sheep. It therefore follows that, had it not been for Butch Cassidy, Hickman would never have been so desperate to have his sheep certified and the case would never have been brought.

That is the story. The question we now have to consider is: is it true? We have not found the origin of this story nor have we found strict proof of it. What we have done is investigate the relevant background to establish the likelihood of its being true.

There were certain difficulties about introducing sheep into what is now the U.S.A. – Indians, wolves, climate, terrain and so on – but sheep were basic to the earliest settlers and, both sheep and settlers being adaptable breeds, sheep were successfully introduced with the earliest colonists. The earliest sheep in North America came up from Mexico in the sixteenth century; and in the seventeenth century the eastern states received breeding flocks with the first colonizers. The spread of sheep westwards was slow until the nineteenth century, when the expansion of sheep breeding coincides with the development of the new states and their federalization. But it should be noted that whilst, at first, the greatest concentration of sheep was in the eastern parts, the balance shifted away from the east to the wild west as the great plains were opened up, especially by the railways.

The breeds of sheep which populated the States were many and various. It seems as if new breeds of sheep are not hard to come by, either by natural selection or even by mutation. The breeding cycle being relatively short it is not difficult to produce, relatively quickly, new strains of sheep which will breed true, by crossing existing breeds. In this way new types of sheep can be produced for economic purposes – for example, to provide better or more wool or better or more meat; or for environmental purposes – for example to provide a type which will suit particular climatic or other geographical circumstances.

In the southern states the sheep were mostly Merinos or local developments of them. In the eastern states Texels, British Downs of many types, Cotswolds and other British breeds were imported and bred from but the commonest sheep were based upon Leicesters. When the British restricted the export of sheep in the eighteenth century, the Americans not only imported more Merinos but bred their own breeds – the Arlington Longwool being bred by George Washington himself. Later in the nineteenth century more British breeds were introduced: Cotswolds, Cheviots, Oxfords, Shropshire and Hampshires, Scottish Blackfaces, Dorset Horns and others. The breed of sheep missing from these lists is the Kent or Romney Marsh, a sheep to which we will return as soon as we have said something about the history of cattle in the USA.

No doubt there were cows kept for purely domestic purposes by all the European settlers from their first arrival in North America. Yet for commercial purposes Texas can be considered to be so much the chief centre of large scale commercial production as to be almost the only relevant cow rearing area until as late as the 1870s. It was from Texas that the great cattle drives took place along the trails to the markets. These markets were, at first, the towns of the eastern states. As the railways moved across the states, the trails moved westward too and the market became the railhead. Some railheads developed into permanent cattle markets largely on account of the meat packing stations founded there. Other markets were temporary – such as a gold rush town. It seems that it was Texas cattle drovers, driving cattle to the market created by the Colorado gold rush, who first discovered that what had, until then, been widely thought of as the Great American Desert, inhospitable to man and beast alike, was in fact not one and that the Great Plains were ideal stock country. As the railroad moved west so did cattle ranching, reaching Wyoming in the 1870s. Thus the cattle came to Wyoming from the south in about 1870; the sheep came to Wyoming from the east in about 1870.

It was treated as gospel in the Great Plains in the 1870s that 'sheep and cattle don't mix'. It was certainly well known that cattle men and sheep herders didn't mix. This rivalry probably started as a racial prejudice, the sheep herders being mainly Mexican and the cattle ranchers mainly north European. It was compounded by their very different styles of life, dictated by the differences in tending sheep and cattle. It was rationalized by the agricultural science of the time. The received wisdom, anyway amongst the cowmen, was based on the fact that cows and sheep graze differently in two main respects. Firstly, cows, because they loop grass into their mouths with their long tongues and then bite it off, do not crop grass as low as sheep which, with a split lip and incisors, can bite it off at ground level or even below, roots and all, thus reducing the grasses' chances of regeneration, especially in hot, dry climates where any remaining roots are burned off in the sun. Secondly, cows spread out widely when grazing and therefore do not strip an area before moving on; sheep graze in tight flocks, stripping whole areas and, with their small and sharp-edged hooves, cut up the ground and compact it solid. As if that were not bad enough, cowmen thought that cattle would not graze where sheep had grazed before or drink where sheep had drunk before. Land which had been affected by sheep in these ways was said to be 'sheeped off'.

Therefore, as sheep and cattle poured into the mid west, conflicts over the use of the range broke out. Despite informal sheep deadlines laid down by the cowmen, some of which held for years, the sheep kept coming and the deadlines were broken. The cowmen spread saltpetre on the ranges; the sheep ate it and died. The cowmen drove herds of sheep over precipices (they simply drove the leaders over and the rest followed). If that did not deter the sheep herders – and it did not – they shot the sheep and then they shot the sheep herders. The sheep herders shot back. Feuds broke out. These episodes of violence, with the cowmen trying to clear the sheep herders off the range, are known as the range wars.

The best of the range wars was undoubtedly the Tonto Basin War, which was conducted in the aptly named Pleasant Valley, Arizona, between the Graham clan, representing the cows, and the Tewksbury clan, representing the sheep. The war began in 1877 and came to a satisfactory conclusion in 1892 when the last of the Tewksburys killed the last of the Grahams.

The range wars lasted longest in Wyoming where the animosity between cowmen and sheep herders was aggravated by the rapid worsening of the grazing land in the last decade of the nineteenth century. The cowmen attributed this to the sheep, though it was more probably caused by general overgrazing by both cows and sheep and by the repeated droughts of the decade. Whatever the cause, the result was that much of the pasture land reverted to sage bush scrub. The last of the range wars did not end until 1909, when the War of the Ten Sleep Country of Wyoming reached its finale. In that last incident cowmen shot dead several hundred sheep, not to mention three sheep herders, piled them all onto a funeral pyre and burned the lot. This so irritated the Wyoming Wool Growers' Association that they offered large rewards for information and, as a result, seven cowboys were convicted of the murders and sent to the state penitentiary for long terms of imprisonment. The effect of the these range wars was to drive the sheep farmers still further west and north west. From Wyoming they spread into Idaho and Utah.

Butch Cassidy was born George Leroy Parker, in Wide Valley, Utah, in 1866, where his father had a cattle ranch, much of the stock for which appears to have been proceeds of rustling. Butch grew up with a great admiration for a cowboy and rustler called Mike Cassidy, who was employed by his father. When Mike Cassidy withdrew to Mexico before the law caught up with him, George Parker changed his name to George Cassidy and left Utah to work in the mines in Colorado. There he fell into bad (or worse) company and joined the McCarthy gang, carrying out his first train robbery in 1887. He already had a reputation as a good shot. The first rodeo in Wyoming, and probably anywhere, was apparently held in the early 1880s at Laramie Plains and was organized by the Two Bar Cattle Company. One of the performers was George Cassidy, who 'put on a fine bit of fancy pistol shooting'.

When the McCarthy gang broke up in 1890 Cassidy worked on several ranches in Wyoming until 1892, when he became a butcher at Rock Springs – and thereby picked up his famous nickname. In 1894 he was convicted of stealing horses (which either indicates that he was back into crime or that the meat in his shop was of dubious quality). When he was released several months before his two-year prison sentence expired, he swore to the Governor of Wyoming that he would commit no further robberies in Wyoming. The story is that he kept this promise: he planned robberies in Wyoming but he did not himself take part in them – he only took part in robberies outside Wyoming. With that judicious interpretation of the promise he doubtless felt free to commit crimes other than robbery in Wyoming.

From about 1896 onwards Cassidy established a stronghold and hideaway at Brown's Hole in the Uinta Mountains, at almost exactly the point where Wyoming, Utah and Colorado meet. In due course he was joined there by the Hole in the Wall gang. It is said that when one hundred or so badmen left the Hole in the Wall to move to Brown's Hole, they pillaged every sheep camp they encountered on the way and killed all the sheep. At about this time Cassidy and the others at Brown's Hole became known as the Wild Bunch. The gang included, of course, the Sundance Kid. From their fortress the Wild Bunch ravaged the neighbourhood and continued to do so until 1900.

It is of passing interest to note that Cassidy left the Wyoming area largely as a result of a novel but misplaced attempt to establish a legal aid system. When one of his confederates, Matt Warner, was arrested on a double murder charge, Cassidy got two of his henchmen to rob a bank. The proceeds were used to pay for Douglas V. Preston to represent Warner. In fact Preston was paid a retainer by Cassidy and represented several of the Wild Bunch before becoming the Attorney-General of Wyoming. But the Bank which had been robbed was a member of the American Bankers' Association, and they set Pinkertons onto the Wild Bunch; from then on the pressure was on. In about 1900 Cassidy left Brown's Hole and mainly used Fort Worth as a centre. After a last train robbery in Montana in 1901, Cassidy went to New York and thence to South America, not to return to the United States again. In 1909 he and the Sundance Kid were killed by Bolivian soldiers in San Vicente. Or not, as the case may be.

The most relevant parts of this story are that Butch Cassidy was pursuing a criminal career (actual participation in robberies excluded) in Wyoming from about 1890 to about 1900; and that he was a cowboy, a cattleman and not a sheep man. He was a gun for hire in Wyoming at the time of the range wars, but we have no evidence that he actually participated in them.[13]

III. Romney Marsh Sheep

One of the least startling of our discoveries in the course of this important research has been that Kent or Romney Marsh sheep come from Romney Marsh, in Kent. Apart from Soay sheep, they may be the oldest breed in the country. They are said to be of Roman origin though there appears to have been an infusion of Leicester and Cheviot stock at some time. No doubt natural selection played a great part in developing their particular characteristics, and the unyielding and unchanging conditions of the Marsh, to which they are ideally suited, has kept them that way.

Most English lawyers know of the Romney Marshes because of the Laws of

[13] This, and the preceding three sections, are based mainly on: M.L. Ryder, *Sheep and Man* (1983); Mari Sandoz, *The Cattle Men* (1961); Paul I. Wellman, *The Trampling Herd* (1958 ed.); Robert Elman, *Badmen of the West* (New York, 1974); Will Henry, *Alias Butch Cassidy* (New York, 1967).

Romney Marsh, a regulatory regime for reclaiming and maintaining marshes and fens, which was the *fons et origo* of much modern drainage law in England. The Romney Marsh (and its neighbouring marshes) were and are flat, low lying, exposed to the ravages of the elements and decidedly bleak in winter but as hot as you get in England in the summer. The pasture was mainly perennial rye grass and wild white clover: a not particularly dainty repast. The sheep are, therefore, of a particularly hardy variety even if, as sheep go, they are not unattractive. The British Wool Marketing Board prosaically describes them as 'hornless sheep with white, broad face, black nose, poll well covered with wool. Compact body with broad neck and shoulders and short, strong-boned legs'. William Cobbett was somewhat more poetic, referring to Romneys as 'white as a piece of paper' and 'very pretty and large . . . With these sheep the Marsh abounds in every part of it and the sight is very beautiful'. In 1796 the Agricultural Society declared the Romney to be 'perhaps the most valuable sheep in the world'.

We have found the following characteristics claimed for this breed:

1. The breed produces a very dense and fine wool, probably the best wool of the longwool breeds.
2. It provides good lamb and mutton.
3. It matures very early and therefore needs less care and protection when young.
4. It is particularly tough and hardy: it can withstand extreme environments, both the cold and wet and the hot and dry; it has particularity hard hooves which resist foot rot and enable it to survive in marshy conditions; it has a high resistance to worms.
5. It is a particularly good grazer. This results from its unusual but characteristic pattern of grazing. Instead of flocking closely together to graze, Romneys spread out and distribute themselves evenly over whatever pasture is available to them. They remain so spread out even at night. But they are not given to straying and require minimal fencing. This means that they are tolerant of tight grazing systems or will get the best out of poor pastures. (We would add, although the standard sheep reference works do not make the point, that this habit of spreading evenly would not only make Romneys good for foldage, but would also have made them appeal to those who supported the theory that close flocks of sheep caused soil compaction, reducing its agricultural value)
6. It is said to be resistant to salt and therefore able to live in a salty seaside atmosphere and to eat salt-laden pasture.

The first five of these characteristics can be established by scientific means; the last characteristic is often claimed but there appears to be nothing to establish it beyond a peradventure. However, the original wild sheep, from which modern domesticated animals derive, were animals of the desert margins and well adapted to a salty diet; and, further, they did not flock together, flocking being a habit which people have bred for. Soay sheep, the most primitive breed in this country, are well able to live off seaweed – and also do not flock. Romneys are a very old breed and do not flock closely. It seems reasonable to suppose that that if a relatively primitive sheep retains one primitive characteristic it would, at least in some measure, retain the other.

These are obviously useful animals. The value of the breed is demonstrated by the fact that is has spread over much of England. Although in Kent they were known as Romney Marsh sheep, outside Kent, and particularly in Smithfield, they were known as Kent sheep. But when they started being exported they were usually known as Romneys, not Kents. Because of the vast numbers of them that were exported all over the world the National Sheep Association refer to them as 'the best known sheep in the world'. The case of New Zealand is particularly striking. The first sale of Romneys to New Zealand was in 1851. Now 80 per cent of the sheep in the North Island are Romneys and 40 per cent of those in the South Island are Romneys. Around Canterbury in the South Island Romney ewes were crossed with Southdown rams to produce fat lambs, the sliced up bits of which are known as Canterbury lamb. Most of the New Zealand lamb now eaten in this country is predominantly Romney.

The characteristics of Romneys would have been particularly attractive to sheep herders of Wyoming or Utah. Clearly Romneys are good wool and meat sheep and would meet all but very specialized requirements on those scores. Their particular hardiness and ability to withstand extremes of climatic conditions would also be useful in the hot wastes of Utah. But their grazing characteristics were also important: their habit of spreading out to graze both met the objections of the cattle men and also ensured that they made the best use of the poorer pastures which would be found in Utah. It seems unfortunate for the case that their resistance to salt cannot be proved; and it also has to be pointed out that not all of Utah is a salt desert. Nevertheless a prospective purchaser from Utah would know that some Utah land was salt affected and would be persuaded, by looking at Romney Marsh, that the sheep must be salt resistant. Having examined the characteristics of many other breeds of sheep, we cannot find one that would clearly be a more attractive prospect for sheep herders recently thrust into Utah. Yet it has to be said that the export records show that there has only ever been a small and occasional sale to the States.[14]

It will be remembered that the story to be tested is that Butch Cassidy shot up the sheep herders of Wyoming so badly that they departed into Utah, where the land was so salty that salt resistant sheep were needed; therefore the sheep they wanted were Romneys and, for the chance of good sales to

[14] This section is based on private communications to the authors and on: British Wool Marketing Board, *Sheep Breeds: Their Wool and Its Uses* (1983); E.H. Carrier, *The Pastoral Heritage of Britain* (1936); Lord Ernle, *English Farming, Past and Present*, 5th ed. (1936); Elizabeth Henson, *British Sheep Breeds* (Princes Risborough, 1986); National Sheep Association, *British Sheep* (1987 ed.); Kenneth A. Ponting, *Sheep of the World* (1980); R. Trow-Smith, *A History of British Livestock Husbandry, 1700–1900* (1959); M.L. Ryder, op. cit.

them, Hickman so desperately needed his sheep certified that he sued the Kent or Romney Marsh Sheep Breeders' Association. How far does the evidence substantiate the story? Did Butch Cassidy affect the development of English law?

There are two possible approaches. One is to accept the facts and to debate causation – to agree that the story is correct in all its details but to assert that one cannot argue from them that Butch Cassidy influenced English law. Using this approach, the case against Butch Cassidy's influence is that the chain of causation is too long. On the reasonable forseeability test the case for Butch Cassidy would fail. Had the officious bystander said to Butch Cassidy as he rode into Wyoming: 'Do you think that if you carry on with what you plan, the English law relating to s. 20 of the Companies Act will be settled?' then, whatever Mr. Cassidy might have said or done by way of response, a reasonable man would doubtless have answered 'No'. That would settle the issue.

Of course, the facts pass the 'but for' test. But for Mr. Cassidy's shooting up the sheep herders, this case would not have been brought. Doubtless if this particular case had not been brought, a similar case would have been, by someone in roughly similar circumstances; but it might well not have been in quite the form it actually took and it may well not have come before Astbury, J. The result might well have been very different. On this view of causation, we think it highly arguable that Butch Cassidy did influence the development of English company law.

The other approach is to accept causation and dispute the facts. Our opinion on the facts, which are of course a matter for the jury, is that the connection is not proved to the criminal law standard of 'beyond reasonable doubt'. We cannot pin the attacks on the sheep men on to Butch Cassidy personally, though it seems likely that he would have been involved; we have no good evidence on the salty part of the story, but it remains a possibility; we have some slight doubts about the dates tying up, as the gap between Butch Cassidy leaving Wyoming about 1900 and the case being brought in 1914 seems a little large.

Yet, if the matter is to be heard by a civil jury and decided upon the balance of probabilities, we would ask for judgement in our favour. It could have been Butch Cassidy and it could have been salt. We would suggest that what may well have happened is that as the sheep farmers spread westward they found that Wyoming and other cattle states were inhospitable. Partly for reasons of economics and pressure on grazing grounds, they went further west, into Utah and other states; they were also encouraged to make this move by the range wars, conducted by cowboys very much of the Butch Cassidy ilk. Clearly they were moving into poorer pasture lands and wanted sheep which could make better use of them. Bearing in mind the received wisdom of the day about the destructive effect of sheep grazing and its causes, the Romney Marsh sheep would look like a very good bet on all counts. Sometime round about 1910, give or take several years either way, there very probably were American sheep herders in Europe looking for a hardy sheep pretty much like the Romney. Doubtless Hickman wanted to get in on the act. The fact that the records show very few exports to the States demonstrates only that the Association thwarted him in the attempt. No doubt a vicious squabble amongst the breeders, based on what sheep were or were not to be considered pure bred Romneys, would have sent the American farmers hurrying elsewhere. Stories of the range wars would have been around in England at the same time as the American farmers were there. The facts would have been woven together and embroidered with the name of one of the most charismatic of the gunmen.[15]

[15] The authors would like to express their thanks to: David Roberts of the Romney Sheep Breeders' Society; Dr. Mike Curran of Wye College, University of London; the library staff of Harper Adams College; the British Wool Marketing Board; Steve Roddie of Wolverhampton Polytechnic. The extent and nature of the authors' indebtedness to Reg Scragg, LL.B., M.Phil., will be obvious.

Chapter 13

The Burdens of Empire and the Legalization of White Supremacy in Canada, 1860–1910*

John P.S. McLaren

'Whereas the incoming of Chinese to British Columbia largely exceeds that of any other class of immigrant, and the population so introduced are fast becoming superior in number to our own race; are not disposed to be governed by our laws; are dissimilar in habits and occupation from our people; evade the payment of taxes justly due to the Government; are governed by pestilential habits; are useless in instances of emergency; habitually desecrate graveyards by the removal of bodies therefrom; and generally the laws governing the whites are found to be inapplicable to Chinese and such Chinese are inclined to habits subversive of the comfort and well being with the community'.[1]

In this preamble to the Chinese Regulation Act 1884 which the Chinese ambassador to the Court of St. James, Lew Ta-Jen, characterized as 'a series of charges such as was never before made in a public document against a people of a friendly nation',[2] the government of British Columbia put on public record its deep antipathy to Chinese immigration to and settlement in Canada's most westerly province.

Although the sentiments might not have been expressed so openly and blatantly, they were shared by the governments of other white colonies and dominions in the British Empire, as well as by those of the western states of the United States of America, especially California.

This essay examines the evolution of anti-oriental legislation in British Columbia. In the process consideration is given to: (a) the legal models developed elsewhere in the British Empire which were employed or appealed to in furthering the policy of anti-Asian discrimination in Canada; (b) the extent to which imperial and metropolitan interests limited or tempered the impulse to institutionalize notions of white supremacy; and (c) the ideological and cultural influences which inspired the legislation and conditioned the reaction to it.

*My thanks are due to Burt Harris for his help with the background research.

[1] Act to Regulate the Chinese Population of British Columbia, S[tatutes of] B[ritish] C[olumbia] 1884, c. 4, preamble.

[2] C.O. 881/8, print 129, 1888, 1–3 (letter from the ambassador to the Earl of Rosebery, British foreign secretary, enclosed with letter from Rosebery to Colonial Office, 5 August 1886).

As was the case in several of the Australian colonies, in New Zealand and in California, the first Chinese in British Columbia went to pan for gold, on the mainland, in 1859–60.[3] Others followed to satisfy the demand for household servants in Victoria, the capital of Vancouver Island, where white female domestics were few and far between. Until the mid 1860s the presence of the Chinese was suffered. Most of them were distant from centres of population, and those who were not, occupied jobs for which there were no white takers. Moreover, as a group they were thought to be 'sojourners' who would pass on in due course and return home.[4] They also received protection at a formal, legal level from the policies of James Douglas, the governor of the twin colonies of Vancouver Island and British Columbia and Matthew Baillie Begbie, the first professional judge, appointed by London to the mainland colony in 1858. These were men committed to British notions of law and order and equal treatment by the law of all who lived under the British flag. They both made it clear that they would not stand for discrimination against the Chinese.[5]

Outward hostilities toward the Chinese began to develop in the mid 1860s, as the gold ran out and white and Chinese workers looked for jobs elsewhere in the economy. Racist attitudes were quick to surface within the white community. Fears deriving from the prospect of competition in the labour market with Chinese soon expanded into a set of economic grievances, including charges that they unfairly vied for trade and business, refused to invest their wages in British Columbia, preferring to send the money home to China, and wilfully eluded payment of local taxes.[6] These materialist concerns fed on an established pattern of racial stereotyping which branded the newcomers as generally uncivilized and inferior.[7] They were picked on because they were seen as remaining socially aloof and culturally distinct in their own quarters. As they resisted attempts at spiritual assimilation by Christian missionaries, the label 'heathen' was readily applied to them. They were charged with being innately immoral, for the few Chinese women who arrived on the west coast seemed in most instances to occupy the role of prostitutes. The sanitary practices of the Chinese community came in for heavy criticism. There was particular revulsion at the custom of exhuming

[3] W.P. Ward, *White Canada Forever* (Montreal, 1978), 23; P. Roy, *A White Man's Province: British Columbia Politicians and Chinese and Japanese Immigration, 1858–1914* (Vancouver, 1989), 4–5.

[4] See comments of Amor de Cosmos, editor of the *Victoria Daily Colonist*, looking forward to the involvement of the Chinese in building a transcontinental railway – 10 May 1860. Shortly thereafter De Cosmos, a future premier of the province, became a leading exclusionist.

[5] B. Gough, 'Keeping British Columbia British: The Law and Order Question on the Gold Mining Frontier', *Huntington Library Quart.*, xxxviii (1975), 269.

[6] Ward, op. cit., 30.

[7] Ibid., 29–30. On the roots and development of the racial stereotyping of Chinese in North America, see S. Miller, *The Unwelcome Immigrant: The American Image of the Chinese, 1785–1882* (Berkeley, 1969).

bodies to return the bones to China in accordance with traditional burial rites. They were also considered to be a social threat because of an apparent addiction to gambling and opium smoking.[8] All this was easily translated into the rhetoric of both physical and moral contagion and provided the basis for continuing and ever more intense demands that the growth of this 'depraved population' be stemmed and existing residents be 'encouraged' to return to their homeland.

During the 1860s and early 1870s there were occasional calls from British Columbia politicians for the imposition of a discriminatory head tax against the Chinese.[9] A tax of this sort had already been introduced in the Australian colonies of Victoria and New South Wales in the mid 1850s and early 1860s (over the expression of some misgivings in London) as a means of discouraging the migration of Chinese to their gold fields.[10] Tension and violence had occurred in both jurisdictions as white miners reacted hostilely to the presence in their midst of the 'celestials', as the Chinese were pejoratively described.[11] The calls for a head tax failed to gain majority support in British Columbia, because, it was supposed, it was beyond the jurisdiction of the province under the British North America Act of 1867, which reserved matters relating to aliens and naturalization, and trade and commerce to the dominion government.[12]

In 1878 (a year when an upsurge of Chinese immigrants to British Columbia occurred) the legislature, following the lead of Queensland in 1877, enacted a discriminatory, quarterly tax against Chinese residents in the province.[13] When this legislation was challenged in *Tai Sing* v. *MacGuire* it was made clear by Justice John Hamilton Gray that the legislation was both *ultra vires* and openly discriminatory.[14] He added that, if special legislation was needed to deal with the immigration of Chinese, then Ottawa would have to enact it under Canadian constitutional arrangements.

The British Columbia authorities seem to have accepted this judicial advice, resorting to lobbying of the federal government, which grew in intensity as large numbers of Chinese labourers were hired to complete the final stages of

[8] M. Zaffroni, *The Great Chain of Being: Racism and Imperialism in Colonial Victoria* (M.A. Thesis, History, Victoria, 1987), 18–23, 152–69.

[9] See report in *Victoria Daily Colonist*, 19 May 1865 on motion introduced in the colonial legislative assembly by G.E. Dennes of Saltspring Island, and B.C., *Journals of the Legislative Assembly*, i, 1872, 15–16 for first motions before the new provincial legislative assembly of John Robson, M.L.A. for Nanaimo.

[10] See Stat. Vict., 1855, no.39; Stat. N.S.W., 1861, no.3.

[11] R. Huttenback, *Racism and Empire: White Settlers and Coloured Immigrants in the British Self-Governing Colonies, 1830–1910* (Ithaca, N.Y., 1976), 59–61.

[12] British North America Act 1867, 30 & 31 Vict., c. 3 (U.K.) s. 91(25) and (2) respectively.

[13] Act to Provide for the Better Collection of Provincial Taxes from Chinese, S.B.C. 1878, c. 35 ss. 2, 8, based on Act to Amend 'The Gold Fields Act' 1874 so far as Relates to Asiatic and African Aliens and in Other Respects, Stat. Q'ld, 1877, no.12.

[14] (1878) 1 B.C.L.R., 101 (S.C.).

the construction of the Canadian Pacific Railway through British Columbia's mountain ranges.[15]

The frustration at resistance by Ottawa to enacting Chinese restriction legislation which, as the Prime Minister, Sir John A. MacDonald said, would mean abandonment of the railroad,[16] led the British Columbia legislature to try the statutory route again in 1884. Both impressed and worried by the fact the United States Congress had closed the door to further immigration by Chinese labourers in 1882 and aware that the Australian colonies were pressing for further restrictions on Chinese entry, the legislature passed a package of bills in 1884, again citing Australian precedents and aspirations. The Chinese Immigration Act,[17] which sought to ban further immigration to British Columbia, was disallowed by the Canadian Governor General, the Marquis of Lansdowne.[18] The Chinese Regulation Act,[19] which purported to impose an annual tax of $10.00 on all Chinese residents of the province, was struck down by Justice Henry Pellew Crease of the British Columbia Supreme Court in *R.* v. *Wing Chong* as unconstitutional, not only because it trenched upon Federal jurisdiction over aliens, and trade and commerce, and was patently discriminatory, but also because it infringed on imperial treaty obligations to China.[20] The Act provoked a strong reaction from the Chinese which induced the Foreign Office in London to issue a letter of apology.[21]

Despite these rebuffs, the primary strategy of the British Columbia authorities, which was to shame Ottawa into action, succeeded. The Conservative government of Sir John A. MacDonald, aware that with the completion of the Canadian Pacific Railway there would be a surfeit of Chinese on the employment market, sought to stem further immigration.[22] The Dominion Chinese Immigration Act of 1885 was modelled on earlier Australian legislation.[23] It introduced a $50.00 head tax. At the same time it incorporated a tonnage limit of one Chinese immigrant per fifty tons on any vessel bringing such nationals to Canada. This latter expedient had first been incorporated into legislation of the state of Victoria in 1855 at the suggestion of the then Colonial Secretary, the duke of Newcastle,

15 P. Roy, 'A Choice between Evils: The Chinese and the Construction of the Canadian Pacific Railway in British Columbia', *The C.P.R. West: The Iron Road and the Making of a Nation*, H. Dempsey, ed. (Vancouver, 1984), 13–34.

16 H.C., *Debates*, 30 April 1883, 905 (MacDonald).

17 S.B.C. 1884, c. 3.

18 *Canada Gazette*, 1884, xvii, no.41, 1586.

19 S.B.C. 1884, c. 4.

20 (1885) 1 B.C.R., pt. II, 150 (B.C.S.C.).

21 See above, n.2.

22 Sir John, ever the wily politician, made sure that he had control of both the agenda and the panacea by appointing a federal Royal Commission on Chinese Immigration with two reliable commissioners, his own Secretary of State, Joseph Chapleau, and B.C. Justice John Hamilton Gray, to examine the problem and make recommendations on legislation, see *Report and Evidence* (Ottawa, 1885).

23 Act to Restrict and Regulate Chinese Immigration into Canada, S.C. 1885, c. 71, based in particular on Act to Restrict the Influx of Chinese into New South Wales, Stat. N.S.W. 1881, no.II.

who professed to be concerned about the conditions in which Chinese were transported to the Australian colonies.[24] It had been avidly seized upon by the Australian colonies and later New Zealand as a means of controlling the pace and flow of those migrating from China.[25] That the Australian colonies had by the 1880s effectively blunted the concerns of the imperial government about the adverse impact of this type of legislation on its treaty relations with China is evident in statements in the debates in Ottawa over the legislation, which indicated that London had no objection to what was proposed.[26] Concern for Chinese sensitivities which had induced the British government to reserve some earlier Australian legislation (especially that from Queensland) was fading.

By 1885 Canada shared with Australia and New Zealand a two-tiered immigration policy embodied in: (a) the Immigration Act with a low entry fees and tonnage ratio, designed to encourage immigration from European countries;[27] (b) the Chinese Immigration Act with a differential and high entry tax and tonnage ratio calculated to reduce Chinese immigration to a trickle.[28] This latter system, it was supposed, would placate anti-Chinese hysteria in British Columbia as well as preserving the tattered vestiges of imperial concern for British treaty obligations to China.

The special dominion legislation was in fact effective in reducing the flow of Chinese to British Columbia, a process assisted by the refusal of the federal government to allow the wives or families of existing Chinese residents to join them in Canada.[29] As a consequence overt anti-oriental feeling faded in British Columbia between 1885 and 1895. It was to revive with a vengeance, as it did in Australia and New Zealand, in the mid 1890s with the realization that a new Asian 'intruder' had established a foothold in the province. A combination of British Columbia employers looking for contract labour, the peregrinations of Japanese fishermen and overcrowding and high taxes in Japan led to a modest migration from that country to the Canadian west coast beginning in the late 1880s.[30] The result was that by 1895 there were the makings of a definable Japanese presence there. As it was initially a male, sojourner community with its own strong cultural identity and resistant to the influence of the dominant social culture, the stereotypes applied to the Chinese were readily transferred

[24] C.O., 411/1, no.12, Newcastle to Governor Latrobe, 29 January 1853; 202/60, no.22, Newcastle to Governor Fitzroy, 5 February 1853.

[25] Stat. Vict., 1855, no.39; Stat. S.A., 1857, no.3; Stat. N.S.W., 1861, no.3; Stat. Q'ld, no.8, 1877; Stat. N.Z., no.47, 1881.

[26] H.C., *Debates*, 2 July 1885, 3004 (Chapleau).

[27] Act Respecting Immigration and Immigrants, S.C. 1869, c. 10, ss. 2, 3, as amended S.C. 1872, c. 28, s. 1; S.C. 1875, c.15, s. 2.

[28] See above, n.23.

[29] The dominion government was only willing to make an exception in the case of Chinese wives of European husbands, see Act to Amend 'The Chinese Immigration Act', S.C. 1887, c. 35, s. 1.

[30] K. Adachi, *The Enemy that Never Was* (Toronto, 1976), 6–16; Roy, above n.3, 81–83.

to it.[31] If anything they were sharpened by concern flowing from the apparent industrial progress and growing military power of Japan.

Dealing with Japanese immigration at a legislative level was more difficult than in the case of the Chinese. Britain had signed a Treaty of Commerce and Navigation with Japan in 1894 which included provisions on free movement of subjects of both countries.[32] Although the treaty was not binding on white self-governing dominions without their accession, the British government was very concerned not to offend the Japanese whose country, in contrast to China, was seen as the rising power in the Far East.[33] When several Australian colonies and New Zealand in 1896 sought to extend their anti-Chinese immigration legislation to 'other Asians' the legislation was reserved for the consideration of London because of a possible conflict with imperial treaty obligations to Japan.[34] The British government was faced with the challenge of how to balance concern for Japanese sensibilities with the conflicting desires of settlers in the white dominions. It was Joseph Chamberlain, the Colonial Secretary in the Conservative government of the marquis of Salisbury who rose to the challenge. Chamberlain, the very quintessence of the high imperialism of the turn of the century, was a firm believer in the supremacy and civilizing mission of the British race and was committed to strengthening both the economic and military links between Britain and its dominions.[35] At the same time he recognized the importance to British interests of placating Japan.

The solution to the immigration problem which he seized upon was readily at hand, recently devised by the legislature of Natal, one of Great Britain's South African colonies, to stem immigration from India. The white population of the colony, which had relied on indentured labour from India for many years, developed increasing antipathy to free Indian immigration, which together with the previously indentured population had produced virtual parity in the Indian and white populations by 1891.[36] The legal solution devised by the whites to cut off further Indian entry was the so-called Natal Act enacted in 1897, which applied a simple language test to all would-be immigrants.[37] The latter were required to fill out an application in 'a language of Europe'. It was correctly supposed that this would be beyond Indian immigrants whose mother tongues were 'non-European' and most of whom were illiterate in any event. From

[31] Ward, op. cit., 97–98, 102–103, 110–14; Roy, above n.3, 81–88.

[32] L. Herslet, *Herslet's Commercial Treaties*, xix (1895), 691.

[33] See W. Langer, *The Diplomacy of Imperialism, 1890–1902* (New York, 1956), 460–61, 472–73, 491, 680–83, 776–77.

[34] Huttenback, op. cit., 156–62.

[35] C. Brown and R. Cook, *Canada, 1896–1921: A Nation Transformed* (Toronto, 1974), 30–32. On Chamberlain's views on race, see W. Mock, 'The Function of "Race" in Imperialist Ideologies: the Example of Joseph Chamberlain', *National and Racialist Movements in Britain and Germany Before 1914*, P. Kennedy and A. Nicholls, ed. (1981), 190.

[36] On the early history of the migration of indentured East Indians to Natal, see Huttenback, op. cit., 52–58.

[37] Immigration Restriction Act, Stat. Natal, 1897, no.1, s. 3.

Britain's point of view the solution was attractive because it made no reference to particular races or peoples.

Chamberlain succeeded in persuading both Australian and New Zealand leaders in London for Queen Victoria's diamond jubilee in 1897 that this was the tack to take.[38] The Natal 'formula' was adopted in New Zealand[39] and became the centrepiece of the 'white Australia' policy with the establishment of the Commonwealth in 1901.[40] The colonial secretary also suggested that the formula might be the answer to Canada's Asiatic immigration problems.

The dominion government under the leadership of Sir Wilfred Laurier, the Liberal prime minister elected in 1896, endeavoured to ignore and, where necessary, to resist what were considered to be the ranting of the 'red-necks' on the Pacific coast.[41] That was easier said than done. Following the lead of Australia and New Zealand, the British Columbia government sought to employ legislation to stem the flow of Japanese immigrants. For the moment accepting that the dominion occupied the field in immigration legislation, the British Columbia legislature was asked to pass labour regulation legislation in 1897 and 1898 designed to cut off employment opportunities for Chinese and Japanese workers in any enterprise established by private act of the legislature; these were typically public works, utilities and transportation operations.[42] When this legislation was passed, and swift and unfavourable reaction was communicated by diplomatic representatives of the Japanese government,[43] Chamberlain sought to intervene, pointing to the adverse affect that such action could have on Anglo-Japanese relations.[44] In further correspondence, while emphasizing the need to remain sensitive to Japanese sensibilities, he also made it clear that a strategy was needed which would placate white anxieties in British Columbia. The answer for Canada lay in the Natal formula for, he said, 'it is not the practical exclusion of Japanese to which the Government of the Mikado objects, but their exclusion *nominatim*, which specifically stamps

[38] Huttenback, op. cit., 162–68; M. Ollivier, *The Colonial and Imperial Conferences from 1887 to 1937*, i (Ottawa, 1954), 138–39, 144.

[39] Act to Place Certain Restrictions on Immigration into New Zealand, Stat. N.Z., 1899, no.33.

[40] Act to Amend the Immigration Acts, 1901–1908, Commonwealth Acts, 1910, no.10.

[41] See e.g. the vigorous response of the Commissioner of Inland Revenue to suggestions from M.P.s from B.C. that the Chinese were 'filth' and only valuable when dead, H.C., *Debates*, 14 September 1896, 1347, 1359 (De Lotbiniere).

[42] Act Relating to the Employment of Chinese or Japanese Persons on Works Carried on under Franchises Granted by Private Acts, S.B.C. 1897, c. 1. As its title indicates, this was a statute designed to establish a general clause to be included in all subsequent private Acts incorporating named companies. When it was reserved by the lieutenant-governor, the B.C. legislature passed the same legislation in 1898, S.B.C. 1898, c. 28.

[43] F. Gisborne and A. Fraser, *Correspondence and Reports of the Minister of Justice and Orders in Council upon the Subject of Provincial Legislation, 1896–1920*, ii (Ottawa, 1922), 531–33 (Letter from Tatszgoro Nosse, Japanese consul general to Governor General Lord Aberdeen, 15 October 1897); 539–40 (Letter from S. Shimuzu, Japanese consul in Vancouver to Aberdeen, 10 May 1898).

[44] Ibid., 531–33 (Letter from Colonial Secretary, Joseph Chamberlain, to Lord Aberdeen, 15 October 1897).

the whole nation as undesirable persons'.[45]

Ironically this advice was adopted by the government of British Columbia and rejected by the dominion authorities. Beginning in 1900 the former introduced legislation which sought to apply a language barrier, both to new entrants to the province from outside Europe and those already resident who were seeking employment in public or semi-public enterprises. In each instance the British Columbia Immigration[46] and Labour Regulation Acts[47] were disallowed by Ottawa. The provincial governments of the period were primarily motivated by a desire to pressure Ottawa into action, although it is also possible that they were encouraged by a more empathetic local judiciary (often drawn from the ranks of former provincial politicians) and the Privy Council's sanitizing of the process of constitutional interpretation to believe that constitutional challenge might succeed.[48]

The Laurier government had for its part concluded that a formal legal approach to the problem of Japanese immigration was not the route to take.[49] The prime minister seems to have been averse to any public stance which would suggest a commitment to curb the free flow of commerce and peoples to and from Canada.[50] Moreover, he was in the process of developing foreign and international trade policies which would increase Canada's visibility and prestige not only within the empire but also within the international community at large. For the dominion government the appropriate way to approach the Japanese problem was by diplomatic means. This strategy was made possible by an official undertaking of the government of Japan in 1900 to ensure that its local prefects limited dramatically immigration from the regions of Japan to Canada.[51] For the Japanese, who had shrewdly observed that legislation cutting off access to those speaking non-European languages was a flimsy attempt at shrouding anti-Japanese legislation, this was an acceptable compromise. For Canada it meant preserving the goodwill of an important military power and future trading partner in the Pacific region.

Laurier was willing to make concessions to British Columbia on Chinese

[45] Ibid., 554–55 (Letter from Chamberlain to Governor General Earl Minto, 23 March 1899).

[46] Act to Regulate Immigration into British Columbia, S.B.C. 1900, c. 11; 1902, c. 34; 1904, c. 26; 1905, c. 28; 1907, c. 21; 1908, c. 23.

[47] Act Relating to the Employment on Works Carried on under Franchises Granted by Private Acts, S.B.C. 1900, c. 14; 1902, c. 38; 1903, c. 14; 1904, c. 30; 1905, c. 81.

[48] The first generation of provincial judges who were sympathetic to the Chinese, including Justice Crease and Chief Justice Begbie, had retired or died by 1900. With them went any significant concern for exposing the discriminatory motives of the provincial authorities in enacting anti-oriental legislation. The illegitimacy of courts commenting on the merits of legislation under constitutional challenge was established in *Union Collieries* v. *Bryden* [1899] A.C. 580 (P.C., Can.) and confirmed in *Cunningham* v. *Tomey Homa* [1902] A.C. 151 (P.C., Can.).

[49] H.C., *Debates*, 14 June 1900, 7408–7409 (Laurier).

[50] See M. Timlin, 'Canada's Immigration Policy, 1898–1910', *Can. Jour. Econ. and Poli. Sci.*, xxvi (1960), 517, 518.

[51] Canada, *Session Papers*, 1909, no. 74b, instructions by Japanese Foreign Office to Local Governors (17 May 1900).

immigration by increasing the head tax first to $100.00 in 1900 and to $500.00 in 1903.[52] He refused, however, to relent on Japanese immigration despite continuing pressure from the west coast. The new three-tiered system of immigration which was the result of Laurier's diplomatic manoeuvres survived as long as the number of oriental immigrants to British Columbia reduced to a trickle. From 1905 to 1907 a dramatic upswing in immigration of Chinese and Japanese occurred.[53] To these were added a new group of Asians, the first East Indian immigrants to British Columbia. The Chinese and Japanese were being lured by contract labour companies to service the needs of Canadian enterprises anxious for additional workers during a period of labour shortage. Although some of the Japanese had arrived via Hawaii and thus were outside the embrace of the diplomatic agreement, it was clear that a significant proportion had come directly from Japan and that the accord was not working.[54] The East Indians were attracted by a combination of hard times in the Punjab, from which most of them came, and the blandishments of the Canadian Pacific Steamship Line concerned to build up its trans-Pacific passenger business.[55] In common with their oriental predecessors they suffered from the same sort of stereotyping. Moreover, because one of the early groups of Sikhs had arrived destitute and suffered privation during an abnormally cold winter (without support from the white community), they were thought to be ill-suited to British Columbia's climatic conditions.[56]

When a serious anti-Asian riot broke out in Vancouver in the summer of 1907, during which extensive property damage was incurred in the Chinese and some damage in the Japanese quarter of the city, it was clear to Ottawa that resolute action was required.[57] The issue of Japanese immigration had become particularly sensitive as Canada had recently acceded to the Anglo-Japanese Treaty of Alliance of 1902. Prime Minister Laurier nevertheless determined that a review of the diplomatic agreement was needed, especially in light of the fact there was some evidence of complicity by Japanese government representatives in the provision of contract labour for Canadian enterprises. To the relief of the dominion government the renewal of the accord was achieved by diplomatic representatives who were despatched to Tokyo early in 1908.[58]

Laurier was now faced with the additional complication of resistance in British Columbia to an immigrant group from within the Empire, the East Indians. Expressing grave doubts about the ability of Canada to legislate specifically against the immigration of British subjects, the dominion government passed

52 Act Respecting and Restricting Chinese Immigration, S.C. 1900, c. 32; S.C. 1903, c. 8.

53 Ward, op. cit., 64–66.

54 Timlin, op. cit., 526.

55 Ward, op. cit., 80; Roy, above n. 3, 164.

56 Ward, op. cit., 82–83.

57 Ibid., 67–70; Roy, above n. 3, 185–226.

58 Ibid., 75; 207–13. That the accord succeeded in its objectives seems to have had more to do with the redirection of patterns of Japanese emigration to Asian destinations than the commitment to it of the government of Japan; see Timlin, 528.

an order-in-council, under the Immigration Act of 1906,[59] giving them the power to exclude at discretion those prospective immigrants not coming into Canada by a 'continuous voyage' from their country of origin or birth.[60] This order was directed at both Japanese coming from ports other than those in Japan (for example from Hawaii) and the East Indians (there was no direct steamship line between India and Canada at that juncture). After a successful court challenge to the continuous voyage order by the Canadian Pacific Railway on behalf of 183 Indians in 1908 in the case of *Re Bahari Lal*,[61] another order was temporarily substituted and then incorporated into the Act itself.[62] For good measure in the matter of 'Hindoo immigration' a further order-in-council was passed requiring that all Asian immigrants not covered by diplomatic arrangements (Japanese hailing from Japan) or special statutes (Chinese) have $200.00 and a ticket to their destination in their possession.[63] When the Immigration Act was recast in 1910 the substance of both orders was included in the statute,[64] together with a provision giving power to the dominion government to make regulations prohibiting for 'a stated period, or permanently, the landing in Canada of immigrants belonging to any race deemed unsuited to the climate or requirements of Canada, or of immigrants of any specified class, occupation or character'.[65]

The Immigration Act of 1910 represented the culmination of Canada's somewhat tortuous attempt to fashion an immigration policy which took account of the sensitivities of Japan, preserved the formal rhetoric of membership in a multi-racial empire and the persistent demands of the white population of British Columbia for the exclusion of Asians. The result was a complicated system which Mackenzie King, one of its architects and himself later Prime Minister, described unctuously as a 'harmony of policies'.[66] What it was in fact was an elaborate exercise in dissimulation which represented an effective capitulation by Canada to racist sentiment in British Columbia.

This study demonstrates that in legislating discrimination on racial grounds there was borrowing among the white dominions of the British Empire. This was natural enough as there were no British precedents or models with which to work. Britain itself had no race problem in the minds of its governors, and thus no tried legal solutions which could be emulated. Moreover, official imperial policy, although at times it seems to have amounted to little more than rhetoric, entertained doubts about the use of the law to create inequality

59 Act Respecting Immigration and Immigrants, S.C. 1906, c. 19, s. 30.

60 Canada, Order-in-Council, no. 27, 1908, Jan. 8.

61 (1908) 8 W.L.R. 129 (B.C.S.C.).

62 Act to Amend the Immigration Act, S.C. 1908, c. 33.

63 Canada, Order-in-Council, no. 932, 1908, June 3.

64 Act Respecting Immigration, S.C. 1910, c. 27, ss. 37, 79.

65 Ibid., s. 38.

66 W. MacKenzie King, *Report on Mission to England to Confer with the British Authorities on the Subject of Immigration from the Orient and Immigration from India in Particular* (Ottawa, 1908), 10.

of treatment of those of other races seeking to live or already resident in British territories.

The transmission of formal legal models was only part of the process of institutionalizing racist policies. More important, because it fostered the social and political climate in which white supremacist legislation became possible, was the sharing of racist ideas and sentiment within and between white settler populations. Especially among the white communities on the Pacific rim, as trade and commerce expanded and seaborne travel became safer and more efficient during the course of the nineteenth century, regular contacts and lines of communication developed. Both in the white dominions and on the United States west coast there were apostles of white exclusivity. The sentiment was passed between them and tailored to fit the particular circumstances of each community.[67]

The agents of racist ideology included the people who moved between and across the various jurisdictions – gold miners, missionaries, traders, sailors, white migrants and even recreational travellers. In the case of communities which were geographically proximate, in particular British Columbia and the west coast American states, institutional links, particularly within the labour movement, engendered strong feelings of common cause and solidarity in the face of the Asiatic intruder.[68] Personal contact, while important, was necessarily limited. It was the press which was probably the single most important factor in the translation and dissemination of racist ideology. In communities in which there was little time to read and absorb information and opinion, let alone to discriminate between conflicting views of the human condition, newspapers and magazines provided the only constant source of news and commentary to which most people were exposed.[69] A significant majority of publications was ill disposed to the Chinese and their editors and contributors made no bones about it. Moreover, the press at large was prone to publishing material drawn from other sources, in particular that which had cultural and scientific pretensions, which was racist in content, without any attempt to comment upon it, let alone call it into question. For white populations already suspicious of oriental 'intruders' their prejudices were confirmed and hardened by what they read in newspapers and magazines.

The existence of strong racist sentiment in the white dominions and the resulting pattern of first restrictive and later exclusionary legislation was not aberrational, an accident, as it were, of geography or the product of a change in the climate or something in the drinking water. The emergence of racism in those jurisdictions was connected to a more profound process of acculturation, the growth of an aggressive form of racial consciousness

67 C. Price, *The Great White Walls are Built: Restrictive Immigration to North America and Australasia, 1836–1888* (Canberra, 1974).

68 For the origins of this connection through the Knights of Labour, see Roy, above n. 3, 54–63.

69 See R. Evans, K. Saunders and K. Cronyn, *Exclusion, Exploitation and Extermination: Race Relations in Colonial Queensland* (Sydney, 1976), 15–16.

in the white Anglo-Saxon world throughout the nineteenth century which was reflected in a strong belief in the political ascendancy and cultural hegemony of the Nordic peoples.[70] Increasingly, assisted by the infusion of social Darwinism and early eugenics discourse, it manifested itself in claims of biological superiority over those of non-Caucasian ancestry.[71] This phenomenon tracked closely the exploitation of non-European societies and cultures by the two leading western capitalist nations. The spectacular growth of the international trade of Great Britain and later the United States brought those countries into contact with social and political systems vastly different from their own. Their nationals, whether official representatives of the state, merchants, missionaries or settlers, inevitably made judgements on what they observed of the political system and social practices of the host communities.[72] To the extent that those attributes were seen as standing in the way of European economic and strategic interests, or were characterized as the mark of an uncivilized people or of a decaying culture, the judgements became increasingly critical and took on the character of negative stereotypes. The latter became firmly imbedded in the thoughts and discourse of white observers and, in turn, of their countrymen.[73] This process of negative characterization was particularly evident in relation to the Chinese, who were increasingly labelled as decadent and perverse. The greatest impact of these racist impulses was felt in the white colonies and dominions which had oriental immigrant populations: it was in these territories that the greatest insecurities about economic survival and strongest competitive urges were to be found. There oriental immigrants were spurned not only because they were deemed culturally inferior, but more importantly because they became enmeshed in a capitalist system in which their cynical exploitation by business as a cheap source of labour meant that they were pitted against and thoroughly detested by white workers.[74]

Feelings of racial superiority were not, however, limited to the white settler communities. They also conditioned to one degree or another the attitudes and actions of imperial and metropolitan authorities in the Anglo-Saxon world. It is this shared ideology which explains the apparent paradox of the representatives of the empire on the one hand preaching the virtues of a multi-racial family subject to British principles of justice and fair play, while on the other progressively accommodating the ultra-racist arguments and discriminatory policies of white settler communities. It is true that imperial and metropolitan politicians and bureaucrats did express serious doubts about

[70] See R. Horsman, *Race and Manifest Destiny: The Origins of American Racial Anglo-Saxonism* (Cambridge, Mass., 1981); C. Bolt, 'Race and the Victorians', *British Imperialism in the Nineteenth Century*, C. Eldredge, ed. (1984), 126.

[71] Zaffroni, op. cit., 26–66.

[72] Miller, op. cit., 16–141.

[73] Ibid., 145–66.

[74] R. Warburton, 'Race and Class in British Columbia: A Comment', *B.C. Studies*, xlix (1981), 79.

the almost fanatical positions of settlers on matter of race. However, their attachment to the benefits of the spread of British institutions and culture and economic expansion associated with settlement made it difficult for them to stand up to the constant barrage of complaint from those who were in the vanguard of this desirable policy of 'anglicanization'.[75] Where individuals took a firm stand against local racism, as it may be argued the early British Columbia judges did, their efforts were forgotten as more compliant individuals were appointed to the bench and the process of constitutional interpretation became sanitized.

Intestinal fortitude on the part of imperial and metropolitan authorities on matters of race decreased as Britain sought to loosen its political control over those parts of the empire in which white settlement had been encouraged and which were thought to be capable of self-government. Part of the problem was that even those who were strong advocates of the imperial ideal did not see the races as equal. For them, though non-white races might well learn to assimilate at some point in the future, in the short term the tutelage and protection of the non-white population by its wiser, more worldly white rulers was necessary. With political devolution within the white empire this meant local white politicians and civil servants. In the event of a crunch developing out of animosity by white settlers and their political representatives towards racially distinct populations in their midst, arguments based on notions of trusteeship of 'lesser' peoples were unlikely to be maintained consistently, or would be qualified in order to appease settler sentiment. In the climate of exaggerated ethnocentricity which marked the British Empire of the late nineteenth – and early twentieth – century, it was natural that in the final analysis the benefit of any doubt would go to those who, despite their obsessive campaigns and boorish tactics, were carrying through a vital, perhaps the most vital, item on the imperial agenda: the expansion of British institutions, economic interests and culture across the globe.

[75] On the development of the 'civilizing mission' in British colonial policy, see J. Manning Ward, *Colonial Self Government* (Toronto, 1976), 233–46.

Chapter 14

Sir Augustus Stephenson and the Prosecution of Offences Act of 1884

Roger Chadwick

During the second half of the nineteenth century radical changes in the demography of Britain were accompanied by equally notable changes in the behaviour of its population. What had once been seen as a 'most turbulent and ungovernable people' became a European model of anxious respectability – a nation of shopkeepers.

The decline of violent crime and its progressive isolation, if not in a criminal under-class as Tobias and others have suggested,[1] at least in the lowest socio-economic strata, was matched by a growing ethical consensus among the respectable majority. In the formation of this consensus government played a reluctant but crucial role. While efforts to revise or even to codify the substantive criminal law failed, changes in the administration of the law brought a rising level of pressure to bear against those who persisted in the traditional spirit of lawlessness. As V.A.C. Gatrell observed:[2]

> In so far as the machinery of law and order had positive effects on Victorian criminality it was because those who broke the law were not well defended against those who sought to bring them to justice. The agencies of the law were, in that sense, appropriate to their task.

Foremost among these agencies were those of police and public prosecution and their spasmodic evolution in Victorian England was sufficient to shift the balance of the legal system significantly against the offender. What may be true of crimes of violence is not, however, necessarily true of all crime and in late Victorian England it was the emergence of new crimes and new criminals which attracted much of what Gatrell called the 'prosecutorial energy' of that society.[3] It was an impetus that had to meet continuing opposition from all parts of the political spectrum fearing the extension of government power. In the hands of a new generation of public servants the Department of Public Prosecutions evolved as a response not to the threat of the 'criminal classes' but of middle-class, white-collar crime. Moriarty not Fagin was the

1 J.J. Tobias, *Crime and Industrial Society in the 19th Century* (New York, 1967).
2 *Crime and the Law*, V.A.C. Gatrell et al., ed. (1980) 258.
3 Ibid., 251.

arch-criminal of the 1880s.

By the 1880s the operation of those detached agencies of government which provided police, prosecution and penal services had come to be controlled by a new generation of officials. They were men who stood somewhat below the highest level of the civil service and thus at a distance from the conservative political pressures which constrained both ministers and their permanent under-secretaries. In the 1860s and 70s the founders of the Victorian criminal justice apparatus gave way to a new cohort of management. Edwin Chadwick, Rowan, Mayne and Jebb had all been outsiders employed at a time when the role of central government was highly suspect. Their successors, Edmund Henderson and Howard Vincent, commissioner of Metropolitan Police and Director of the Criminal Investigation Department respectively, Edmund DuCane, the first director of a national Prison Commission,[4] and A.K. Stephenson, from 1866 the Treasury Solicitor, were more securely seated. All of them showed what, for Victorian civil servants, was an uncharacteristic boldness and drive for executive efficiency. They had few inhibitions about the extension of central government authority.

Stephenson inherited an office which served not only the Treasury but the Home Office as well; by 1875 the latter's work far exceeded that done on behalf of the Treasury. Between 1875 and 1879 Stephenson also acquired the civil and criminal business of the Admiralty, the Office of Works, the War Office and the Queen's Proctor's Department. He was later proud to point out that his 'take-overs' had reduced staff in these offices from twenty-one to ten and more than halved their legal expenses.[5] By 1879 the treasury solicitor had become the effective director of prosecutions for the Metropolitan area. In his own characteristic phrase he had begun to 'take charge' when the ends of justice were at stake. He had also begun to act as adviser to police authorities throughout England and Wales and, even more significantly, to accept a growing volume of prosecution costs in difficult cases. It is this budgetary shift which is the key to the changing character of public prosecution in the Victorian criminal justice system.

The traditional mechanism for recompensing the prosecutors of criminals had been a 'reward'; a reward not merely offered for 'information leading to conviction' but for the successful prosecution of specific offences. By Acts of William & Mary, William III, Anne and George III rewards were granted out of the hereditary revenues of the Crown to persons who 'prosecuted to conviction' highwaymen, coiners, robbers, housebreakers and

[4] An appointment which arose under the Prisons Act 1877, amalgamating the already 'nationalized' Convict Prisons (for long-term prisoners) with local prisons, hitherto devoted to those with lesser sentences.

[5] 'Report of the Committee Appointed to Inquire into the Office of Public Prosecutor . . .' (May 1884), *Parl. Papers*, xxiii (1884). Henceforth cited as 'Report (1884)'.

cattle thieves.[6] These rewards were not payable in the event of acquittals and bore no relationship to the actual cost of prosecution. The first example of an allowance from public funds to cover the actual cost of prosecution was an Act of 1752 (25 Geo. II c. 36) which permitted the successful prosecutor of a felony to recover 'a reasonable amount of compensation for his expenses' from county funds. Subsequent legislation, and most notably Bennet's Act of 1818 (50 Geo. III c. 70) extended this principle to cover failed prosecutions, allowances to witnesses and costs incurred at preliminary investigations. This shift from the private purse to the local rates, even if occasionally helped by the Crown, was not popular. In 1836, following a parliamentary inquiry into local rates, it was agreed by a vote of the House, rather than an Act of Parliament, that half of the reasonable expenses of prosecuting felonies might be recovered from the Exchequer. A decade later, in 1846, this compromise was extended to cover the full cost. Not only did such a concession require an annual vote but it left a long list of excluded offences including many of rising concern to the society of early Victorian England, including conspiracy to obtain by false pretences, keeping disorderly houses and libel. It was, nevertheless, not these exclusions which exercised early Victorian law-reformers but the lack of equity and the inefficiency of the prosecutorial system.

When, in 1856, a Select Committee reported on a proposed Bill to appoint a public prosecutor the prevailing system was criticized in roundly utilitarian terms. Lord Brougham declared in his evidence:[7]

> The existing law is by no means as effectual as it ought to be: the duty of prosecution is usually irksome, inconvenient and burthensome. The injured party would often rather forego the prosecution than incur expense of time, labour and money. Entrusting the conduct of the prosecution to a private individual opens a wide door to bribery, collusion and illegal compromise.

The law laid no onus on either the Crown or the individual victim to prosecute a criminal offender although both had been, in different senses, the victims of that offence. On the other hand it was open to any private individual to prosecute and, under the legislation referred to above, for courts to award expenses. It was this 'privilege' which permitted the emerging police authorities progressively to assume the role of prosecutor in the 1840s and 1850s. It was an uncertain expedient which depended heavily on the resources of the local police authority. In the relatively well-organized Metropolitan area the Home Office itself disposed of an extensive police force. By 1860 there were more than two policemen to every 1000 of London's population, a Criminal Investigation

[6] Ibid., appendix.

[7] 'Report of the Select Committee to whom the subject of the Prosecutions Bill was referred . . .' (May 1856), iii, *Parl. Papers*, vii (1856).

Department that was already over 200 strong in 1860 and which, under Howard Vincent's leadership, was to grow in the following decade to over 800 men.[8] In the office of the Treasury Solicitor it had by the 1870s not only the energetic Stephenson but three experienced assistant-solicitors and access to the agency services of Wontner's, a major London law firm. Through its financial resources it was able to recruit the specialized forensic services needed in difficult cases: medical advisers, scientific specialists and even ballistic experts.[9] After committal, occasionally even at preliminary proceedings, the services of experienced and competent treasury counsel were available. There were only two in the 1870s, H.B. Polland and Montagu Williams, but their number rose to six by the end of the century.

The major cities and large new boroughs of industrial England began to follow this model in the early 1840s. Leeds, for example, was an innovator in the prosecution of crime. Two 'respectable' prosecuting attorneys were appointed to handle all criminal cases and an inspector of police invariably bound over to prosecute on the understanding that he would employ one or other of them. It had been a very successful experiment as the town clerk reported to the criminal law commissioners in 1845.[10] In less prosperous and go-ahead places the system did not work so well and continued to depend on the efforts of a mixture of police and private individuals aided by local attorneys, often 'in low practice and on the look-out for the expenses allowed by the county'.[11]

Mid Victorian England thus exhibited a patchwork of variations on the traditional concept of private and personal prosecution. While for the most part sufficient to deal with the mass of traditional felony, it could not keep pace with the characteristic crimes of a rich new urban society; the society which Trollope attacked in 1875 in *The Way We Live Now*.[12]

It was the emergence both of new forms of crime and new types of defence which pointed up the inadequacies of the system. When the issue of a public prosecutor for England and Wales was revived by a Conservative government in 1879 it was in response to a series of complex banking and insurance company frauds, not the least of which sprang from the failure of the City of Glasgow Bank in 1878 and the subsequent and effective prosecution of its directors initiated by that city's procurator fiscal and leading to their indictment before the High Court of Justiciary.[13] The bankruptcy laws and even the

[8] 'Judicial Statistics for England & Wales', *Parl. Papers*, lvi (1862).

[9] Purdy, the leading London gun-maker, appeared as a specialist prosecution witness in the trial of Charles Pearce in 1878.

[10] 'The Commission . . . on the Criminal Law', 8th Report (1847), appendix A, 221, *Parl. Papers* (1847).

[11] Ibid., appendix A, 330.

[12] Anthony Trollope, *The Way We Live Now* (1875), which is built around the gigantic frauds of Melmotte and Cohenlupe.

[13] Mr. Mitchell Henry, *Hansard* (14 March 1879) at col. 988.

new Food and Drug Acts[14] began to give rise to new offences which could not easily be prosecuted by members of the public alone, or even by a single police authority. The assembly of witnesses and the cost of counsel in protracted proceedings put such prosecutions beyond the reach of the victims of the crime, already impoverished by their losses.[15] As a member of Parliament noted in the debate on the Bill:[16]

> There was a class of offences in which a large number of persons conspired to commit extensive frauds and by means of 'long firms' succeeded in doing so in many parts of the country at one & the same time. The duty of prosecuting such criminals was so onerous that no private person could be expected to undertake it.

Increasing awareness of the limitations on criminal liability through insanity had led to some important mid nineteenth-century cases in which a verdict of not guilty by reason of insanity had been obtained. Prosecutors were increasingly aware of the need for specialist medical evidence in such cases. Not surprisingly the middle-classes were best equipped to grasp such defences. A judge, Baron Martin, noted in a contemporary case, 'a poor person was seldom inflicted with insanity but it was common to raise such a plea when people of means were charged with the commission of a crime'.[17] Poison cannot be claimed to have been an exclusively middle-class expedient but it was certainly widely used by affluent men and women and it presented many problems to the prosecution in Victorian murder cases. The list of those who gained acquittal is as well known as that of those convicted.[18]

Both Scotland and Ireland had well established systems of public prosecution but R.A. Cross, the Home Secretary, and his Tory colleagues did not propose to try to create such an extensive bureaucracy in England. The scheme which was offered was modest both in terms of its staff and their powers. The Attorney-General described the measure as 'only to be tentative',[19] and he declared that the existing system 'as a rule works remarkably well'.[20] Even so the Bill aroused characteristic opposition from both sides of the House. The proposed powers of the Home Secretary and the Attorney-General to

14 The first such Act was passed in 1860 and depended on the initiative of the individual consumer. It was reinforced in 1872 by the Adulteration of Food, Drinks and Drugs Act which allowed public analysts to bring prosecutions. A further Act of 1875 tried to set standards for pure food and drugs. See A.S. Wohl, *Endangered Lives: Public Health in Victorian Britain* (Cambride, Mass., 1983).

15 The most celebrated example of the cost of prosecuting such fraud was the case of Orton, the Tichbourne Claimant, whose criminal prosecution, after the failure of his civil suit, was said to have cost the government over £100,000. See below, at n. 24.

16 Mr. Bulwer, *Hansard* (14 March 1879) at col. 969.

17 The case of Christiana Edmunds, *The Times*(17 Jan. 1872). Baron Martin's experience of affluent insanity included the notorious case of George Victor Townley in December 1863, where parental money and complaisant medical men allowed the convicted man to escape the gallows.

18 The cases of Dr. Smethurst (1859), Adelaide Bartlett (1866) and Florence Bravo (1876), who were all acquitted, are as celebrated as those of Florence Maybrick (1889) and Fanny Oliver (1869) who were not.

19 Sir John Holker, *Hansard* (14 March 1879) at col. 983.

20 Ibid.

appoint an apparently unlimited number of local prosecutors was seen as an egregious opportunity for patronage.[21] It was an example, in Sir William Harcourt's words, of 'one of the most growing evils in this country, the centralization of patronage in the hands of the Executive Government'.[22] In the eyes of one member it was an attempt to create a Ministry of Justice under another name.[23] It would be inefficient declared another since: 'All Treasury prosecutions partook more or less of jobbery and always cost too much'.[24] In the mind of one Tory member it would strike at the heart of the national character:

> There was nothing which could be more prejudicial to the English character than to imitate the example of various foreign countries, and teach people to look to the Government for everything. If people would not look after their own property, it was not right that they should be able to ask the Government to do it for them.[25]

There was opposition too from special interests and Harcourt declared that an earlier Liberal Bill had broken down because it had been opposed by:[26]

> the most formidable body except the Licensed Victuallers, in the country – for everybody knows that they exercise an influence over hon. Members which is not equalled by any except Licensed Victuallers – I mean Solicitors.

There was nevertheless, by this time, recognition among leaders on both sides of the House that action was needed and that, while traditional anxieties must be met, there was an overriding duty on Parliament to exercise the law. Farrer Herschell, later a Liberal Chancellor, reminded the House that 'every act which the law constitutes a crime is, as such, an offence not against the individual injured but against the community or State'.[27]

The compromise which emerged from the committee stage on the Prosecution of Offences Bill in 1879 was indeed a 'tentative' measure. When Sir John Blossett Maule Q.C. began work as the first Director of Public Prosecutions in January 1880 he, a single assistant,[28] and four clerks were temporarily housed in the Home Office building and empowered 'to institute, undertake and carry on such criminal proceedings as might be prescribed by regulations under the act or, in a special case, be directed by the Attorney General'. The Act imposed a further duty upon the Director to give advice to chief officers of police, clerks to justices and other persons in accordance

21 Mr. Williams, ibid., at col. 967.

22 Sir W.V. Harcourt, ibid., at col. 978.

23 Mr. Mitchell Henry, ibid., at col. 987.

24 Mr. Williams, ibid., at col. 967. Williams went on to cite the Tichbourne case citing the cost at over £100,000. In fact it only cost the still massive amount of £60,000, Report (1884), Evidence of A. Stephenson.

25 Mr. Floyer, *Hansard* (14 March 1879), at col. 984.

26 Sir W.V. Harcourt, ibid., at col. 978.

27 Sir F. Herschell, ibid., at cols. 973–74.

28 The Act did in fact authorize a maximum of six such assistants.

with the regulations.

The regulations under that Act authorized the Director to assist prosecutors or police authorities responsible for prosecutions by incurring special costs in the preparation of scientific evidence, plans, models, and extra fees to counsel. They were, however, remarkably vague in that they did not list the categories of crime for which he would be responsible. Issued by the Secretary of State in January 1880, they set out circumstances under which the Director might intervene in prosecutions. Cases 'as appear to be of importance or difficulty, or as from special circumstances, or the refusal or failure of a person to proceed with a prosecution . . .'[29] It was made clear in a Home Office circular to the chairmen of Quarter Sessions that this function was intended 'not to supplant but only to supplement the system now in use'.[30] It had, however, supplanted the authority of the Treasury Solicitor as the principal civil service adviser to the government on criminal justice affairs, even if a great deal was left to the initiative of his successor.[31]

It is clear that the role which Maule chose to adopt was consultative and passive. Unlike Stephenson, he was no fighter. All the cases previously referred to the Criminal Department of the Home Office for advice or help were now referred directly to him. In cases where he thought prosecutions should be instituted he merely referred them to the Treasury Solicitor in exactly the same way as the Home Office staff had earlier done. Those cases that had gone directly to the Treasury Solicitor, also went to the Director, only to be returned to the Treasury Solicitor for action, since the new Department of Public Prosecutions had no resources for actually handling cases and made no attempt to create them. It was not a good solution and it did not work.

In June 1883, urged on by the complaints of both Stephenson and his own Home Office staff,[32] Harcourt, now Home Secretary, assembled a departmental committee to reexamine the office of public prosecutor.[33] It carried out a humiliating investigation into the relaxed daily routine of Maule and his small staff. It concluded that 'at present the Director of Public Prosecutions is consulted and determines upon prosecutions but takes no practical part in their conduct, a duty which is remitted by him to the Solicitor of the Treasury'.[34] During his evidence Maule was able to offer little defence of this position and betrayed a painful ignorance of practical detail being unaware, for example, of his own department's costs or even of

[29] 'Rules as to Prosecutions under 42 & 43 Vict. c. 22, s. 8', Report (1884), appendix.

[30] Ibid., appendix.

[31] The Attorney-General remained, of course, the nominal political authority in such cases.

[32] The failed prosecution of Hannah Dobbs, the 'Euston Square murderess', provided an outstanding example. Maule refused to pursue Dobbs despite the pressure of both Stephenson and Howard Vincent, Home Office H.O. 144 Series, Case 84111 (1879–80).

[33] Its members were formidable, including Henry James, Farrer Herschell, Randolph Churchill, J.R. Gorst and Henry Fowler.

[34] Report (1884).

his assistant's salary.[35] The evidence of this assistant, B.A. Sparks, was even more damaging. He considered some two or three cases a day, the reading of whose particulars would, he agreed, 'take [him] about a quarter of an hour to read through from beginning to end' after which they would normally be sent to the Treasury Solicitor for an opinion or action.[36] By contrast Stephenson's evidence was both detailed and aggressive.[37] He first described the network of agency arrangements and 'approved' prosecuting solicitors which he had earlier established around the country, and the rigorous scale of costs which he maintained. He went on to outline a scheme for amalgamation of the new department with his own, complete in all respects except that of the name of the combined Director and Treasury Solicitor. An independent Department of Public Prosecutions was he declared 'a fifth wheel on the coach of Justice'.[38] His solution was one which the committee readily accepted and in the autumn of 1884 it was incorporated in a further Prosecution of Offences Act.

This new Act not only effectively established Stephenson, the existing Treasury Solicitor, as Director of Public Prosecutions but made a modest attempt to define his additional powers. The Director became responsible for the prosecution of all offences punishable by death, and for all those offences which he had hitherto undertaken as Treasury Solicitor – effectively for those which any independent authority thought too difficult to handle. To murder cases were added coinage offences; bankruptcy offences and company frauds referred by the Board of Trade; and a continuing volume of requests for help from clerks to justices, coroners, police authorities and other government departments.[39] The volume of work grew rapidly in the ever more regulated life of late Victorian England and by 1908 it became necessary to reestablish an independent Department of Public Prosecutions.

In 1880 Sir John Maule had reviewed fewer than 500 cases of which the Treasury Solicitor prosecuted less than forty per cent. In 1899 the combined department handled over 1300 cases and prosecuted 519. These included fifteen murder cases and eight other offences against the person, including three under the recent Criminal Law Amendment Act.[40] It prosecuted 116 currency offences on behalf of the Treasury and nineteen major frauds on behalf of the Board of Trade. The balance of its work addressed an astonishing mixture of corporate and private misconduct. Montgomery County Council was prosecuted for offences against the Quarries Act of 1894, a ship's captain for importing a parrot contrary to the Foreign Animals Order, two East Europeans for incitement to murder the Emperor of Russia and a farmer for

35 Ibid., minute 1.

36 Ibid., minute 608.

37 Ibid., minute 209.

38 Ibid., minute 228.

39 E. Tindal Atkinson, 'The Department of Public Prosecutions', *Canadian Bar Rev.*, xxii (1944), 416.

40 An early twentieth century Director of Public Prosecutions, Atkinson, noted how his department began to take responsibility for sexual offences against children and young persons, where traditional community attitudes remained more tolerant than the legal establishment.

contravening the Contagious Diseases (Animals) Act. The highly-respected firm of Steel, Peech and Tozer were prosecuted for possessing illegal die-stamps with which to press 'standard' markings on non-standard bridging steel.[41] It was a workload which reflected not only the prosecutorial energy but the changing priorities of the late Victorian criminal justice system.[42]

[41] The prosecution appears to have been at the instance of the Colonial Office and the girders destined for East Africa. In the event it was established that this very 'contemporary' offence was the responsibility of certain of the company's staff and not of the directors.

[42] 'Report of the Director of Public Prosecutions', (Public Accounts Committee), *Parl. Papers* (1899), 279.

Chapter 15

Paul Vinogradoff as Legal Historian

V.G. Grafsky

Pavel Gavrilovich Vinogradoff comes first in the list of Russian scholars who have chosen research into English history as their professional vocation and have remarkable achievements in this area to their credit. Reminiscences of those who knew him and assessments of him by his contemporaries preserve for us an excellent impression of this respected teacher of many generations of historians in the universities of Moscow and Oxford as well as of a highly gifted public figure.

He was born in 1854 in Kostroma, a provincial city on the banks of the river Volga about 300 kilometres from Moscow. It is interesting to note that the name of his city comes from the name of an ancient Slavonic god and to draw attention to a point of resemblance between the god, Kostroma, and the Scottish John Barleycorn: both could be born again after their death. As a scholar his ideas on history and law were formed at the time when the study of social history was beginning to flourish. In the introduction to his monograph on the social history of medieval England which appeared in 1887 he wrote: 'If, in general, scientific investigation into history is a concern of the entire nineteenth century, social history belongs mainly to the second half of that century'.[1] One should bear in mind that, in Vinogradoff's opinion, the historical explanations and interpretations of the eighteenth century were confused and one-sided when compared with the scientific methods of the nineteenth century. Vinogradoff did not share their ideas of a revolutionary remaking of society. In his estimation the programmes of revolutionary innovation produced in the eighteenth century looked like 'utopias of political rationalism'. These views succumbed in the face of competition from Savigny's conception of the role of historical tradition and the spirit of the people, what is called in German the *Volksgeist*.

His father was a teacher in a grammar school and Vinogradoff in his later years recalled the value of his upbringing in a patriarchal and god-fearing milieu. He also felt the beneficial influence of the political and intellectual discussions in which he took part during his school and university years. As the guiding stars of his intellectual development he named the Russian

[1] Published in St. Petersburg it appeared in translation as *Villeinage in England* (Oxford, 1892).

historian Vasily Kluchevsky, the German Romanist Theodor Mommsen and that master of the history of the English common law, Frederick William Maitland. In Vinogradoff's own words Vasily Kluchevsky was, 'a product of mysterious forces hidden in the very centre of the Russian plains, for he was the son of a poor village priest'. He was 'sensitive, concentrated, endowed with the artistic genius of a painter, a kind of Rembrandt, revealing the essence of historical character and movements by a combination of intuition and keen criticism'. Mommsen was 'the eagle with his piercing look, a man of devouring industry who gathered all the shreds of evidence as to the past of Rome and made them part of his personal life'. Of Maitland he said that he was 'almost uncanny in the triumph of his mighty mind over weakness of his body, impatient of unproved assumption and hasty generalization, carrying the practical sense of the common law into the past and illumining the past with the flame of his quaint humour'[2] One may say that to him these three great historians were the best personifications of the vocation of the scientific historian.

Here it may be pointed out that, by his own confession, Vinogradoff's inclination towards the study of English law and society was related to certain peculiarities of English life which in his opinion always appealed strongly to the interest of foreign observers, notably the rule of law and the manly spirit of freedom. In his inaugural lecture delivered in Corpus Christi College in the University of Oxford on 1 March 1904 he said, 'Like so many others I began by studying political institutions, but was insensibly led to inquiries as to legal and social history. This brought me into contact with some of the best representatives of English thought and learning and more especially with the Oxford intellectual centre'.[3] When he himself started teaching in Oxford one of the most influential teachers and authorities there was Henry Sumner Maine. Of him he said:[4]

> His was one of those minds which radiate far beyond their immediate surroundings: the whole of my generation of students of law and history have had to deal directly or indirectly with the ideas propagated by him or similar to his. . . . [he was] a scholar, who before all strove to be a thinker; a lawyer, who was more interested in the origins of legal rules than in the rules themselves; a man of the world, who brought all the resources of his shrewd common sense to the investigation of antiquarian problems; a sociologist, who never dealt in names nor played with words.

In relation to Maine as a leader of legal thought he made the very profound and just observation that: '. . . such a leader always personifies in his life and work, with more or less individual colouring, some combination of the aims and ideas of his time'.[5]

2 Quoted by H.A.L. Fisher in the memoir which he prefaced to *The Collected Papers of Paul Vinogradoff* (Oxford, 1928; rptd. London, 1964), i, 70.

3 'The Teaching of Sir Henry Maine', *Law Quart. Rev*., xx (1904), 119; *Collected Papers*, ii, 173.

4 Ibid., 119–20; 174.

5 Ibid., 120; 174.

According to Vinogradoff legal history dealt with:[6]

> . . . streams of doctrines and institutional facts which pass through the ages and cross national boundaries from one historical formation to another. These constitute what may be called the current of *cultural tradition*. Again, the solutions of legal problems on different occasions fall into groups according to similarities and contrasts, for which there is a common basis in the nature of the problems themselves. This gives rise to the application of the *comparative method*. The continuity of culture and comparative jurisprudence produce the atmosphere of what might have been called International Law had not the term been appropriated to other uses.

It was not necessary to dwell at length on the progress which had been made in tracing cultural continuity in the history of legal systems. A classic example had formerly been drawn from the reception of Roman law by medieval and modern Europe but others could be identified in the history of Roman law itself. Law was a historical phenomenon and hence any general theory of law of necessity needed some historical input. The question which was more important – systematic theoretical construction or explanation of the historical development of the law – was futile because in any case a systematic general theory of law would always require treatment of theories which had been replaced under the promptings of reflection on the tasks of the human race and the environment which conditions its response. The law as a social fact and as a component of social experience was a very important element of social existence and social relationships. Its function in regulating private relationships was no less important than its function in regulating state institutions or the division of power in a state.

Two principal methods have dominated the field of jurisprudence so far as it has been concerned with abstract studies of law and rights: the analytical method and the historical one. Vinogradoff considered that this contrast was inaccurate. Logically the antithesis of the analytical approach is the synthetical one; the counterpart of dissection is amalgamation. Abstract concepts and terms, Vinogradoff wrote, were often treated by analytical jurists like questions concerning logical terms and formal classifications. They believed that these two formed the essence of jurisprudence and could be employed without making any connection with social realities. In this way the so-called 'world of concepts' was created. Rudolf Ihering ridiculed such a paradise of concepts (*Begriffshimmel*) but, as Vinogradoff noted, the works of Bierling, Kelsen and Stammler provided many illustrations of this kind of scholasticism. In England analytical positivism was represented chiefly by Austin and his followers.

Vinogradoff's own method and the task which he proposed was to show that legal facts and ideas could be studied from a point of view which disclosed new vistas for the student of language, folklore and religion. Comparative research,

6 'The Study of Jurisprudence', *Collected Papers*, ii, 205–6.

he wrote, seemed to offer the prospect of bringing order into the mass of impressions gained from contemplation of life in society. We may reasonably attempt to distinguish between cultural types, to note recurring sequences of development and to suggest reasons why these types and sequences present themselves not on identical, but on parallel or divergent lines.[7] The early positivists, Comte and Spencer, proclaimed the advent of a sociology destined to encompass the whole range of natural sciences as the crowning effort of human knowledge. Later thinkers in Vinogradoff's day, including Vinogradoff himself, were not so optimistic but made many reservations and restrictions. As he put it: 'The world of human relations does not have the same immutable laws and ever-recurring sequences characteristic of natural sciences. Rather they are like a stream, originating from inconspicuous sources, which flows along various courses to an unknown sea. Social combinations, even when similar, are never alike'.[8] The rules of conduct in a given society are usually the result of converging ideas of various kinds, every single one of which would be powerless to produce the effect required on its own. 'Neither the life of a family nor that of a nation nor that of a state depends entirely or mainly on the faultless regularity of its logical construction'.[9] In the case of the family, for example, it is not the contract of marriage that ensures the happiness and mutual devotion of the married couple. Marriage is a complex experience and an institution to which many heterogeneous elements contribute. It may be analyzed with regard to various component factors: sexual attraction, moral sentiment, care for children, political utility, economic solidarity, traditional habits, conventional habits, sacramental beliefs. Each of these factors in turn may be subjected to separate observation and deductions. If we want to study it as a living whole we are bound to speculate on the binding force or synthesis which brings and holds together the various elements in the average case or discloses dangerous centrifugal tendencies. This is a problem for a synthesizing sociology and a synthesizing jurisprudence.

One of his contemporaries described Vinogradoff as the best known figure in the learned world of the continent and his description was correct. Take, for example, his activities in his capacity as university lecturer and popularizer of the knowledge of history and legal science. From the memoirs of the Russian academician Bogoslovsky, a pupil of Vinogradoff at Moscow University, may be quoted a letter describing how the *lex Salica* was studied:[10]

> We were given the task of making ourselves acquainted with the text and with the relevant literature and then commenting on certain articles of the law or presenting one of the cases dealt with in complete and convincing form. . . . Pavel Gavrilovich summarized the papers submitted after going through them thoroughly and then started to interpret the most difficult passages with the students participating. He

[7] *Custom and Right* (Oslo, 1925), 2, 8.

[8] Ibid.

[9] Ibid., 12.

[10] M.M. Bogolovsky, *Istoriografiia, Memuaristika, Epistolariia* (Moscow, 1987), 76–77.

had a gift for inspiring their interest. Comparisons of different texts were made and the meaning of each was explained. After this critical analysis the whole picture of the mode of life of the Salian Franks which was being studied was reconstructed. It was a great pleasure to participate in the work and watch it.

In the nineties of last century educational establishments were founded in Moscow. Their aim was to disseminate scientific knowledge widely throughout the population. On the initiative of the historian Professor Milyukov a Home Study Committee was set up. The idea was comparable to some extent with university extension courses in England. In the first decade of its existence the editorial board of the committee, with the active assistance of Paul Vinogradoff, published significant works on law and government. These included translations of A.V. Dicey, Léon Duguit, Gabriel Tarde and of many other prominent scholars. In the same period Vinogradoff wrote a textbook for secondary schools and prepared a book of readings on history in four volumes for which he was later awarded the Major Prize of Peter the Great by the Academy of Sciences.

At the beginning of this century Vinogradoff was engaged in gathering together and summing up the results of his long life of research. The idea was to bring everything together in a great treatise under the title *Outlines of Historical Jurisprudence*. Historical jurisprudence, he thought, might be covered under the following scheme: 1. Origins in Totemistic Society; 2. Tribal Law; 3. Civic Law [the law of city states]; 4. Medieval Law, in its combination as Canon and Feudal law; 5. Individualistic jurisprudence; and 6. Beginnings of socialistic jurisprudence.[11] The first volume published in fact contained the introduction and the section on tribal law. The second, published in 1923,[12] contained the section on the jurisprudence of the Greek city states but, although a third volume on the medieval jurisprudence of Western Christendom was announced in it as being in preparation, Vinogradoff was able to finish and publish only the two volumes; he died in 1925.

The introduction set out compactly and lucidly the views and theories of Vinogradoff's predecessors and surveyed the whole field of jurisprudence. In the first part he dealt with the interrelation of law and other human sciences: logic, psychology, social science and political theory. In the second he described the different methods and schools of jurisprudence: rationalists, nationalists, evolutionists and modern tendencies. From his stance he was critical of Marxist doctrine for its materialistic fatalism and for depriving law of moral authority, as well as for considering law as merely a reflection of the domination of one or other of the classes into which society is divided. He saw this as a great simplification, especially in relation to sociological interpretation of the nature of law and the social functions of law.[13]

Vinogradoff took the view that learning law without organizing ideas is

11 *Outlines of Historical Jurisprudence*, i (London, etc., 1920), 158.

12 *Outlines of Historical Jurisprudence*, ii (London, etc., 1923).

13 'Historical Types of International Law', *Collected Papers*, ii, 255–58.

useless. Jurisprudence was bound to be a historical discipline in so far as it must take stock of the social conditions which call forth legal principles; succession and ownership, possession and contract did not start from specific laws or from actual conflicts. Succession had its roots in the necessary arrangements for the household on the death of the householder; ownership began with taking occupation; possession was reducible to *de facto* detention; the origins of contract went back to the practice of barter. Jurisprudence was also bound to be analytical in so far as it must examine the logical consequences of legal principles and their rational combinations. As Vinogradoff wrote:[14]

> The results are never quite rational or simple: various side influences and cross-currents bring in unexpected turns and complicate actual developments. Opposition and compromises between conquerors and conquered, psychological peculiarities, industrial discoveries, the pressure of economic needs, produce all sorts of variations which it would be impossible to reduce by dialectic process to the evolution of one or the other principle. As a matter of fact the governing principles of jurisprudence, such as tribal solidarity, the City State, the Catholic Church, individualism, socialism, are synthetic in their nature and therefore subject to disruption and combination as well as to evolution.

In conclusion, it may be of interest to cite first of all a significant generalization made by Vinogradoff:[15]

> . . . in trying to understand the history of human society in its legal aspects we must begin by ascertaining the *leading themes* which recur in jurisprudential thought. As in music, they are not stereotyped in their manifestations, they vary in the course of conflicts and harmonizing attempts, but they are not numerous and are therefore amenable to definite observation and to reflective estimates.

I should like to add that the scope of the vision and the clarity of the analysis in Vinogradoff's studies were, as in chess, the outcome of a complex and all-embracing survey of all the participants in legal relations and conflicts. The survey also embraced the critical zones of social tension and a careful consideration of all possible perspectives. Today when we discuss the problems of continuity and change in the development of legal knowledge it is very hard to get rid of the impression that we have not usually been able to come up to the high achievements of our predecessors. How often are our bold pretensions to originality the result of our ignorance of the achievements of those who had advanced so far beyond the horizons visible to us. Not infrequently the feeling that we lack a sufficient apparatus of ideas arises from the fact that we are not familiar enough with the vast experience of our predecessors. I am deeply convinced that the heritage of Paul Vinogradoff is still of great importance because of its potential to advance our knowledge and I believe that it is worthy of thorough and attentive study and discussion both now and in the future.

[14] *Outlines of Historical Jurisprudence*, i, 368–69, quoted by H.A.L. Fisher, *Collected Papers*, i, 65.

[15] Ibid., 369; 66.